Contents

Abbreviations

Introduction   i

1 Overview   1

A right to strike?   2
Development of the law   2
International obligations   4
Scheme of the law   8
Industrial action   10
Pressure on the employer   11
Concerted action   12
Strikes   13
Industrial action short of a strike   14

2 Liability for industrial action   17

Union liability in tort   17
Liability under statute   18
Repudiation   19
Endorsement of unofficial action   21
Liability under common law   21
Breach of contract   22
Exceptions   23
Legal consequences   25
The industrial torts   26
Rejection of the unified theory   27
Statutory immunity   28
Direct v indirect action   29
Defences to the industrial torts   30
Procuring or inducing a breach of contract   30
Causing loss by unlawful means   36
Intimidation   41
Conspiracy   42
Economic duress   43
Criminal liability   44

3 Trade union immunities   45

Scope of immunity   46

'Is not actionable in tort on the ground only...'   47
Double liability   48
Trade dispute   49
Subject-matter of dispute   52
'Wholly or mainly'   58
Overseas disputes   60
Acas conciliation   61
'In contemplation or furtherance'   61

4 Loss of immunity   65
Ballots and notice of industrial action   66
Secondary action   66
Definition of secondary action   66
Employer in dispute   67
Lawful secondary action   69
Dismissals during unofficial action   69
Unlawful picketing   70
Union-only and recognition clauses   71
Union-only clauses   71
Industrial pressure to impose union-only clauses   71
Union recognition clauses   72
Industrial pressure to impose union recognition   73
Enforcing union membership   73

5 Industrial action ballots   75
Preliminary considerations   77
Notice of ballot to employer   78
Sample voting paper   89
Independent scrutineer   89
Entitlement to vote   92
Determining the balloting constituency   92
Denial of entitlement to vote   96
'Small accidental failures'   98
New union members   98
Existing members – new jobs   99
Separate workplace ballots   100
Reasonable belief in single workplace   101
'Common factor' across different workplaces   101
Overseas members   103
Ballot requirements   104
Content of the voting paper   104
Conduct of the ballot   108

Industrial Action

Employment Law Handbook

April 2010

IDS

Industrial Action

Employment Law Handbook

Previous edition 1999

Incomes Data Services Ltd
Finsbury Tower, 103-105 Bunhill Row, London EC1Y 8LZ
Tel: 020 7429 6800 Fax: 020 7393 8081
Website: www.incomesdata.co.uk

ISBN 978-1-847-03990-3

IDS Employment Law Handbook, 'Industrial Action', is published by Incomes Data Services Limited (Registered in England & Wales, Company No 913794. Registered Office and address for service: 100 Avenue Road, London NW3 3PF).

The information contained in this journal in not intended to be a substitute for specific legal advice and readers should obtain advice from a qualified adviser in relation to individual transactions or matters.

No natural forests were destroyed to make this product: only farmed timber was used and re-planted.

A CIP catalogue record for this book is available from the British Library.

Typeset by DC Graphic Design, Swanley Village, Kent BR8 7PA
Printed by St Austell Printing Co, 41 Truro Road, St Austell, Cornwall PL25 5JE

Informing employer of ballot result 111
Notice of industrial action to employer 112
Calling industrial action 118
Period of effectiveness 119
Intervening legal proceedings 121

6 Picketing 125

Statutory protection for picketing 126
'In contemplation or furtherance of a trade dispute' 126
Purpose of picket 127
Place of picket 128
Number of pickets 131
Pickets, marches and demonstrations 133
Loss of protection 134
Civil liability 135
Trespass to the highway 135
Private nuisance 136
Union liability 138
Criminal liability 138
Public nuisance 138
Obstruction of the highway 139
Offences under S.241 TULR(C)A 140
Aggravated trespass 142
Public order offences 142
Dispersal orders 147
Breach of the peace 147
Conspiracy 149
Protection from Harassment Act 1997 150
Offence of harassment 150
Tort of harassment 151
Putting a person in fear of violence 152
Harassing a person at home 153
Secondary picketing 153

7 Remedies for unlawful action 155

Injunctions 156
Basis on which interim injunctions are granted 156
Grounds on which injunctions normally sought 159
Judicial discretion 161
Scope of injunction 162
Procedure 162
Contempt of court 165

Damages   166
   Heads of damage   168
Action by union members   169
Action by individuals   171

8 Industrial action dismissals   175
Dismissal during unofficial action   176
   Unofficial action   177
   Authorisation and endorsement   179
   Timing of dismissal   181
   No action in support of employees dismissed under S.237 181
   Effect of S.237 on unofficial action   182
   Employer-provoked strikes   182
   Health and safety issues   183
Dismissal during 'protected' official action   184
   Automatically unfair dismissal   184
   'Protected' industrial action   185
   The protected period   186
   Reasonable steps for resolution of dispute   186
   Reinstatement   188
   Tribunal procedure   188
   Qualifying period   188
   Time limits   188
Dismissal during 'non–protected' official action   189
   Strikes, lock-outs and other industrial action   190
   Industrial action and trade union activities   198
   Relevant employees   199
   Timing of complainant's dismissal   206
   Dismissal of relevant employees   208
   Selective re-engagement   210
   Reasonableness of dismissal   213
   Compensation   215
   Time limits   216

9 Industrial action and employment rights   217
Detriment short of dismissal   217
Pay   220
   Withdrawal of goodwill   222
   Payment for partial performance   224
   Remedies   225
Redundancy payments   227
   Reason for dismissal   227

Redundancy and misconduct 228
Industrial action during the notice period 229
Extension of notice period after strike 230
Lay-off and short-time 231
Guarantee payments 232
Involvement in industrial action 232
Causation 233
Continuity of employment 234
Meaning of 'strike' 234
Dismissal of strikers 235
'Taking part' in a strike 236
Effect of strikes on period of continuous employment 237
Lock-outs 238
Agreement concerning continuity 239
Notice rights 240
Time-off rights 241

10 Industrial pressure to dismiss 243
Reason for dismissal 243
Pressure to dismiss 244
Redeployment 245
Causation 247
Contributory conduct 247
Joinder of third parties 248
Right not to be subjected to detriment 248

Abbreviations

Courts

ECJ	European Court of Justice
ECHR	European Court of Human Rights
PC	Privy Council
HL	House of Lords
CA	Court of Appeal
Ct Sess	Court of Session
NICA	Northern Ireland Court of Appeal
QBD	Queen's Bench Division
Div Ct	(Queen's Bench) Divisional Court
KBD	King's Bench Division
ChD	Chancery Division
NIRC	National Industrial Relations Court
EAT	Employment Appeal Tribunal
ET	Employment Tribunal

Case references

AC	Law Reports, Appeal Cases
All ER	All England Law Reports
BNIL	Bulletin of Northern Ireland Law
Ch	Law Reports, Chancery Division
CMLR	Common Market Law Reports
COET	Employment Tribunal folio number
EAT	Employment Appeal Tribunal unreported case number
ECR	European Case Reports
ET	Employment Tribunal unreported case number
EWCA	Court of Appeal unreported case number
ICR	Industrial Cases Reports
IRLR	Industrial Relations Law Reports
ITR	Industrial Tribunal Reports
KB	Law Reports, King's Bench Division
QB	Law Reports, Queen's Bench Division
SCOET	Scottish Employment Tribunal folio number
TLR	Times Law Reports
WLR	Weekly Law Reports

Legislation

DDA	Disability Discrimination Act 1995
EqPA	Equal Pay Act 1970
ERA	Employment Rights Act 1996
ERelA 1999	Employment Relations Act 1999
ERelA 2004	Employment Relations Act 2004
ETA	Employment Tribunals Act 1996
RRA	Race Relations Act 1976
SDA	Sex Discrimination Act 1975
TULR(C)A	Trade Union and Labour Relations (Consolidation) Act 1992

Statutory references. unless otherwise stated, are to the Trade Union and Labour Relations (Consolidation) Act 1992 (TULR(C)A).

Many cases in this Handbook were decided under legislation that preceded the TULR(C)A. Reference is made throughout to the corresponding provisions in the later consolidation statute and not to their antecedents in repealed legislation.

Introduction

This Handbook aims to provide a clear and comprehensive account of the law governing industrial action. Since 16 October 1992, that law is contained in the Trade Union and Labour Relations (Consolidation) Act 1992 (TULR(C)A), which consolidated all the provisions governing collective labour law previously found in various statutes dating back to 1875. The TULR(C)A has been amended several times since then, in particular by the Employment Relations Act 1999, which made significant changes, especially in relation to industrial action ballots and industrial action dismissals. Following a review in February 2003 by the Department of Trade and Industry (now the Department for Business, Innovation and Skills), further amendments were implemented by the Employment Relations Act 2004. All statutory references in this Handbook are to the TULR(C)A unless otherwise stated.

The Handbook is set out as follows:

- Chapter 1 provides an overview of the law governing industrial action, taking into account its legislative history, and addresses the question of whether there is a 'right to strike' under domestic or European law. It also explains how the various strands of the law, both collective and individual, pull together and examines the definitions of 'strike' and 'industrial action', which are fundamental to the whole scheme of industrial action law

- Chapter 2 discusses the circumstances in which trade unions will be held vicariously liable for the actions of their officers and members and explains the legal liabilities – in contract, tort and, in certain cases, under the criminal law – that may be incurred by unions and those taking industrial action

- Chapter 3 looks at the basic statutory immunities for trade unions organising industrial action

- Chapter 4 examines the circumstances in which unions' basic legal immunity is forfeited

- Chapter 5 covers the statutory requirements for conducting secret ballots before taking industrial action and sets out the notice provisions that must be complied with

- Chapter 6 explains the law on picketing

- Chapter 7 sets out the remedies available in respect of industrial action that is not protected by statutory immunity. The most common remedy sought is an injunction against the union involved to prevent or curtail the action. However, union members and individuals are also entitled to seek orders restraining industrial action in certain circumstances

i

- Chapter 8 details the law governing the dismissal of participants taking part in either official or unofficial industrial action

- Chapter 9 deals with the legal impact of strikes and other industrial action on continuity of employment and on various employment rights, such as the right to wages or to redundancy pay

- Chapter 10 covers the special case of dismissals made in response to actual or threatened industrial action.

The law is stated as at 1 March 2010. This Handbook completely replaces IDS Employment Law Handbook, 'Industrial Action' (1999), which should now be discarded.

This publication aims to provide accurate, authoritative information and comment on the subjects it covers. It is offered to subscribers on the understanding that the publisher is not in business as a lawyer or consultant.

1 Overview

A right to strike?

Scheme of the law

Industrial action

Strikes

This Handbook is concerned with the legal implications of industrial action in **1.1** the workplace. The law relating to industrial action is a minefield which unions must negotiate with great care if they are to avoid exposing themselves and their members to legal proceedings brought by employers and others.

In this chapter we provide an overview of the law governing industrial action, starting with a brief history of industrial action law before focusing on the concept of a 'right to strike' under domestic and international labour provisions. We then turn to the current scheme of the law in this country, highlighting the steps unions must take to avoid incurring legal liability for industrial action. In the final sections of the chapter we examine the broad concept of 'industrial action' and explain the meaning of the term 'strike'.

But first some statistics. The Labour Disputes Statistics produced by the Office for National Statistics (ONS), which has carried out the annual Labour Disputes Survey since 1891, show that overall there has been a downward trend in the number of strikes over the past 20 years, with the number of working days lost in 2009 recorded at 438,000. Strike activity during the 1970s and 80s had been comparatively high, with 23.9 million working days lost in 1972, 29.5 million in 1979 (ending in the 'Winter of Discontent') and 27.1 million in 1984. These figures are dwarfed, however, by the industrial disputes of the 1910s and 20s. The number of working days lost during the first of those decades peaked at 35 million in 1919; while 85.9 million days were lost to stoppages in 1921 and 162.2 million in 1926, the year of the General Strike.

The vast majority of strikes are for three days or less. The latest complete yearly **1.2** figures from the ONS show that in 2008 48 per cent of the working days lost were for strikes lasting two days; 37 per cent were for one-day strikes; and 13 per cent were for strikes lasting three days; meaning that strikes of more than three days were responsible for only two per cent of stoppages during that year. However, while these statistics are useful for identifying overall trends, it should be noted that the ONS figures exclude action involving fewer than ten workers unless that action lasts for 100 working days. Consequently, the actual number of strikes in any given year will almost certainly be higher. Furthermore, these statistics only record work stoppages and exclude other forms of industrial action.

1

1.3 A right to strike?

There is no overarching right to strike under UK law. Instead, statutory protection for trade unions, which were legalised in 1871, has taken the form of immunities from prosecution. Trade unions first began to flex their industrial muscle in the 1890s. However, two seminal decisions of the House of Lords in the early 1900s resulted in unions being almost totally unable to take industrial action within the boundaries of the law. The first was Taff Vale Railway Co v Amalgamated Society of Railway Servants 1901 AC 426, HL, in which their Lordships held that unions could be liable for the employer's losses during a strike. The second, heard just weeks later, was Quinn v Leathem 1901 AC 495, HL, which established liability in tort where unions use industrial action to put pressure on an employer. In response to these decisions the Liberal Government of the day passed the Trade Disputes Act in 1906, which gave trade unions immunity from liability in tort provided the action taken was 'in contemplation or furtherance of an industrial dispute' (the so-called 'golden formula'), which is now contained in S.219 of the Trade Union and Labour Relations (Consolidation) Act (TULR(C)A). This did not amount to a positive right to strike, which has never existed in British law, but rather immunity from the legal liabilities which would otherwise flow from taking industrial action.

To supplement the trade union immunities, individuals who take part in industrial action have been given limited statutory protection from unfair dismissal. At common law an employee taking part in industrial action will almost always be in breach of his or her contract of employment, leaving him or her potentially liable for damages and – more commonly – vulnerable to dismissal. However, under the TULR(C)A employees are protected from unfair dismissal for taking part in industrial action in certain strictly defined circumstances – see further Chapter 8.

1.4 Development of the law

Until the late 1960s, governments of all political persuasions adopted a relatively laissez-faire approach to industrial relations, officially encouraging collective bargaining but not imposing any rigid legislative framework. Certain measures were passed to overcome particular difficulties – for instance, when the application of the ancient tort of intimidation to the industrial context was confirmed by the House of Lords in Rookes v Barnard 1964 AC 1129, HL, the then Labour Government promptly extended the scope of the statutory immunities to cover this tort – but otherwise legal intervention was minimal in this area. By the end of the 1960s, however, an increasing incidence of industrial unrest, coupled with concern about the level of inflation, led governments to adopt a far more interventionist approach. The first legislative manifestation of this was the Conservative Government's Industrial Relations Act 1971, which repealed the Trade Disputes Act 1906 and was an ambitious attempt at comprehensive 'root and branch' reform of the British industrial relations system. Trade unions adopted a policy of wholesale non-compliance with this Act and, with economic conditions far more favourable to unions at that time than in the 1980s and 1990s, the Act became unworkable and was repealed by the Labour Government in 1974.

The interventionist approach was continued by Labour in the 1970s, extending the scope of the statutory immunities to protect various forms of secondary action and limiting the circumstances in which injunctions could be obtained by employers in trade disputes. However, the Conservative Government elected in 1979 believed that the scope of the immunities had been extended too far and that in too many instances trade unions were 'above the law'. But rather than attempt comprehensive reform of the law and possibly suffer the same fate as the earlier Conservative Government responsible for the 1971 Act, Margaret Thatcher's Government expressly adopted a step-by-step approach to the reform of the law regulating industrial action. During the 18 years the Conservative Government was in power, a number of Acts were passed which had the dual effect of severely circumscribing the scope of the statutory immunities and creating a number of procedural hoops through which unions must pass if they are to take lawful industrial action. The most important of these were the balloting requirements, first introduced by the Trade Union Act 1984 and consolidated into the TULR(C)A in 1992. Additional balloting requirements were added by the Trade Union Reform and Employment Rights Act 1993 (TURERA), which significantly amended the 1992 Act.

In May 1997 a new Labour Government was elected and the following year a **1.5** White Paper on employment law reform, 'Fairness at Work' (Cm 3968, May 1998), was published, setting out a number of important proposals for reform of the law on industrial action. These proposals led to the enactment of the Employment Relations Act 1999 (ERelA 1999), which introduced, among other things, the right not to be dismissed for taking part in 'protected' official industrial action (see Chapter 8). The Act also aimed to 'clarify and simplify' the law on industrial action ballots, but unfortunately the resulting balloting and notice requirements were far from simple and have done nothing to reduce the overall burden on unions – see Chapter 5. Further amendments were introduced by the Employment Relations Act 2004 (ERelA 2004), which, among other things, extended the protected period for unfair dismissal purposes from eight weeks to 12.

The end result of all the changes to the law is that the freedom of trade unions and individuals to take industrial action is more constrained now than it was under the Trade Disputes Act 1906. However, trade unions and other labour movement organisations and individuals continue to campaign for reform. In 2005 the Trades Union Congress voted to mark the centenary of the Trade Disputes Act 1906 by backing a new Bill to restore some of the freedoms that the 1906 Act had provided. That Bill – the Trade Union Rights and Freedoms Bill – was introduced in the House of Commons as a Private Member's Bill by Labour MP John McDonnell but did not survive beyond its first reading.

1.6 International obligations

The restrictions on the freedom to take industrial action, including the complex balloting requirements and the limited protection for workers taking such action, has led to repeated criticisms of the UK Government for failing to comply with its international obligations. Those obligations are found in the International Labour Organisation (ILO) Conventions (the ILO is the United Nations (UN) body responsible for drawing up and overseeing international labour standards); the UN's International Covenant on Economic, Social and Cultural Rights 1996 (ICESCR); and the European Social Charter. (Also of relevance are the EU Treaty on the Functioning of the European Union (formerly the EC Treaty or Treaty of Rome) and the European Convention on Human Rights and Fundamental Freedoms – see below.)

Criticism has been voiced not only by trade unions and bodies such as the Institute of Employment Rights (see, for example, the IER's submission to the Joint Committee on Human Rights Inquiry into the Concluding Observations of the UN Committee on Economic, Social and Cultural Rights, March 2004), but also by the supervisory bodies of the ILO and ICESCR themselves. Both the UN Committee on Economic, Social and Cultural Rights and the ILO Committee of Experts consider that restrictions on the right to strike and the right to collective bargaining under UK law place undue limitations on the exercise of those rights.

1.7 However, the obligations under the ILO Conventions and ICESCR do not create legally enforceable rights and their effectiveness appears to rely on the influence they bring to bear on the European Court of Justice (ECJ) and the European Court of Human Rights (ECtHR). Certainly, recent judgments of the ECtHR demonstrate that the Court is increasingly citing the findings of the UN Committee and the ILO in its interpretation of the right to freedom of association guaranteed by Article 11 of the European Convention on Human Rights (see below). This was noted by the Joint Committee on Human Rights in its First Report of session 2009–10, in which it reiterated its predecessors' recommendations that the UK Government review the law in this area.

1.8 **The Treaty on the Functioning of the European Union.** While European Union law in the employment field has generally been concerned with matters such as discrimination, family rights, 'atypical' workers and transfers of undertakings, it does appear to have some relevance in the industrial action arena. At the end of 2007 the ECJ decided two cases in quick succession under the then EC Treaty (now the TFEU) in which it seemed to recognise that trade unions and their members have a fundamental right to take industrial action –

but that that right is qualified. The first case was International Transport Workers' Federation and anor v Viking Line ABP and anor 2008 ICR 741, ECJ, where trade unions initiated collective action against Viking Line, a Finnish shipping company, when it sought to 'reflag' one of its vessels in order to crew it with cheaper Estonian workers. Viking sought an injunction in the High Court restraining the collective action on the ground that it would encroach upon its rights to freedom of establishment under Article 43 of the EC Treaty (now Article 49 TFEU). On appeal to the Court of Appeal, the issue was referred to the ECJ, which held that while the action might indeed restrict Viking's Article 43 rights, that restriction could in principle be justified by an overriding reason of public interest such as the protection of workers, provided the action did not go beyond what was necessary to achieve that objective. It would have been for the Court of Appeal to do the balancing exercise in order to determine whether that action was justified in the circumstances but the parties settled before it had the opportunity to do so.

The Viking Line case was followed a week later by Laval un Partneri Ltd v Svenska Byggnadsarbetareförbundet and ors 2008 IRLR 160, ECJ. In that case, Swedish trade unions took collective action in the form of a blockade, aimed at forcing a Latvian company to abide by a Swedish collective agreement governing the terms and conditions of building workers in respect of Latvian workers posted to Sweden. The ECJ found that the unions' action constituted a restriction on the Latvian company's freedom to provide services under Article 49 of the EC Treaty (now Article 56 TFEU). However, as in Viking, the ECJ held that such a restriction could in principle be objectively justified. But given that the Swedish government had already enacted legislation providing for minimum conditions of employment in respect of posted workers, as required by the EU Posted Workers Directive (No.96/71), and the fact that Swedish law makes no provision for a minimum wage or the applicability of Swedish collective agreements to posted workers, collective action aimed at obliging the Latvian company to observe the terms of a collective agreement providing for better working conditions could not be objectively justified in this case.

1.9 Thus, while the ECJ appears to recognise that there is a fundamental right to strike, such action will have to be justified to be lawful. It is interesting to note in this regard the ECJ's decision in Laval that collective action could not be justified where national legislation implementing the Posted Workers Directive already provided a minimum level of protection for cross-border workers. This would seem to suggest that European employment legislation may have the unintended effect of restricting the circumstances in which collective action will be justified.

1.10 **The European Convention on Human Rights and Fundamental Freedoms.** The Human Rights Act 1998 (HRA) incorporates the European Convention on Human Rights and Fundamental Freedoms (ECHR) into domestic law. Under the Act, an individual can bring a claim against a public body arguing that his or her Convention rights have been violated but there is no provision to claim a breach of the HRA against a private organisation or individual. However, courts and tribunals must interpret, so far as it is possible to do so, Acts of Parliament and statutory instruments in a way compatible with the Convention rights – S.3 HRA. This includes, of course, the TULR(C)A, which governs the circumstances in which industrial action in this country is lawful and provides limited protection from dismissal for those taking part.

The most important Convention right in so far as industrial action is concerned is the right to freedom of assembly and association contained in Article 11(1). This states that 'everyone has the right to freedom of peaceful assembly and to freedom of association with others, including the right to form and to join trade unions for the protection of his interests'. However, Article 11(2) sets limits on the scope of this right by providing that 'no restrictions shall be placed on the exercise of these rights other than such as are prescribed by law and are necessary in a democratic society in the interests of national security or public safety, for the prevention of disorder or crime, for the protection of health or morals or for the protection of the rights and freedoms of others. This Article shall not prevent the imposition of lawful restrictions on the exercise of these rights by members of the armed forces, of the police or of the administration of the State.'

1.11   Thus, the right to freedom of assembly and association is what is known as a 'qualified right'. Its scope was considered by the ECtHR in two recent cases. The first was Demir and anor v Turkey 2009 IRLR 766, ECtHR, where the Court held that a Council's refusal to collectively bargain with a trade union on behalf of its employees amounted to a breach of the union's rights under Article 11. In reaching its decision the Court held that specialised international instruments such as the ILO Conventions – regardless of whether the respondent state had ratified them – and the practice of European states were relevant. It rejected the idea that civil servants could be treated as 'members of the administration of the state' for the purpose of Article 11(2) in order to limit their right to organise and form trade unions. It noted that those restrictions must not impair the essence of the right to organise. The applicants had been prevented from enjoying their trade union rights and this could not be justified as 'necessary in a democratic society' within the meaning of Article 11(2). The Court went on to say that the right to bargain collectively has become one of the essential elements of the right to form and to join trade unions for the protection of individual interests.

This judgment was quickly followed by Enerji Yapi-Yol Sen v Turkey (Application No.68959/01), ECtHR, which concerned a ban on public sector workers from taking part in a one-day national strike. Enerji Yapi-Yol Sen is a union of civil servants and member of the Federation of Public Sector Trade Unions. The Federation organised a one-day national strike in support of the right to a collective bargaining agreement but five days before the planned day of action the Turkish Government issued a circular prohibiting civil servants from taking part. Those who did so were disciplined. The ECtHR held that the disciplinary action taken on the strength of the circular was capable of discouraging trade union members and others from exercising their legitimate right to take part in strikes or other actions aimed at defending the interests of Enerji Yapi-Yol Sen's members. The Turkish Government had failed to justify the need for such a restriction and the adoption and application of the circular did not answer a 'pressing social need'. There had therefore been a disproportionate interference with the union's rights which amounted to a violation of Article 11.

Since the Enerji Yapi-Yol Sen case the ECtHR has considered the application of Article 11 to cases where individuals have been subject to a detriment by their employer for taking part in industrial action (against which there is no statutory protection in this country – see Chapter 9). The Court has held that national law permitting the imposition of a detriment for exercising the right to strike is an impermissible impediment and amounts to an unjustified breach of Article 11(1). (See, for example, Danilenkov v Russia (Application No.67336/01), ECtHR, where the detriment involved the assignment of less work, resulting in reduced income, and discriminatory selection for redundancy; and Kaya and Seyhan v Turkey (Application No.30946/04), ECtHR, where the detriment took the form of a written disciplinary warning 'to be more attentive to the accomplishment of his/her functions and in his/her behaviour'.)

The question of whether the complex balloting and notice provisions contained **1.12** in Part V of the TULR(C)A amount to an unlawful restriction on unions' and their members' rights under Article 11 has recently arisen in Metrobus Ltd v Unite the Union 2010 ICR 173, CA, where the Court of Appeal was concerned with possible breaches by the union of the balloting and notice requirements. As part of its defence, Unite argued that the restrictions imposed on it by the TULR(C)A presented obstacles so numerous and complex that errors on its part were almost inevitable, and that for this reason its rights under Article 11 in relation to taking industrial action were so constrained that they could not be effectively exercised. The Court rejected this argument, holding that, although the statutory requirements are detailed, they are not so onerous as to make the exercise of the right to freedom of association contained in Article 11 so restricted as to be disproportionate. The rules were of a type permitted under Article 11(2), which allows for restrictions on the exercise of the right, and fell within the United Kingdom's 'margin of appreciation'.

British Airways plc v Unite the Union 2009 EWHC 3541, QBD, also concerned breaches of the balloting and notice requirements. In that case the High Court granted an interim injunction preventing the union from proceeding with strike action despite support from more than 90 per cent of those who had voted (which constituted 80 per cent of union members). The Court held that the union had failed to comply with the balloting and notice requirements because it had included a number of members who had taken voluntary redundancy and consequently would have left the company before the strike actually took place. In reaching her decision, Mrs Justice Cox acknowledged the United Kingdom's international obligations contained in a number of instruments, including ILO Convention No.87 on the Freedom of Association and Protection of the Right to Organise, and commented that 'sooner or later, the extent to which the current statutory regime is in compliance with those international obligations and with relevant international jurisprudence will fall to be carefully reconsidered'.

That said, it seems unlikely that the UK Government will grant a positive right to strike under domestic law unless it is forced to do so – as it was in relation to protection for employees penalised for failing to give up their trade union rights. That issue came before the ECtHR in the combined cases of Wilson and anor v United Kingdom; Palmer and ors v United Kingdom; Doolan and ors v United Kingdom 2002 IRLR 568, ECtHR, where the employers had offered additional pay increases to employees who agreed to accept individual contracts in place of collectively agreed terms and conditions. The ECtHR held that, by permitting employers to use financial incentives to induce employees to surrender important union rights, the UK Government had failed in its positive obligation to secure the enjoyment of rights under Article 11. That failure was a violation of Article 11 in respect of both unions and individual applicants. This ruling led to new Ss.145A–145F being inserted into the TULR(C)A by the ERelA 04, prohibiting employers from inducing workers to give up their union membership or activities or their right to collective bargaining rights.

1.13 Scheme of the law

Industrial action can expose trade unions and their members to a variety of civil and – in the case of individuals – criminal legal proceedings. In addition, workers dismissed while taking part in industrial action may find that any protection from unfair dismissal is severely curtailed – see Chapter 8. Below we give a brief overview of how industrial action can be rendered unlawful, who is liable for such action, and the remedies available to persons affected by unlawful industrial action. We also look at the types of criminal offence that may be committed during industrial action.

Industrial action almost invariably involves the commission of one or more torts exposing the union and its members to civil legal liability if the action is not otherwise lawful. To determine whether industrial action is lawful, a three-stage inquiry is needed:

- does the industrial action involve the commission of a tort for which there would be liability at common law? (See Chapter 2)

- if there is liability at common law, does S.219 TULR(C)A confer immunity? (See Chapter 3.) S.219 confers immunity on certain acts done 'in contemplation or furtherance of a trade dispute' (the so-called 'golden formula'). The protected acts are the 'industrial torts' of procuring or inducing a breach of contract, causing loss by unlawful means (also known as unlawful interference or interfering with business by unlawful means), intimidation, or conspiracy to commit one of these torts. Torts such as trespass and nuisance are not protected. If S.219 does not apply, then the industrial action will be unlawful and legal remedies can be sought by employers and others. However, even if S.219 does on the face of it confer immunity, the organisers of industrial action will not automatically be in the clear. The next stage often determines liability

- does anything in the TULR(C)A remove S.219 immunity and restore liability at common law? (See Chapter 4.)

Immunity conferred by S.219 is lost where: 1.14

- a union has taken industrial action without the support of a valid ballot or without giving the employer due notice of industrial action (see Chapter 5)

- there is unlawful secondary action (see Chapter 4)

- action is taken in support of workers dismissed while taking part in unofficial industrial action (see Chapter 4)

- there is unlawful picketing (see Chapter 6)

- a union has taken industrial action to impose union-only labour clauses or union recognition (see Chapter 4)

- a union has taken industrial action to impose union membership (see Chapter 4).

If immunity is lost for any one of these reasons, then the industrial action will be unlawful.

Both unions and their members may be held legally responsible for unlawful industrial action. The vicarious liability of a union for the acts of its officials and members depends on which tort has been committed. Vicarious liability for the industrial torts turns on S.20 TULR(C)A, which specifies the circumstances in which a union will be held to have endorsed or authorised industrial action. In the case of any other tort, vicarious liability is determined according to common law principles. Vicarious liability is discussed in Chapter 2.

Once liability has been established, the most common and effective remedy   1.15
available to employers is an interim injunction to restrain industrial action from commencing or continuing (as this will bring an end to the industrial dispute for all practical purposes). Employers also have the option of bringing

civil proceedings for damages, although this is far less common. Trade union members may also seek an injunction against their union to restrain unlawful action that does not have the support of a ballot or is in breach of the union's rules. In addition, individual members of the public may in certain circumstances apply for an injunction to restrain unlawful industrial action. If the terms of an injunction are broken, individuals may be punished by an unlimited fine and/or imprisonment. Unions may be exposed to an unlimited fine and/or sequestration of assets. Remedies for unlawful action are considered in Chapter 7.

Industrial action almost invariably involves a breach of contract by the union members participating. Although employers could theoretically sue their workers for breach of contract, the most common sanction against individual employees is dismissal. Employers may also be entitled to withhold the wages of employees taking part in industrial action. Breach of contract is dealt with in Chapter 2, unfair dismissal is covered in Chapter 8, and the withholding of pay is discussed in Chapter 9.

Finally, employees participating in industrial action may also commit a number of criminal offences. These are most commonly committed during the course of picketing and include: public nuisance; obstruction of the highway; intimidation offences under S.241 TULR(C)A; and offences under the Public Order Act 1986 and the Criminal Justice and Public Order Act 1994. It should also be noted that a criminal offence will be committed if certain classes of employee take industrial action – for example, members of the armed forces. The criminal law operates independently of the civil law and the fact that a union member commits a criminal offence in connection with industrial action will not render that action unlawful for the purposes of any civil proceedings. Unions are not vicariously liable for criminal offences committed by their members. Criminal liability is considered in Chapters 2 and 6.

1.16 Industrial action

'Industrial action' is a generic term which describes a multitude of actions that can be taken by either employees or employers with the aim of pressuring the other party to concede or withdraw a demand made in an industrial context. The demand made will usually concern 'industrial matters' (i.e. matters going to the terms and conditions of employment) but can also be of a political or social nature. However, note that the immunities relating to industrial action mentioned above only apply to acts done 'in contemplation or furtherance of a trade dispute' and will not cover action taken purely for political purposes. Examples of industrial action range from extreme 'all-out' action such as strikes and lock-outs to lesser forms of action, including bans on compulsory or voluntary overtime, go-slows, work-to-rule campaigns and boycotts.

Although the term is used throughout the TULR(C)A, there is no statutory definition of 'industrial action'. In Seaboard World Airlines Inc v Transport and General Workers' Union and ors 1973 ICR 458, NIRC, Sir John Donaldson said that 'the forms of industrial action are limited only by the ingenuity of mankind'. That comment was in the context of the Industrial Relations Act 1971, which made 'irregular industrial action short of a strike' unlawful if it was in breach of contract, although strikes were lawful if appropriate notice was given. Sir John said that almost all forms of industrial pressure short of a strike fell within the definition of 'irregular industrial action' and, as a safe working rule, there was no alternative to either striking or doing the full job which employees were employed to do. Anything in between would constitute irregular industrial action short of a strike. Specific instances he gave were any concerted form of working without enthusiasm, taking prolonged tea breaks and even 'departures for the relief of natural pressures'. And in Midland Plastics v Till and ors 1983 ICR 118, EAT, a case concerning the industrial action dismissal provisions which were then contained in S.62 of the Employment Protection (Consolidation) Act 1978, the EAT said that the kinds of activity which might constitute 'other industrial action [short of a strike]' included go-slows, working to rule, overtime bans and picketing.

1.17 The Industrial Relations Act 1971 was repealed in 1974 and the TULR(C)A contains no equivalent provision making irregular industrial action short of a strike unlawful. However, Sir John Donaldson's statements in the Seaboard case are still applicable in so far as they provide a guide to what will amount to industrial action. Generally speaking, industrial action is action which is:

- taken in order to put pressure on an employer in an industrial context, and

- concerted.

Pressure on the employer

1.18 If employees decide in concert to knock off work early in order to go to the pub or to a football match, they are taking action which would probably be in breach of their contracts of employment, but it would not be 'industrial' action unless it is accompanied by some demand on the employer. However, the demand need not be limited to matters concerning the terms and conditions of the workforce in question; it could be a political or environmental demand, for example.

In Chapter 8 we discuss a number of cases concerning the definition of industrial action in the context of industrial action dismissals. The dismissal provisions are contained in Part V of the TULR(C)A and cases on their interpretation have relevance to the collective industrial action provisions, also contained in Part V. In the unfair dismissal context there have been a number of cases on the meaning of 'intention' for industrial action purposes, and tribunals have placed emphasis on the need for employees to have the intention of applying pressure on the employer or of disrupting the business. Thus, depending on the

11

employees' intentions, a refusal to do non-contractual overtime may not be industrial action – Butterworth and anor v FA Gill Ltd COET 1854/141; similarly, the organisation of a deputation to discuss grievances with management may fall outside the term – Singh and ors v Pennine Fur Fabrics Ltd ET Case No.15418/85.

1.19 **Concerted action**
It used to be assumed that action taken by an individual employee could not be classified as industrial action – see, for example, Bowater Containers Ltd v Blake EAT 552/81. However, in Lewis and Britton v E Mason and Sons 1994 IRLR 4, EAT, the EAT upheld a tribunal's decision that, for the purposes of the industrial action dismissal provisions of Part V of the TULR(C)A, a single employee acting alone could be involved in industrial action. The EAT justified this decision by saying that whether or not there was industrial action was a question of fact for the tribunal to decide; that in order to constitute industrial action there 'must be conduct designed to coerce the employer to improve the terms and conditions of employment'; and that on the facts the tribunal was entitled to make the finding that it did. This decision is, however, undermined somewhat by the EAT's failure to refer to any authorities in deciding whether industrial action requires some form of concerted behaviour by more than one employee, and is of dubious precedential value. Furthermore, the fact that the industrial action dismissal provisions are found in Part V of the TULR(C)A, where the definition of 'strike' expressly requires a concerted stoppage of work, arguably supports the view that industrial action generally implies some form of action by employees in concert.

Industrial action does not necessarily have to involve a breach of the employment contracts of the individual employees taking part, although in the majority of cases it will do so. Similarly, the fact that there has been a breach of individual employment contracts is not of itself a defining characteristic of industrial action – Glenrose (Fish Merchants) Ltd v Chapman and ors EAT 245/89. What matters is whether the action in question is taken by employees acting in concert with the aim of putting pressure on the employer to concede a demand made by the employees. This is made plain in the following case:

• **Power Packing Casemakers Ltd v Faust and ors** 1983 ICR 292, CA: F and two other employees were dismissed for refusing to work non-contractual overtime. The question arose as to whether this constituted 'industrial action': if it was industrial action, the tribunal would have no jurisdiction to hear their claims for unfair dismissal. In dismissing the employees' appeals on this point, the Court of Appeal held that there was no requirement that there had to be a breach of the individual employees' contracts of employment in order for industrial action to have taken place.

Important questions can arise, particularly in the context of the unfair dismissal **1.20** provisions, as to the timing of industrial action. When, for example, does a threat to take industrial action become industrial action, so that the unfair dismissal provisions apply? This controversial issue is dealt with in detail in Chapter 8. There are also several issues concerning the timing of industrial action for the purposes of the balloting provisions; these are considered in Chapter 5. For the other collective industrial action provisions in Part V, particularly S.219, which confers immunity on trade unions for certain types of action, it is sufficient to note here that the tort of intimidation is committed when industrial action is threatened. However, this tort is expressly covered by the S.219 immunities. Intimidation is considered in Chapter 2 under 'The industrial torts'.

Strikes
1.21

There is generally little need to distinguish between a strike and other forms of industrial action. The statutory provisions relating to the trade union immunities and to industrial action dismissals apply equally to both. The distinction is important, however, for the purposes of the balloting provisions, since when balloting its members a trade union must obtain separate approval for strike action and for industrial action short of a strike – S.229(2) TULR(C)A (see Chapter 5 for further details). The distinction between a strike and other forms of industrial action is also important for the purposes of calculating continuity of employment under S.216 of the Employment Relations Act 1996 (ERA), which provides that any week in which an employee was participating in a strike shall not count for the purposes of continuity (see Chapter 9 for details). Finally, the distinction can be important outside the context of the statutory framework – for example, when the provisions of a collective agreement give one of the parties certain rights in the event of a strike.

The term 'strike' can have different meanings for different purposes. A general definition was provided in Tramp Shipping Corp v Greenwich Marine Inc 1975 ICR 261, CA, a case which concerned the meaning of 'strike' for the purposes of a clause in a shipping charterparty. The facts were that dock workers refused to work a 24-hour day in three shifts, and worked a single eight-hour shift each day instead. The Court of Appeal held that this was a strike, although the periods of absence from work were discontinuous and the dock workers, apparently, were not in breach of contract. Lord Denning MR noted the paucity of guidance as to the meaning of the term 'strike', and then proceeded to define it as follows: '[A] strike is a concerted stoppage of work by men done with a view to improving their wages or conditions, or giving vent to a grievance or making a protest about something or other, or supporting or sympathising with other workmen in such endeavour. It is distinct from a stoppage which is brought about by an external event such as a bomb scare or by apprehension

13

of danger.' Lord Justice Stephenson, in the same case, agreed with these comments, saying that a strike 'must be a stoppage intended to achieve something or to call attention to something... a rise in wages, improvement of conditions, support for other workers or for political changes; an expression of sympathy or protest'. (Note, however, that secondary action is now unlawful under S.224 TULR(C)A – see Chapter 4.)

1.22 Similarly, in Anderson and ors v British Coal Corporation, unreported 28.1.93, QBD, the High Court held that, for the purposes of a guaranteed wage provision in a collective agreement, a ban on compulsory overtime was a 'strike'. In support of this conclusion the Court referred to Lord Denning's definition in the Tramp Shipping case, and to Stephenson LJ's statement that, in order to constitute a strike, a stoppage need only be of a few hours' duration provided it was concerted.

1.23 ## Industrial action short of a strike
For the purposes of Part V of the TULR(C)A, which contains the provisions conferring immunity on trade unions for acts done in contemplation or furtherance of a trade dispute (see Chapter 3), the balloting provisions and the industrial action dismissal provisions, 'strike' means 'any concerted stoppage of work' – S.246. In the context of Part V, 'strike' must be distinguished from less extreme forms of industrial action, otherwise the phrase 'industrial action short of a strike' would be rendered otiose.

The S.246 definition of a 'strike' was considered by the Court of Appeal in Connex South Eastern Ltd v National Union of Rail, Maritime and Transport Workers 1999 IRLR 249, CA. In that case the RMT balloted train conductors on taking industrial action in the form of a ban on overtime and rest-day working. The ballot-paper asked the conductors to vote 'Yes' or 'No' to strike action, making no mention of industrial action short of a strike. Having obtained a majority 'Yes' vote, the RMT then gave the employer notice of the proposed action. The employer alleged that the action planned was, in fact, industrial action short of a strike, for which the union had no lawful mandate. The Court of Appeal referred to the decisions in Tramp Shipping and Anderson (above) and held that the definition of a 'strike' in S.246 as 'any concerted stoppage of work' was broad enough to cover any mutually planned refusal to work, including a ban on overtime and rest-day working. It followed that the union had asked its members the correct question in the ballot.

1.24 Arguably, the effect of the Connex decision was that only those forms of industrial action which do not actually involve any stoppage of work, such as a withdrawal of goodwill, a go-slow or a work-to-rule, would fall outside the S.246 definition of a 'strike'. Although the union in the Connex case benefited from a wide definition of the term 'strike', in many cases it would be the unions that had the most to fear from the decision. This is because it is generally easier

14

to obtain a vote in favour of action short of a strike than strike action. In any event, the Connex decision was reversed by statute in so far as it relates to the definition of a 'strike' for balloting purposes. A new S.229(2A) TULR(C)A, inserted by ERelA 1999, provides that for the purposes of framing the question on the ballot-paper under S.229(2), an overtime ban and a call-out ban both constitute 'industrial action short of a strike'. A similar amendment was made to the definition of strike in S.246, providing that a strike 'means (except for the purposes of S.229(2)) any concerted stoppage of work'. However, the wide definition of a strike in S.246 TULR(C)A as 'any concerted stoppage of work' remains unchanged, with the result that other forms of limited industrial action involving a stoppage of work – including, oddly, bans on rest-day working – presumably still constitute strike action for balloting purposes. Furthermore, the amendments apply only in relation to the balloting provisions. Presumably, the broad definition of a 'strike' adopted in the Connex case will still be relevant in relation to the provisions on trade union immunity and industrial action dismissals. As noted above, however, these provisions apply whether the action in question is an all-out strike or some other form of industrial action, so in practice it will probably be unnecessary to make the distinction.

An additional requirement, derived from the cases on industrial action dismissals, is that the action is taken with the purpose of disrupting the employer's business. In Rasool and ors v Hepworth Pipe Co Ltd 1980 ICR 494, EAT, for example, the EAT held that a one-hour meeting held in working time without the employer's consent was not a 'strike or other industrial action' for the purposes of S.238 TULR(C)A because it was held for trade union reasons rather than to disrupt the employer's business.

1.25 A narrower definition of 'strike' than that found in S.246 TULR(C)A can be found in S.235(5) ERA. This states, in effect, that a strike is a concerted stoppage of work done as a means of compelling an employer to accept or not to accept terms or conditions of or affecting employment. This would exclude political and sympathy strikes. However, the Court of Appeal in Express and Star Ltd v Bunday and ors 1988 ICR 379, CA, confirmed that this definition is not of general application and is limited to the statutory provisions that deal with the effect of strike action on the computation of periods of continuous employment – a subject that is dealt with in detail in Chapter 9.

2 Liability for industrial action

Union liability in tort

Breach of contract

The industrial torts

Criminal liability

In this chapter we consider the extent to which unions, union officials and **2.1** individual employees are liable in civil and criminal law for acts committed during the course of industrial action. We begin by examining the statutory and common law principles whereby unions are held to be legally responsible for the tortious acts of their members. Then we consider in detail the three main forms of legal liability that individual employees, union officials and unions may incur through taking industrial action: namely, liability for breach of contract, the 'industrial' torts and criminal acts.

Examples of torts that may be committed by union officials include the tort of inducing breach of contract when they induce members to take strike action in breach of the members' employment contracts. And individual employees often commit torts during picketing; for example, trespass. Even where a union is liable for such tortious acts under the statutory or common law principles of vicarious liability discussed below, the individual union officials and members who actually committed the torts in question are not absolved from liability to legal proceedings. However, for reasons explained in Chapter 7, an employer or third party affected by a tort will generally proceed against the union concerned.

Union liability in tort   2.2

In almost every situation involving industrial action the organisers of such action commit one or more tortious acts. The principles that determine the liability of trade unions for torts committed by union members organising or taking part in industrial action will vary according to the tort in question. Liability for the main 'industrial' torts is covered by S.20 of the Trade Union and Labour Relations (Consolidation) Act 1992 (TULR(C)A). These torts, which are discussed at length later in this chapter, are:

• inducing breach of contract

• interfering with, or inducing interference with, the performance of a contract

17

- threatening that a contract will be breached or its performance interfered with, or threatening that the union will induce another person to breach a contract or interfere with its performance

- conspiracy to commit or procure one of the above torts – S.20(1).

If one of these torts is committed, the union may be able to claim immunity from legal proceedings if it can bring itself within the protection provided by the statutory immunities – see Chapter 3 for further details. Liability for other torts is governed by common law principles on vicarious liability. Examples of such torts include interference with trade or business, defamation, trespass, and public and private nuisance. The last three torts are often committed in the course of picketing.

2.3 Liability under statute

Section 20 makes trade unions legally responsible for industrial torts that have been authorised or endorsed by the union. Under this provision, an act is taken to be authorised or endorsed by a union if it was done, authorised or endorsed:

- by any person empowered by the rules of the union to do, authorise or endorse such an act, or

- by the principal executive committee (PEC), president or general secretary, or

- by any other committee of the union or any other official of the union (whether employed by it or not) – S.20(2).

In order to determine whether a particular individual (such as a branch officer) is empowered to authorise or endorse certain acts (the first category of persons referred to above) it is necessary to consider the union's rules. But acts done by the second and third category of persons will render the union liable to legal action notwithstanding any provision to the contrary in the union's rules or in any contract or rule of law – S.20(4). Acts done by the third category of persons may be repudiated by the union, however, with the result that the union is not legally responsible for any industrial torts which have been committed by these persons. (Repudiation is discussed below.)

2.4 In relation to the third category in S.20(2), 'committee of the union' is defined in S.20(3) as 'any group of persons constituted in accordance with the rules of the union'. The same subsection goes on to provide that 'an act shall be taken to have been done, authorised or endorsed by an official if it was done, authorised or endorsed by, or by any member of, any group of persons of which he was at the material time a member, the purposes of which included organising or co-ordinating industrial action'. For this purpose a 'group of persons' need not be a committee constituted in accordance with the union's rules: it may be a wholly unofficial strike committee. 'Official' is defined in

S.119 as '(a) an officer of the union or of a branch or section of the union, or (b) a person elected or appointed in accordance with the rules of the union to be a representative of its members or of some of them, and includes a person so elected or appointed who is an employee of the same employer as the members or one or more of the members whom he is to represent' (e.g. a shop steward).

Section 20(7) defines 'rules' in relation to a trade union as the 'written rules of the union and any other written provision forming part of the contract between a member and the other members'. In British Railways Board v National Union of Rail, Maritime and Transport Workers, unreported 17.9.92, QBD, the High Court had to determine whether members of a 'Local Departmental Committee' were officials of the union. The Court looked at the union rules and decided that the men in question were not elected to any office in accordance with the rules of the union; their election as committee members had been carried out in accordance with the terms of a collective agreement, which was not incorporated into the union rule book. Furthermore, the men's function was to represent staff members, including non-union members. Even if they had been appointed to the committee within the terms of the union's rules, the men were not, in any event, within the definition of 'official' since they were not elected or appointed to be representatives of members of the RMT, as required by S.119.

It follows from these provisions that if a union official, e.g. a shop steward or **2.5** a lay person elected or appointed in accordance with the rules of the union, calls a strike or other industrial action, the union will be liable for any of the industrial torts listed in S.20(1). Similarly, if any member of a group which includes a shop steward calls industrial action, the shop steward will be deemed to be responsible and the union will be liable for his or her deemed actions.

The union is liable notwithstanding anything in the rules of the union, or in any contract or rule of law – S.20(4). It makes no difference to the union's deemed liability that the unofficial industrial action was not authorised or was expressly forbidden by the union's rule book, or that the relevant official did not support the call for industrial action or was not even at the meeting at which the call for industrial action was made. In these circumstances, the union can only avoid liability by repudiating the action.

Repudiation   2.6

The act of a committee or official will not be regarded as having been authorised or endorsed by a union if it is repudiated by the PEC or the president or the general secretary of the union 'as soon as reasonably practicable after coming to the knowledge of any of them' – S.21(1). Repudiation requires the union to do three things:

• it must give written notice of the repudiation to the committee or shop steward 'without delay'

- it must 'do its best' to give individual written notice of the fact and the date of the repudiation – again 'without delay' – to every union member who it has reason to believe is participating, or might participate, in industrial action as a result of the act that is being repudiated, and

- it must give similar written notice to the employer of every such union member – S.21(2).

In addition, the notice of repudiation given to union members must contain the following statement:

'Your union has repudiated the call (or calls) for industrial action to which this notice relates and will give no support to unofficial industrial action taken in response to it (or them). If you are dismissed while taking unofficial industrial action, you will have no right to complain of unfair dismissal' – S.21(3).

2.7 A purported repudiation will be treated as ineffective if any of the above conditions is not complied with – S.21(4). In Balfour Kilpatrick Ltd v Acheson and ors 2003 IRLR 683, EAT, for example, the union sent written notice of repudiation to the employer and the shop steward which was then read out to the employees in the canteen and posted by the clocking station. The EAT upheld the tribunal's finding that the union had not 'done its best' to give written notice to each individual and that the industrial action had therefore not been repudiated. The official could have attended the site and given out individual notices; alternatively, the shop steward could have been instructed to photocopy the letter and hand it out to individual employees.

Even if the union does comply with all the above conditions, the repudiation may still be ineffective or it may subsequently be rendered ineffective. First, a repudiation will be ineffective if the PEC or president or general secretary of the union behaves in a manner which is inconsistent with the purported repudiation – S.21(5). Thus, a written repudiation will be ineffective if it is accompanied by oral encouragement. Secondly, an act will not be treated as repudiated by the PEC, president or general secretary if they do not forthwith confirm that repudiation in writing after a request made to them by a person who is a party to a commercial contract that has been, or may be, interfered with as a result of the act in question and who has not already been given written notice by the union of the repudiation. The request must be made within three months of the purported repudiation – S.21(6).

2.8 Finally, S.20(6) gives a court hearing injunction (or, in Scotland, interdict) proceedings against a union concerning industrial action for which the union is deemed to be liable by virtue of S.20 the power to order the union to take such steps as the court considers appropriate in order to ensure:

- that there is no, or no further, inducement of persons to take part or to continue to take part in industrial action, and

- that no person engages in any conduct after the granting of the injunction because he or she was induced to take part or continue to take part in industrial action before the injunction was granted.

The court could presumably order the union to take disciplinary action – e.g. by withdrawing the credentials of shop stewards – against those who carry on with the industrial action.

Endorsement of unofficial action 2.9

A union may well sympathise with unofficial industrial action and wish to endorse it by holding a ballot and turning it into official action supported by a ballot. However, this is prohibited by the TULR(C)A. If there is unofficial action which is not repudiated, it will be deemed to have been called by the union. But the action will not have the support of a ballot so that the union will have no immunity in tort.

The union cannot legitimise the action by holding a ballot because S.233 provides that action shall not be regarded as having the support of a ballot if the action to which the ballot relates has been called, authorised or endorsed by the union *before* the date of the ballot. Unrepudiated unofficial action will be deemed to have been called by the union so that a subsequent ballot will be ineffective. Nor can the union repudiate the action and then call a ballot relating to the same dispute. A repudiation is ineffective if the subsequent behaviour of the union is inconsistent with the purported repudiation. It would seem to be inconsistent with repudiation of industrial action to follow it up with a ballot asking members if they support similar industrial action. The upshot is that a union must either repudiate unofficial action or incur liability in tort.

Note that one important effect of a union repudiating action is that it completely 2.10 removes an employee's right to complain of unfair dismissal if at the time of dismissal he or she was taking part in unofficial strike or other industrial action (see Chapter 8 for details).

Liability under common law 2.11

For torts other than the industrial torts listed in S.20(1), union liability will depend on the common law principles governing vicarious liability. A union will be liable for torts committed by union officials, employees and other persons acting within its express or implied authority. In Heatons Transport (St Helens) Ltd v Transport and General Workers' Union 1972 ICR 308, HL, the House of Lords held that the union was liable for the tortious acts of shop stewards who organised industrial action – the shop stewards had a general implied authority to act in the interests of the members they represented and, in particular, to defend and improve rates of pay and working conditions.

21

Their Lordships concluded that the union had not taken enough steps to stop the industrial action: the union should have unequivocally withdrawn the shop stewards' authority or taken disciplinary action.

In News Group Newspapers Ltd and ors v Society of Graphical and Allied Trades '82 and ors (No.2) 1987 ICR 181, QBD – a case in which pickets committed the tort of nuisance – the High Court held that a union is not vicariously liable simply because it organises a march or picketing during the course of which tortious acts are committed by third parties, even though such acts could have been foreseen. However, the Court added that a union may be taken to have authorised the commission of a nuisance or other torts or to have continued the nuisance, where the union continues to organise events, which in the light of experience amount to a nuisance or other torts and in the knowledge or presumed knowledge that such nuisance or torts are being committed by those whom it organises. This is the case notwithstanding the fact that the union might condemn the tortious conduct.

2.12 The Court went on to hold that if a union can control the event and the conduct of those taking part, but fails to take any, or any adequate, steps to do so, it is likely that a court will find the union to be vicariously liable for the acts of its representatives. In this particular case the Court held that the conduct of the pickets had been the same since the start of the dispute and it was clear that those who organised the pickets must have been aware of their conduct. The union could exercise substantial control over its members but there was no evidence that the use of disciplinary powers had ever been threatened, let alone used, against those who stepped out of line. There was therefore a strong arguable case that the union had authorised or continued the nuisance involved.

Both of these cases appear to place a heavy onus on unions to control the activities of their members – possibly through appropriate disciplinary action – so as to avoid incurring liability in tort. However, courts will have regard to all the circumstances and each case will turn on its facts.

2.13 Breach of contract

An all-out strike will almost certainly be a repudiatory breach of the striker's employment contract – Simmons v Hoover Ltd 1977 ICR 61, EAT. As such it will amount to gross misconduct entitling the employer to dismiss the striking employee summarily (i.e. without notice) – see Chapter 8 for an explanation of the law on industrial action dismissals. Industrial action short of a strike will also involve a breach of the worker's employment contract in the vast majority of cases and may, in some circumstances, amount to gross misconduct if the breach is serious enough.

Exceptions
2.14

There are two possible exceptions to the general rule that a strike will involve a breach of contract. First, in rare cases, there may be no actual breach – for example, if the action consists of a refusal to work overtime where there is no contractual obligation to do so. However, in such cases there may be a breach of the implied contractual term to render faithful and loyal service to the employer if there is a long-standing practice of working at weekends and this is essential for the efficient functioning of the employer's business.

The second exception is if all workers involved give due contractual notice to terminate their contracts of employment and the industrial action commences upon the expiry of that notice. In such cases, the withdrawal of labour will not involve a breach of contract since the contracts will already be terminated at the time the action begins. If the employees' trade union purports to give notice of termination on their behalf, then the union will need to make sure that it has the express authority (preferably in writing) of the employees to do so – otherwise the notices will be ineffective.
2.15

These exceptions are discussed in greater detail below.

Implied terms. As stated above, most forms of industrial action that fall short of an all-out strike will entail a breach of individual employees' contracts of employment. Indeed, action that does not involve a breach of contract is unlikely to be effective action in the context of an industrial dispute – the whole purpose of industrial action is to put pressure on the employer to concede an industrial demand, and such pressure is best achieved by the employees' refusal to carry out the whole or part of their normal contractual duties. However, one form of industrial action that can prove effective entails employees sticking rigidly to the express terms of their contract; for example, by refusing to work overtime or adhering strictly to workplace rules. In such circumstances, the question arises: does this action entail a breach of any implied terms in the contract of employment?
2.16

The starting point is the Court of Appeal's decision in Secretary of State for Employment v ASLEF and ors (No.2) 1972 ICR 19, CA. There, the union instructed its members to 'work to rule' and to ban overtime, rest day and Sunday working. Following this instruction, the employees worked meticulously in accordance with a literal interpretation of British Rail's rule book. The industrial action had the intended consequence of causing chaos on the rail network. The union argued that the action did not entail a breach of contract because its members were simply complying with the rules set out in the rule book. However, the Court of Appeal held that, although the action did not breach an express contractual term, the entire course of the employees' conduct had to be viewed as a whole. In so viewing the conduct, all three judges in the Court concluded that the employees had breached an implied term in their contracts.

23

2.17 Although the judges in the ASLEF case were agreed that the employees' conduct was in breach of an implied contractual obligation, the three judgments explain the nature of this implied obligation rather differently. Lord Denning MR, considering the employees' motive to be pivotal, held that an employee must not wilfully obstruct his or her employer's business; Lord Justice Buckley held that there was an implied term that an employee would serve an employer faithfully within the requirements of the contract; while Lord Justice Roskill held that an employee must not obey lawful instructions in an unreasonable way if the result was the disruption of the system in which he or she was employed. However, while the terminology may differ, all three of these implied terms can be viewed as establishing a duty of cooperation on the part of the employee.

In the later case of British Telecommunications plc v Ticehurst and anor 1992 ICR 383, CA, T, a union official and manager with BT, had taken part in a campaign of withdrawal of goodwill, non-cooperation and two one-day strikes. When she presented herself for work after the strikes, BT asked her to sign a declaration that she would undertake to work normally in accordance with the terms of her contract, and would take no further part in the industrial action. When she refused to sign the declaration, T was sent home. This happened for a number of days until the dispute was settled. T's claim for wages deducted by BT in respect of the days on which she was sent home was upheld by the High Court. However, the Court of Appeal held that BT had been entitled to deduct the wages and its appeal would be allowed. Pivotal to this decision was the finding that T had breached the implied obligation to serve her employer faithfully within the requirements of the contract – the formula adopted by Buckley LJ in ASLEF.

In the Ticehurst case the Court of Appeal placed emphasis on the fact that T occupied a managerial position and this arguably heightened the nature of her implied duty of faithfulness and cooperation. It is settled law that the nature of the implied duty varies according to the position held by the employee, and it could therefore be argued that the decision in that case depended to some extent on its particular facts and that the duty to serve the employer faithfully within the terms of the contract may be less onerous in the case of non-managerial employees. The Court of Appeal also specifically rejected T's argument that industrial action had to be effective for a breach of contract to have occurred. According to Lord Justice Ralph Gibson, the breach of the implied term occurred when the employee did an act, which was discretionary in contractual terms, 'not in honest exercise of choice or discretion for the faithful performance of her work but in order to disrupt the employer's business or to cause the most inconvenience that can be caused'.

2.18 Arguably, the effect of the ASLEF and Ticehurst cases is that industrial action, even if it consists of rigid adherence to the express terms of the contract of employment, will almost always constitute a breach of the implied duty of cooperation. However, a Privy Council decision in a Bermudan case – Burgess and ors v Stevedoring Services Ltd 2002 IRLR 810, PC – suggests that simply refusing to work non-obligatory overtime may not be a breach of the duty of cooperation, even where the refusal is motivated by an industrial dispute. The key factor in that case was that the individual employees were not contractually obliged to accept any overtime. In their Lordships' opinion, implied duties of cooperation and faithfulness do not require employees to do anything outside the terms of the contract, and contrary to the view of Lord Denning MR (but not the other members of the Court) in ASLEF, it is not necessary to examine an employee's motive for refusing to do something which is outside the contract of employment. Although, as a Privy Council decision, Burgess is merely of persuasive authority, the fact that the decision concerns the application of common law principles should mean that it is highly persuasive.

Action on expiry of notice. In Boxfoldia Ltd v National Graphical Association **2.19** (1982) 1988 ICR 752, QBD, the union gave the employer 14 days' notice that its members would withdraw their labour. The union's members duly went on strike, no ballot having been held. The employer sued the union for inducing breaches of employment contracts. The union denied that there had been any breaches of contract and claimed that it had given due notice of termination of its members' contracts. Mr Justice Saville stated that there was no rule that a strike notice must be construed as notice of breach of contract rather than notice of termination. On the facts, however, the union had no authority to act as its members' agents to terminate their contracts and, in any case, the wording of the union's letter to the employer could only be construed as giving 14 days' notice of an official strike. Accordingly, if a union and its members wish to pursue this route the form in which the strike notice is given is crucial: the union must expressly state that it is giving lawful notice of termination of the employees' contracts of employment on their behalf.

In practice, it is very rare that employees and unions take the drastic step of terminating the employees' contracts of employment. It is a tactical move that a union might encourage its members to take only if the union was very confident that the employer would cave in to its demands and re-employ the employees.

Legal consequences
2.20

The law confers no statutory immunity for breach of contract. Statutory immunity is confined to actions in tort – and breach of contract is not a tort (although inducing a breach of contract is a tort and the one most commonly committed when a strike or other industrial action is called – see below). If breaches of contract are committed, the employer is free to sue for damages for breach of contract. In practice, however, this is not a particularly attractive option.

25

First, it is unlikely that there will be any claim against a union for breach of contract. This is for the simple reason that the employer will almost certainly have no contract with the union since collective agreements virtually never take the form of legally binding contracts, but instead are expressed as being binding in honour only. Indeed, collective agreements are conclusively presumed *not* to be intended to be legally enforceable unless they state the contrary in writing – S.179 TULR(C)A.

2.21 Secondly, civil actions for breach of contract against individual employees are fraught with practical difficulties and unlikely to be rewarding. The employer would have to identify the individuals concerned and, more difficult, quantify the financial loss sustained from each individual breach. If this is large – as where a few key workers close down a factory – damages are likely to be irrecoverable. Bankrupting employees will not be conducive to good industrial relations. In practice, therefore, civil action is hardly ever taken against individual employees in the context of industrial action, the employer's remedy, if any, being against the union involved by way of an action in tort. (It should be noted, though, that the employer will be entitled to withhold the wages of employees taking part in industrial action – see Chapter 9 under 'Pay'.)

Note that S.236 TULR(C)A prohibits the courts from compelling an employee to work by ordering specific performance of the employment contract or by granting an injunction to restrain the breach of contract.

2.22 The industrial torts

The 'industrial torts' are those that most commonly occur during industrial action. They are not statutorily defined but have developed through case law. These torts are often referred to as the 'economic torts' because effective industrial action has a significant financial impact on an employer's business. However, the label 'economic torts' can refer to a wider range of torts than those which occur during industrial action and for this reason we have used the term 'industrial torts' throughout this chapter to avoid any confusion. It should also be noted that industrial action may involve the commission of the 'non-economic' torts of trespass and nuisance. These are discussed in Chapter 6.

The industrial torts represent a difficult area of the law, not least because they have developed in a piecemeal fashion in the context of interim injunction proceedings where the employer need only establish that there is 'a serious issue to be tried' rather than prove the case on the balance of probabilities – the civil standard of proof at full trial. Owing to the nature of industrial action, an interim injunction will frequently bring about the end of the dispute and consequently few cases actually proceed to full trial. As a result there has, until recently, been little detailed judicial analysis of the principles and reasoning underpinning the industrial torts. (Injunctions and other remedies are discussed in detail in Chapter 7.)

The industrial torts do not enjoy any special status in the common law and the **2.23** principles that inform tort liability for industrial action have often been developed in cases concerned with a completely different area of law whose facts do not touch on industrial action. One example of this can be found in the important House of Lords decisions in OBG Ltd and ors v Allan and ors and other cases 2007 IRLR 608, HL, which were concerned with, among other things, insolvency proceedings and intellectual property rights.

Rejection of the unified theory **2.24**
It is now impossible to discuss the industrial torts without considering the judgments of the House of Lords in OBG Ltd v Allan. In that case, their Lordships considered three appeals in which the claimants alleged the commission of various economic torts, none of which concerned industrial action or trade unions. For present purposes, it is not necessary to examine the factual background to any of the appeals; what really matters is the extensive consideration given to the state of the economic torts in the speeches of Lord Hoffmann and Lord Nicholls.

Both opinions recognised that, in the years following the Court of Appeal judgment in DC Thomson and Co Ltd v Deakin and ors 1952 Ch 646, CA, there had been a blurring of the dividing line between the two most prominent of the industrial torts: procuring a breach of contract, otherwise known as the tort in Lumley v Gye 118 ER 749, Court of Queen's Bench; and causing loss by unlawful means, often called unlawful interference. From Deakin and the later case of Merkur Island Shipping Corporation v Laughton and ors 1983 ICR 490, HL, there developed a 'unified theory' of economic torts, which took the view that the tort of procuring a breach of contract was but one species of a more general tort of actionable interference with contractual relations. Influenced by this unified theory, the courts – usually in the context of interim proceedings – identified a number of species of economic and industrial torts: direct inducement or procurement of breach of contract; indirect inducement or procurement of breach of contract by unlawful means; direct interference with contract; indirect interference with contract by unlawful means; and interference with business by unlawful means.

However, their Lordships in OBG Ltd v Allan rejected the unified theory of the **2.25** economic torts. Lord Hoffmann and Lord Nicholls were both opposed to the adoption of a unified theory, instead stressing that the tort in Lumley v Gye should be confined to procuring or inducing a breach of contract. Lord Walker, Lord Brown and Lady Hale were all in agreement on this point (although they did not agree on all points, as explained under 'Causing loss by unlawful means' below). The tort in Lumley v Gye is, their Lordships explained, distinct and

27

separate from the tort of causing loss by unlawful means and there is no 'middle ground' tort of interference with contract arising where there have been no unlawful means used and there is no breach of contract.

In the aftermath of the Allan decision, it seems that the industrial torts can be broadly identified as:

- procuring or inducing a breach of contract (the tort in Lumley v Gye)

- causing loss by unlawful means (also known as unlawful interference or interfering with business by unlawful means)

- intimidation

- conspiracy

- economic duress.

In previous editions of this Handbook we identified eight industrial torts, rather than just five. This reduction reflects the structure of the economic and industrial torts as identified by the House of Lords in OBG Ltd v Allan in that there are no longer distinct direct and indirect forms of the tort of inducing a breach of contract and the previously identified torts of direct interference with contract, indirect interference with contract by unlawful means, and interference with business by unlawful means can now be considered manifestations of the tort of causing loss by unlawful means. We discuss each of the above torts in turn below. However, before doing so, there are a number of preliminary matters to consider.

2.26 Statutory immunity

The statutory immunity granted by S.219 TULR(C)A only protects actions that give rise to liability for the torts of inducing breach of contract, interfering with the performance of a contract (a form of the tort of causing loss by unlawful means), intimidation, and conspiracy to commit one of these torts. Statutory immunity is dealt with in Chapter 3. Even if actions appear to be protected by statutory immunity, note that the 'claw-back' provisions contained in the Act may remove such immunity and restore liability at common law. These provisions are discussed at length in Chapters 4–6.

In most industrial action scenarios there will be no argument about whether a tort has been committed. The debate will normally centre on whether the action falls within the scope of the statutory immunities (see Chapter 3), whether the balloting and notice provisions have been complied with (see Chapter 5), or whether the action is rendered unlawful for some other reason (see Chapter 4). However, it remains important to understand the scope of the industrial torts and to be aware of their possible limitations and they are therefore discussed in detail below. First, however, it is helpful to consider the distinction between direct and indirect industrial action and the effect this has on the industrial torts.

Direct v indirect action

2.27

Direct action occurs when a union induces or exerts pressure on one of the parties to the contract of employment or commercial contract (or on the owner of the business affected by the dispute) directly. A (the union) induces B (the employee(s) or supplier) to break a contract with C (the target employer). The classic example of this is a primary strike. Direct action can be represented by the following diagram:

Diagram A

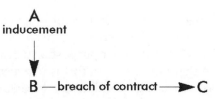

The hallmark of indirect action is that the union exerts pressure on one or both of the parties to a commercial contract, or on a company's business generally, via a third party (i.e. a person who is not a party to the contract). The classic scenario is secondary action aimed at the target employer: A (the union) induces B (the employees of the third party) to break their contracts of employment with C (the third party), the necessary consequence of which is that C's commercial contract with D (the target employer) is breached or otherwise interfered with. Indirect action can be represented by:

Diagram B

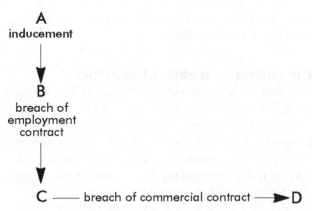

Prior to the decision in OBG Ltd and ors v Allan and other cases (above), the **2.28** question of whether allegedly tortious conduct was direct or indirect action could be of crucial importance. For example, the Court of Appeal in DC Thomson and Co Ltd v Deakin and ors 1952 Ch 646, CA, indicated that there was a tort of indirectly inducing or procuring a breach of contract, which, unlike the direct version of the tort, required that the breach was induced or procured by unlawful means. However, their Lordships in Allan disapproved of the distinction between directly and indirectly procuring or inducing a breach of contract. Lord Hoffmann was of the view that it should not make any difference 'whether there was communication, directly or through an agent, between the defendant and the contract-breaker'. He went on to say that focusing on such matters hides the real questions that a court must ask: 'did the defendant's acts of encouragement, threat, persuasion and so forth have a sufficient causal connection with the breach by the contracting party to attract accessory liability?'

So, as a result of Allan, it is no longer necessary to talk of indirect and direct versions of the industrial torts (although the distinction between direct and indirect action is still relevant for a number of other purposes, such as statutory immunity). Instead, the distinction that now exists in tort is between *accessory* liability – in the form of the tort of procuring or inducing a breach of contract – and *primary* liability, in the form of the tort of causing loss by unlawful means. The former tort can arise from either direct or indirect action, while the latter is likely to be of relevance – at least as far as industrial action is concerned – only where indirect action has taken place.

2.29 Defences to the industrial torts

Justification is theoretically available to unions as a defence to actions in tort but in practice this defence has virtually never succeeded. The only case in which it appears to have been raised with some success as a defence to legal action following a strike was in Brimelow v Casson 1924 1 Ch 302, ChD, where the union called a strike because its members (chorus girls) were so badly paid that they were forced to resort to prostitution to earn a living. Accordingly, we do not consider the defence further.

2.30 Procuring or inducing a breach of contract

Although, as identified earlier, the tort of procuring or inducing a breach of contract has its origins in the case of Lumley v Gye 118 ER 749, Court of Queen's Bench, the classic exposition of the tort is contained in the following passage from the speech of Lord Watson in Allen v Flood and anor 1898 AC 1, HL: 'He who wilfully induces another to do an unlawful act, which, but for his persuasion, would or might never have been committed, is rightly held to be responsible for the wrong which he procured.'

In the context of industrial action, this tort occurs when a trade union that is in dispute with an employer calls for its members who are employees of that employer to take strike or other industrial action – in other words, primary industrial action. By its call for action, the union is inducing those employees to break their contracts of employment to the detriment of the employer. This tort can also occur, albeit rarely, in the form of secondary action. For example, a tort will be committed if a union that is in dispute with an employer directly persuades or induces a third party to breach a supply or other commercial contract with that employer, knowing of the existence of that contract and with the intention of causing harm to the employer. (Subject to the exception of lawful picketing, secondary industrial action is rendered unlawful by S.224 – see Chapter 4. However, action of the kind described above may not be secondary action for the purposes of S.224 because the union may not have instructed its members who are employees of the third party to break their contracts of employment or threatened that those contracts of employment will be broken.)

In OBG Ltd and ors v Allan and ors and other cases 2007 IRLR 608, HL, Lord **2.31** Hoffmann described the tort as a form of 'accessory liability', which Lord Nicholls then referred to as 'secondary or supplemental to that of the third party who committed a breach of his contract'. Thus, it is an essential component of the tort that a breach of contract occurs. Earlier cases which suggested otherwise – most notably Torquay Hotel Co Ltd v Cousins and ors 1969 2 Ch 106, CA, and Merkur Island Shipping Corporation v Laughton and ors 1983 ICR 490, HL – can no longer be considered good law on this point. Mere interference with contract (as opposed to breach) will only be tortious if it can be shown that the interference was brought about by unlawful means – see 'Causing loss by unlawful means' below.

In the context of industrial action, an employer seeking to establish that a union or union official has committed the tort of inducing or procuring a breach of contract must show that:

- the union or the official had knowledge of the existence of the contracts of employment or commercial contract (although not necessarily of the precise terms of those contracts)

- the union or the official intended to persuade the employees or the third party to breach their contracts of employment or the commercial contract with the target employer

- the union or the official intended to cause loss to the target employer, and

- the target employer thereby suffered loss.

Civil Service cases. In the context of disputes in the Civil Service, the TULR(C) A **2.32** makes special provision to ensure that the tort of inducing or procuring a breach of contract will lie against action involving persons, such as 'office holders', who are not generally regarded as being employees in the usual sense. S.245 provides that where any person 'holds any office or employment under the Crown on terms which do not constitute a contract of employment... those terms shall... be deemed to constitute such a contract for the purposes of' the torts based upon inducing breach of, or interference with, a contract.

2.33 Inducement or procurement of breach. Claims made under this tort almost invariably involve *inducement* of breach. The distinction between 'inducement' and 'procurement' is that while inducement involves some choice on the part of the employees (or third party) in question in determining whether or not to breach their contracts, procurement occurs when the person who commits the breach had no choice in the matter but was compelled to breach his or her contract. This is more likely where the industrial action is indirect, though direct procurement would occur when a union forcibly prevented an employee or a third party from carrying out a contract by, for example, stealing tools, kidnapping an employee, or incapacitating a truck that was to be used to make deliveries.

In order to commit the tort of inducement of breach of contract, the union must have used words or actions which can be said to amount to an inducement. The mere provision of information, in the absence of any attempt to persuade someone that a particular course ought to be adopted, will not amount to inducement. For example, in DC Thomson and Co Ltd v Deakin and ors 1952 Ch 646, CA, the defendant officials of the union had informed the third party that its drivers (members of the union) might not be prepared to make deliveries to the target employer. The Court of Appeal held that this amounted to mere advice and not any 'pressure, persuasion or procuration' that would make the union liable in tort. However, the Court noted that in certain circumstances it would be obvious that the advice was intended to be acted upon and in those cases it would be equivalent to persuasion (i.e. inducement). Although the legal status of much of the Deakin decision is unclear following criticism by the House of Lords in OBG Ltd v Allan (see above), this aspect of the decision remains a valid example of the distinction between inducement and mere advice.

2.34 Knowledge and intention. In OBG Ltd v Allan Lord Hoffmann stated that: 'To be liable for inducing breach of contract, you must know that you are inducing a breach of contract. It is not enough that you know that you are procuring an act which, as a matter of law or construction of the contract, is a breach. You must actually realise that it will have this effect.' For a person to knowingly procure or induce a breach of contract, therefore, he or she must know that that contract exists. However, it is no defence for a defendant to assert that he or she did not know the exact terms of the contract: it is sufficient to show that he or she had enough knowledge to know that the result of his or her action would be to induce a breach – JT Stratford and Son Ltd v Lindley and anor 1965 AC 269, HL.

In industrial action cases, the knowledge requirement will generally be easy to satisfy since trade unions are likely to be aware of the employment contracts of their members, and through those members they are also likely to be aware of any commercial contracts a supplier has with the employer. In some cases, courts have been willing to hold that a union should be *deemed* to have knowledge of the existence of a contract where actual knowledge has not been proved. The classic statement of the law in this regard – subsequently endorsed by the House of Lords in the OBG Ltd v Allan case – came from Lord Denning MR in Emerald Construction Co Ltd v Lowthian 1966 1 WLR 691, CA:

'Even if they did not know the actual terms of the contract, but had the means of knowledge – which they deliberately disregarded – that would be enough. Like the man who turns a blind eye. So here, if the officers deliberately sought to get this contract terminated, heedless of its terms, regardless whether it was terminated by breach or not, they would do wrong. For it is unlawful for a third person to procure a breach of contract knowingly, or recklessly, indifferent whether it is a breach or not.'

2.35 The House of Lords in Allan recognised that the above standard set by Lord Denning is clearly consistent with the general legal principle that 'a conscious decision not to enquire into the existence of a fact is in many cases treated as equivalent to knowledge of that fact'. Lord Denning's standard is, however, unquestionably higher than that which applies in negligence or gross negligence, a fact which their Lordships demonstrated by reference to the well-known case of British Industrial Plastics Ltd and ors v Ferguson and ors 1940 1 All ER 479, HL. There, F made enquiry of patent agents as to D's legal entitlement to a secret process developed during his time with a previous employer and, on discovering that the process was patentable, mistakenly believed that the process must belong to D and no one else. The House of Lords upheld a judge's decision that F was not liable because of his honest but mistaken belief that inducing D to disclose the process did not entail a breach of contract. In Allan, Lord Hoffmann distinguished the facts of Ferguson – in which he considered that F 'negligently made the wrong enquiry' – from circumstances where a person deliberately abstains from enquiring as to any relevant legal obligations.

Establishing that a defendant should be held to have deemed knowledge of a contract is a difficult task, as the following case demonstrates:

- **TimePlan Education Group Ltd v National Union of Teachers** 1997 IRLR 457, CA: the NUT was in dispute with TimePlan, a teachers' supply agency, over the terms and conditions of teachers recruited from Australia and New Zealand and supplied by the agency. The NUT became aware that the New Zealand Education Institute (NZEI) was carrying advertisements for TimePlan in its fortnightly magazine and wrote informing it of the dispute and suggesting that it might consider it inappropriate to carry TimePlan advertising in the future. NZEI suspended the advertisements and TimePlan brought proceedings against the NUT, claiming that the union had unlawfully interfered with a continuing contract between NZEI and the agency for the publication of the agency's advertisements. The High Court upheld the claim but its decision was overturned on appeal by the Court of Appeal, which held that there was no evidence that the NUT knew

33

of the existence of a continuing contract between NZEI and the agency. At no time during its correspondence with NZEI was the NUT informed of any such contractual arrangement and, although it was a reasonable assumption that the agency would have paid for the advertisements that it had placed in NZEI's magazine in the past, there was no evidence that it had ever occurred to the NUT that there was a subsisting contract extending to future advertising. The Court did not accept that the NUT was under a duty to make enquiries as to whether there was a contract, or that the union had been reckless as to whether or not such a contract existed. Moreover, the mild language used by the NUT in its correspondence could not be naturally interpreted as showing any intention to persuade, procure or induce NZEI to break its contract with the agency.

Although knowledge and intention are closely linked and are often considered together, they are two distinct requirements. A union that has knowledge of the contracts of its members will not be liable in tort if it can establish that it did not *intend* to procure or induce a breach of contract. Furthermore, as explained by Lord Hoffmann in Allan, an intention to cause loss is not enough in itself to establish the tort, as it is possible to intend to cause loss without intending to procure a breach of contract. Conversely, it is possible to intend to procure a breach of contract without intending to cause loss – South Wales Miners Federation and ors v Glamorgan Coal Co Ltd 1905 AC 239, CA. In that case, a miners' union ordered its members – whose pay would vary according to the price of coal – to stop work for a day with the intention of preventing merchants bringing about a reduction in the price of coal. The fact that the action led to a higher price and therefore higher profits for the employer was held to be no defence to the tort of inducing the miners to break their contracts.

2.36 The restatement of the tort of procuring or inducing a breach of contract by the House of Lords in OBG Ltd and ors v Allan and ors and other cases 2007 IRLR 608, HL, raises question marks over some past decisions addressing the degree of intention that is necessary to establish the tort. Foremost among these is Metropolitan Borough of Solihull v National Union of Teachers 1985 IRLR 211, ChD. There, the NUT instructed its members to refuse to perform school meal duties. When sued for inducing breach of contract the NUT attempted to argue that, since the union genuinely (albeit mistakenly) believed school meal duties were not contractual, no tort had been committed because the tort required that the union knew that the conduct induced was in breach of contract. The High Court rejected this argument, holding that so long as the union knew of the relevant facts the tort was made out, despite the fact that the union may have been genuinely mistaken as to the legal effect of its actions. The High Court's decision does not, however, seem compatible with the judgment of Lord Hoffmann in Allan, which requires that a person actually realise that he or she is procuring a breach of contract. Thus, a union's genuine mistake as to the legal effect of its actions will, it seems, provide a defence to an allegation of inducement.

It is no defence for a union to state that its intention was to bring the employer to the negotiating table, and inducing members to breach their contracts was merely a means of achieving this intended goal. On the contrary, Allan makes it clear that a breach of contract will be intended where it is the means to an end or the end itself. However, their Lordships also endorsed the view that the claimant must have been 'targeted' by the inducement. Thus, if the breach of contract was neither a means nor an end but merely a foreseeable consequence, then it cannot be said to have been intended.

Procuring or inducing a breach of non-contractual obligations. As noted 2.37 above, the classic exposition of the tort in Lumley v Gye can be found in Allen v Flood 1898 AC 1, HL, where Lord Watson said: 'He who wilfully induces another to do *an unlawful act* which, but for his persuasion, would or might never have been committed, is rightly held to be responsible for the wrong which he procured' (our emphasis). It is clear from this statement that the scope of the tort is capable of extending to the inducement or procurement of a breach of *non-contractual obligations* and in recent years it has been found to include inducement of a breach of statutory duty or equitable obligation.

The existence of the tort of inducing a breach of statutory duty was confirmed by the Court of Appeal in Associated British Ports and ors v Transport and General Workers' Union 1989 ICR 557, CA and HL, a case concerning a breach of a statutory duty allegedly imposed on dock workers by the Dock Workers (Regulation of Employment) Order 1947 SI 1947/1189. However, this extension of the tort is limited by the requirement (also confirmed in the Associated British Ports case) that the statutory duty must be independently actionable at the suit of the claimant. In other words, it is not enough simply to point to a statutory duty which the employees taking the action have breached by that action; the breach of that duty must give the claimant employer or company an independent right of action.

In Wilson v Housing Corporation 1998 ICR 151, QBD, an employee of a 2.38 housing association sought to extrapolate from the tort of inducing a breach of statutory duty a further tort of inducing unfair dismissal. He brought proceedings against the Housing Corporation, a regulatory body, alleging that the Corporation had induced his employer to breach his employment contract. During the trial he applied to amend his statement of claim to add an allegation that the Corporation had induced his employer to commit an act of unfair dismissal. The High Court refused his application on the ground that there was no such tort as inducing unfair dismissal. It was one thing to recognise as a cause of action the inducing of a breach of statutory duty which was actionable in the courts. It was quite a different matter to recognise as a cause of action the inducing of a breach of statutory duty which was capable of redress only by

35

a specialist tribunal and subject to specialised and limited remedies and tightly defined time limits. The Court also pointed out that many people are employed in large organisations by subsidiary companies and that dismissals often occur as a result of a parent company's instructions. A tort of inducing unfair dismissal would open the door for employees in such a situation either to evade the unfair dismissal provisions of the Employment Rights Act 1996 altogether by suing the parent company or, as in the instant case, to recover compensation from the employer in the tribunal and then seek top-up damages from the alleged inducer of the breach.

In the context of industrial action, the tort of procuring or inducing a breach of statutory duty could, in limited circumstances, provide a means through which an employer could seek to prevent industrial action. This is because the statutory immunity in S.219 expressly refers to procuring or inducing a breach of contract, rather than a breach of another actionable obligation. So, if a union induced its members to take part in industrial action that breached an actionable statutory obligation, it would not enjoy immunity from suit under S.219 and would therefore be liable for the employer's losses. The principles that underpin statutory immunity are considered further in Chapter 3.

2.39 Causing loss by unlawful means

As explained above under 'Rejection of the unified theory', the House of Lords in OBG Ltd and ors v Allan and ors and other cases 2007 IRLR 608, HL, drew a sharp distinction between the tort of inducing a breach of contract, which it termed a form of accessory liability, and the tort of causing loss by unlawful means, which is a form of primary liability. It is to the latter tort that we now turn.

Over the years the tort has been variously identified as 'causing loss by unlawful means', 'unlawful interference with business', 'interference with trade' and 'interference with contract'. However, following Allan, these many torts are now to be viewed as but examples of the single tort of causing loss by unlawful means. Even in Allan, however, the terminology was inconsistent: Lord Hoffmann adopted the phrase 'causing loss by unlawful means' (which we use in this Handbook), while Lord Nicholls preferred 'interference with business by unlawful means'. However, it is clear from their Lordships' speeches that they were referring to the same tort, and that at its essence it has two elements:

- unlawful interference by A with the actions of a third party (B), in which the claimant (C) has an economic interest, and

- an intention on the part of A to cause loss to C.

2.40 Whereas the tort of inducing a breach of contract can be committed by a union through both direct and indirect industrial action, the tort of causing loss by unlawful means will only arise where the action is *indirect*. A classic example is the targeting of goods – the union (A), in dispute with company C, instructs union members employed by company B to refuse to handle or deal with goods belonging to company C, resulting in loss to C.

Interference with an economic interest. The terminology adopted in Allan – an 'economic interest' – is deliberately broad and can cover interference with a trade, business or contract. Although in many cases the interference will be with the performance of commercial or employment contracts, it should be noted that the tort of causing loss by unlawful means does not depend on a breach of contract, or even the existence of a contract between the claimant and the third party. A defendant can commit the tort simply by unlawfully interfering with a claimant's economic expectations. This is illustrated by the facts in Hadmor Productions Ltd and ors v Hamilton and anor 1982 ICR 114, HL. In that case, H Ltd, an independent producer of television programmes, had an understanding with Thames Television that H Ltd's programmes would be broadcast under licence. However, there was no contractual agreement between the two. The ACTT union instructed its members at Thames Television who were television technicians to refuse to broadcast H Ltd's programmes in order to protect jobs. The House of Lords held that, despite the lack of a contract between H Ltd and Thames Television, the union's actions interfered with H Ltd's commercial expectations and were, as such, an unlawful interference with its business. **2.41**

Unlawful means. In OBG Ltd and ors v Allan and ors and other cases 2007 IRLR 608, HL, the House of Lords was at pains to stress that mere interference with a claimant's economic interest, no matter how spiteful or ill-intentioned, will not found liability in tort. On the contrary, the tort of causing loss by unlawful means depends, as the name suggests, on the defendant having used some unlawful means against a third party in order to interfere with the claimant's interest and thereby cause loss. Regrettably, 'unlawful means' is an imprecise term and in Allan two distinct interpretations were put forward. **2.42**

The first, and wider, interpretation of 'unlawful means' encompasses 'all acts which a defendant is not permitted to do, whether by the civil law or the criminal law'. This view – first expressed by Lords Reid and Devlin in Rookes v Barnard 1964 AC 1129, HL – was endorsed by Lord Nicholls in Allan, albeit subject to the proviso that 'the function of the tort is to provide a remedy where the claimant is harmed through the *instrumentality* of a third party' (his emphasis).

However, Lord Nicholls' view was in the minority, as Lady Hale and Lord Brown concurred with Lord Hoffmann's statement that unlawful means 'consists of acts intended to cause loss to the claimant by interfering with the freedom of a third party in a way which is unlawful as against that third party and which is intended to cause loss to the claimant'. Lord Hoffmann went on to clarify that his interpretation of unlawful means excludes 'acts which may **2.43** be unlawful against a third party but which do not affect his freedom to deal with the claimant'.

The fifth and final Law Lord in Allan, Lord Walker, appeared to sit on the fence, taking the view that neither Lord Nicholls' nor Lord Hoffmann's opinions would be 'the last word on the subject'. He did, however, add that the 'control mechanism' – the means of preventing the reach of the tort extending too far – was to be found 'in the nature of the disruption caused, as between the third party and the claimant, by the defendant's wrong (and not in the closeness of the causal connection between the defendant's wrong and the claimant's loss)'. Lord Walker also cautioned against extending the ambit of unlawful means beyond the examples currently found in case law.

As Lord Hoffmann's interpretation of unlawful means had the support of a majority of the House of Lords, it is the approach courts are now bound to follow. It necessarily excludes two categories of unlawful act from the definition of the tort. The first category covers those acts that, although unlawful, are not actionable at the suit of the third party. This would include the oft-cited example of a courier business that harms the interests of a rival business by regularly breaking the speed limit in order to deliver parcels to a third party quicker than the rival business. Although the breach of the speed limit is unlawful under statute, the third party does not have a cause of action arising from that breach, and so the tort is not made out. Lord Hoffmann did, however, identify one instance where an unlawful act would not be actionable at the suit of the third party, but would still satisfy the definition of unlawful means. This is where the *only* reason for it not being actionable is that the third party has suffered no loss.

2.44 The second excluded category covers those acts which, although unlawful and actionable at the suit of the third party, do not affect the third party's freedom to deal with the claimant. To understand what Lord Hoffmann was getting at here, it is necessary to consider the pre-Allan case law. In RCA Corporation v Pollard 1983 Ch 135, CA, P had been selling bootleg Elvis Presley recordings, in violation of the rights of the estate of Elvis Presley under the Dramatic and Musical Performers' Protection Act 1958. However, RCA – Presley's record label – was unable to gain an injunction restraining the sale of the bootlegs because the infringement of the 1958 Act did not interfere with the liberty of the Presley estate to perform the contract it had with RCA: it merely potentially reduced the profits that RCA could make as a result of the estate's performance of its obligations.

Viewed in light of the RCA case, it becomes apparent that Lord Hoffmann's definition of unlawful means protects business dealings – the freedom of the claimant and third party to enter into trade – but does not protect the value of the assets of the business, such as the exclusive record contract. Generally, indirect and secondary industrial action will target a business's dealings, and so will satisfy that aspect of Lord Hoffmann's definition. However, a canny trade union might be tempted to take action designed to harm the value of an employer's assets rather than interfere with his business dealings in the hope of sidestepping liability.

Unlawful means in industrial action context. Given that the appeals in OBG Ltd and ors v Allan and ors and other cases 2007 IRLR 608, HL, did not concern trade unions or industrial action, it is necessary to put their Lordships' musings on unlawful means into context. In the typical case of secondary action, the unlawful means requirement will be satisfied by the union committing the tort of inducement or procurement of breach of contract against the third party – i.e. by instructing its members employed by the third party to break their contracts of employment (the 'unlawful means'), thereby procuring a breach of the third party's commercial contract with the target employer. However, it should be noted that the inducement of breach of the employees' contracts of employment will not constitute unlawful means if that inducement is protected by the trade union immunities. But this is unlikely to be the case in most instances of secondary action as the trade dispute will be with the target employer (see Chapter 3).

We would argue that inducing a breach of a statutory duty or equitable **2.45** obligation is also capable of amounting to unlawful means, subject to the caveat that the duty or obligation must be actionable at the suit of the third party to whom it is owed. In this respect, Allan clearly overrules the earlier obiter view – expressed by the Court of Appeal in Associated British Ports and ors v TGWU 1989 ICR 557, HL – that any breach of a statutory obligation, whether actionable by the third party or not, can amount to unlawful means.

More controversial is the question of whether the mere breach of the employment contracts themselves could be said to constitute unlawful means. If so, the consequences for individual strikers would be dramatic: in every primary strike the strikers involved would potentially be liable to any person or business whose trade was interrupted or inconvenienced by the action.

Unfortunately, the case law in this area does not provide a definitive answer. In Rookes v Barnard 1964 AC 1129, HL, the House of Lords thought that a breach of a contract of employment could not be unlawful means for this purpose. However, that case was decided in the context of intimidation (see below) and the issue was not finally settled. In Barretts and Baird (Wholesale) Ltd and ors v Institution of Professional Civil Servants and ors 1987 IRLR 3, QBD, on the other hand, Mr Justice Henry thought it was an arguable point, but he also expressed the view that what is now S.236 TULR(C)A, which prohibits a court from making an order that has the effect of forcing an employee to work, might prevent the courts from granting injunctions against employees on this basis.

2.46 Turning to the House of Lords decision in OBG Ltd v Allan, we would argue that Lord Hoffmann's definition of unlawful means does not necessarily exclude a mere breach of contract – such a breach is actionable at the suit of the third party and may interfere with the freedom of the third party and claimant to deal with one another. However, due consideration should be given to Lord Walker's warning against extending the tort of causing loss by unlawful means beyond its current boundaries.

2.47 **Lawful interference.** It follows from the discussion of unlawful means above that if, in the context of industrial action, a trade union interferes with the economic interests of an employer by *lawful* means, there will be no liability in tort. An example:

- **Middlebrook Mushrooms Ltd v Transport and General Workers' Union and ors** 1993 ICR 612, CA: MM Ltd employed about 300 employees who were TGWU members. 89 of the employees took industrial action and were subsequently dismissed. The TGWU then decided to carry out a propaganda campaign involving the distribution of leaflets by its members outside supermarkets which stocked the company's mushrooms. The leaflets urged consumers to exercise their freedom of choice not to buy MM Ltd's product. Since the supermarkets took mushrooms from a number of suppliers and there was no distinction between the mushrooms on display as to origin, consumers could only show their support for the TGWU's stance by either not buying mushrooms at all or by boycotting the supermarkets in question. MM Ltd was concerned that the supermarkets might refuse to stock its mushrooms and sought an interim injunction against the TGWU, restraining it from interfering with the supply contracts with the supermarkets. However, the Court of Appeal held that MM Ltd was not entitled to an injunction because the TGWU had not used any unlawful means – members were free to persuade shoppers to boycott a product in support of their cause.

2.48 **Intention.** The final element of the tort of causing loss by unlawful means is that the defendant must have intended to cause loss to the claimant. In most industrial action cases intention will be relatively straightforward to establish. There are, however, potential grey areas. For the meaning of 'intention', we must again turn to the House of Lords decision in OBG Ltd v Allan (above), although fortunately their Lordships were in agreement on this subject.

The House of Lords' view was that the concept of intention for the purposes of the tort of causing loss by unlawful means is essentially the same as for the tort of inducing a breach of contract. Thus, a defendant does not intend to cause a claimant loss if he or she is merely reckless or negligent about whether loss will result from his or her actions. Lord Hoffmann reasoned that a person intends to cause loss whether it is an end in itself or the means through which that person seeks to achieve another aim, such as personal enrichment or a political statement. However, intention will not be made out where loss to the claimant is neither an end nor a means to an end, but merely a foreseeable consequence of the defendant's actions. An example:

- **Barretts and Baird (Wholesale) Ltd and ors v Institution of Professional Civil Servants and ors** 1987 IRLR 3, QBD: the IPCS represented Fatstock Officers (FOs) employed by the Meat and Livestock Commission (MLC) who were responsible for issuing certificates required to export meat and claim subsidies. There was a dispute between the FOs and the MLC over pay and the FOs carried out a strike ballot which authorised a series of one-day strikes. B and B, which ran a meat trade business that would be affected by the strikes, sought an injunction restraining the union from interfering in its business by unlawful means. The High Court, however, determined that the strike was a primary strike for better pay and that, although the union foresaw that the industrial action would prevent certificates being issued and harm businesses in the meat trade, damage to B and B's business was neither the purpose of the strike nor the means of achieving that purpose, which was to put pressure on the Government.

Relationship with statutory immunity. One consequence of the House of Lords' re-statement and re-labelling of the economic torts in Allan is that the statutory immunities in S.219 TULR(C)A do not accurately reflect the current state of the torts. In particular, there is no reference in S.219 to the tort of 'causing loss by unlawful means', but plenty of references to the tort of interfering with contract. However, as explained in Chapter 3, the Allan decision does not mean that the statutory immunities are ineffective. As we saw above, interference with contract is not a tort in and of itself, but interfering with a contract by unlawful means is a species of the tort of causing loss by unlawful means. It therefore follows that the immunity in S.219 covers the tort of causing loss by unlawful means when that loss is brought about by the union interfering with a contract between the claimant and a third party, but would not apply when the interference is merely with the claimant's economic expectations. **2.49**

Intimidation
2.50

Intimidation consists of *threatening* to act unlawfully, usually by inducing breaches of employment contracts. The ingredients of the tort are:

- that there is a threat to commit an unlawful act in order to coerce a person into acting in a particular way

- that the person threatened must act in that way

- that the person making the threat must intend and cause harm either to the person threatened or to a third party.

The operation of the tort is illustrated by the leading case of:

- **Rookes v Barnard** 1964 AC 1129, HL: R was a non-union employee working in a closed shop at BOAC. Union officials told BOAC that their members would strike if R was not dismissed and BOAC dismissed him with proper notice. The union members had (unusually) a no-strike clause incorporated into their individual employment contracts. The House of Lords held that the union officials, having threatened BOAC with breaches of the employees' contracts of employment, were liable to R under the tort of intimidation.

2.51　It should be noted that the union had not induced a breach of R's contract because he was dismissed with proper notice. Also, it would not have been liable if it had actually induced a breach of its members' employment contracts because the inducement of breach of contract would have been protected by statutory immunity. The significance of the case was that intimidation by threatening to induce breaches of contract was not covered by statutory immunity. The Government promptly rectified this through the Trade Disputes Act 1965. Intimidation, which will be committed in almost every instance of industrial action, is now protected by immunity from legal proceedings if the act threatened would be protected – the scope of this immunity is discussed in greater detail in Chapter 3.

The essence of the tort of intimidation is in the threat to induce the breaches of contract. As with inducement, a distinction needs to be drawn between threats and the mere provision of information and advice. Similarly, the person threatened must prove that the threats were intended to coerce and cause harm. For example, in News Group Newspapers Ltd and ors v Society of Graphical and Allied Trades '82 and ors (No.2) 1987 ICR 181, QBD, the High Court expressed the view that swearing and shouting would not necessarily by themselves amount to threats; however, words such as 'Scab, we'll get you' amounted to threats of violence.

2.52　Conspiracy

The civil tort of conspiracy consists of concerted action pursuant to an agreement between two or more persons. It is rarely relied on now that it is possible to sue unions directly in tort, since suing a union will be considerably more fruitful than suing an alleged conspiratorial combination of union officials.

The tort of conspiracy takes two forms:

- conspiracy to injure by lawful means; and

- conspiracy to injure by unlawful means.

2.53　**Conspiracy to injure by lawful means.** The important point here is that the predominant purpose of the conspiracy must be injury to the claimant. If the conspirators, who will normally be union officials, are pursuing legitimate union interests there will be no actionable tort – this was decided in the leading case of Crofter Hand Woven Harris Tweed Co Ltd v Veitch and anor 1942 AC 435, HL. Legitimate union interests will be those matters that can be the subject of a trade dispute and which are listed in S.244 TULR(C)A – see Chapter 3. It is plain that a strike or other industrial action is likely to injure the employer, but if the action is in pursuit of a genuine trade dispute there can be no cause of action for conspiracy. However, action in pursuit of a personal grudge and with the predominant intention of furthering that grudge will not be in pursuit of legitimate self-interest, even if the subject-matter is ostensibly that of a trade dispute.

Conspiracy to injure by unlawful means. While the conspirators must intend 2.54 to injure the claimant and must use unlawful means to do so in order for this tort to be actionable, it is not essential that they act with the predominant purpose of causing injury to the claimant – Lonrho plc v Al-Fayed and ors 1991 3 All ER 303, HL. Thus, the tort is actionable irrespective of whether the defendants can justify their actions by showing that they had a legitimate purpose. For this reason this form of conspiracy is not protected by the statutory immunities.

The scope of this tort is somewhat uncertain as it is unclear what amounts to unlawful means in this context. Arguably the term should be interpreted consistently with the definition given by Lord Hoffmann in OBG Ltd and ors v Allan and ors and other cases 2007 IRLR 608, HL (see 'Causing loss by unlawful means – unlawful means' above), although their Lordships in that case did not directly address the tort of conspiracy.

Economic duress   2.55
The facts which give rise to intimidation may also give rise to liability in duress. Duress is said to occur where the injured party has been forced by illegitimate pressure to hand over money or other property, or enter into a contract, against his or her will. The remedy provided for economic duress is restitution, i.e. the return of the money or property exacted or paid under any contract.

The leading case is Universe Tankships Inc of Monrovia v International Transport Workers' Federation and ors 1982 ICR 262, HL, where the ITF 'blacked' the claimant's ship and prevented it from sailing until the claimant paid £80,000 to the ITF (most of which represented a backdated wage settlement for the crew). The House of Lords held that the ITF was liable because the pressure applied was not 'legitimate' in that it was not within the scope of the immunities established by S.219 TULR(C)A – see Chapter 3. This decision was subsequently confirmed by the House of Lords in Dimskal Shipping Co SA v International Transport Workers' Federation 1992 ICR 37, HL.

2.56 Criminal liability

There are some special cases in which striking or taking industrial action short of a strike constitutes (or may constitute) a criminal offence:

- the armed forces, as might be expected, have no right to strike. Industrial action would be punishable under military law as mutiny or desertion

- the police also have no right to strike or, indeed, to join a trade union other than the Police Federation. If, however, a person is a member of a trade union before he or she enlists in the police force, then he or she may retain his or her union membership – S.64 Police Act 1996. It is a criminal offence under S.91 to induce a member of the police service to withhold his or her services

- merchant seamen and women have no right to strike while at sea and it is a criminal offence to be in breach of duty endangering a ship, life or limb under S.58 of the Merchant Shipping Act 1995. They may, however, lawfully strike between voyages

- some public sector employees may be committing a criminal offence by striking – e.g. postal and telecommunications workers

- it is a criminal offence under S.3(2) of the Aliens Restriction (Amendment) Act 1919 for an alien to promote industrial unrest unless he or she has been engaged in the industry concerned for at least two years.

Further, it is a criminal offence if a person wilfully and maliciously breaks a contract of employment, knowing or having reasonable cause to believe that the probable consequences will be to endanger life or cause serious bodily injury, or to expose valuable property to serious injury or destruction – S.240 TULR(C)A. A person guilty of this offence is liable on summary conviction to three months' imprisonment or to a fine not exceeding level 2 on the standard scale (currently a maximum of £500) or to both. This offence does not apply to seafarers, although, as noted above, they are subject to the criminal offence contained in S.58 of the Merchant Shipping Act 1995.

2.57 Criminal offences committed in the course of industrial action – e.g. assault or criminal damage – will simply be dealt with by the criminal law in the normal way. No question of statutory immunity arises for criminal conduct. Apart from offences committed during picketing (see Chapter 6), it is extremely rare for the criminal law to be invoked against employees taking industrial action.

3 Trade union immunities

Scope of immunity

Trade dispute

'In contemplation or furtherance'

The law recognises a right to organise strikes and other industrial action by **3.1** granting statutory immunity from liability at common law for the civil wrongs or torts that are most frequently committed in the course of taking industrial action. The basic immunity is contained in S.219 of the Trade Union and Labour Relations (Consolidation) Act 1992 (TULR(C)A), which specifies a number of industrial torts that attract immunity, provided the acts are done in contemplation or furtherance of a trade dispute.

To determine whether industrial action is lawful, a three-stage inquiry is needed:

- does the industrial action involve the commission of a tort for which there would be liability at common law? If the answer is 'No', the action will not be unlawful. However, effective industrial action will almost invariably involve (at the very least) the tort of inducing breaches of employment contracts, so the answer will almost certainly be 'Yes'

- if there is liability at common law, does S.219 TULR(C)A as worded confer immunity? If it does not, then the industrial action will be unlawful in any event. But even if S.219 does on the face of it confer immunity, the organisers of industrial action will not automatically be in the clear. The last stage of the inquiry is crucial

- do the 'claw-back' provisions in the TULR(C)A apply so as to remove S.219 immunity and restore liability at common law?

Torts that attract S.219 immunity are not actionable by anyone unless the Act's **3.2** 'claw-back' provisions apply. These provisions are discussed at length in Chapters 4–6. It should be noted, however, that even if the tort in question does attract immunity and is therefore lawful, the courts still have an overriding discretion to grant an interim injunction to restrain industrial action (see Chapter 7, 'Remedies for unlawful action', for details).

This chapter explains the scope and limitations of the basic immunities conferred by S.219. We consider first the industrial torts that the section covers. Then we explain the requirements of S.219 which specify that immunity is only conferred on tortious acts *done in contemplation or furtherance of a trade dispute*. This phrase is conventionally referred to as the *'golden formula'*. If

45

there is no trade dispute as defined, a strike or other industrial action will enjoy no immunity. Furthermore, the tortious acts must be done in contemplation or furtherance of such a dispute in order for the immunity to apply.

3.3 Scope of immunity

As noted above, the basic immunity conferred on unions is provided by S.219 TULR(C)A. This reads:

'(1) An act done by a person in contemplation or furtherance of a trade dispute is not actionable in tort on the ground only – (a) that it induces another person to break a contract or interferes or induces another person to interfere with its performance, or (b) that it consists in his threatening that a contract (whether one to which he is a party or not) will be broken or its performance interfered with, or that he will induce another person to break a contract or interfere with its performance.

(2) An agreement or combination by two or more persons to do or procure the doing of an act in contemplation or furtherance of a trade dispute is not actionable in tort if the act is one which if done without any such agreement or combination would not be actionable in tort.'

To summarise, the industrial torts that attract protection under S.219 are:

- *inducement of breach of contract* – S.219(1)(a). It is immaterial for these purposes whether the contract concerned is a contract of employment or a commercial contract

- *interference with contract* (or inducement of such interference) – S.219(1)(a)

- *intimidation* – S.219(1)(b). This involves threatening to induce a breach of contract or to interfere with a contract

- *conspiracy* – S.219(2). A conspiracy to do an act in contemplation or furtherance of a trade dispute is not actionable as such if the same act would not be actionable if done by an individual. So if an act is protected by S.219(1) – because it is an inducement of breach of contract or an interference with contract or intimidation – it will not be rendered actionable if there is a conspiracy to commit such an act.

3.4 (Note that the industrial torts were recently revisited and reassessed by the House of Lords in OBG Ltd and ors v Allan and ors and other cases 2007 IRLR 608, HL. As a result, the list of industrial torts covered by S.219 is somewhat outdated. That said, the discrepancy between the industrial torts as set out by the House of Lords and those listed in S.219 is unlikely to be of any practical consequence. This important House of Lords decision is discussed in detail in Chapter 2, 'Liability for industrial action' under 'The industrial torts'.)

Section 219, as worded, covers both *primary* and *accessory* liability for the torts of procuring a breach of contract and interfering with a contract. (The distinction is explained in Chapter 2 under 'The industrial torts – direct v indirect action'.) It should be noted, however, that procurement or interference that attracts accessory liability will normally be *secondary* action and, as such, deprived of protection by Ss.219(4) and 224(1). (For further discussion of secondary action see Chapter 4, 'Loss of immunity'.) S.219 does not cover the tort of interference with trade or business by unlawful means.

Protection applies to *'an act done by a person'*. No distinction is drawn between official and unofficial action, nor is there any distinction made between the acts of a union and those of its officers and members. Provided an act is done in contemplation or furtherance of a trade dispute it will be protected to the extent set out in S.219. (The statutory provisions which govern union liability in tort for official and unofficial action are discussed in Chapter 2.)

'Is not actionable in tort on the ground only...'   3.5
In Hadmor Productions Ltd and ors v Hamilton and anor 1982 ICR 114, HL, the House of Lords ruled that the words 'shall not be actionable' (the original wording contained in the precursor to S.219) meant 'shall not be actionable by anybody'. They were not, as had been suggested in some earlier decisions, limited to meaning 'shall not be actionable only by the employer who is a party to the primary dispute'. Thus, if an act is protected it is a lawful act and it cannot be relied upon by a third party as constituting unlawful means against that third party.

In the Hadmor case the ACTT union threatened that its members would break their contracts of employment with Thames Television by refusing to transmit programmes produced by Hadmor, an independent production company. That constituted the tort of intimidation against Thames Television. But S.219(1)(b) gives statutory protection to intimidation if carried out in contemplation or furtherance of a trade dispute. The House of Lords decided that there was a trade dispute between the union and Thames Television. This meant that the intimidation was not actionable either by Thames Television or by Hadmor because it was, in effect, lawful. The union had interfered with Hadmor's business by means which were 'not actionable'. Accordingly, it was not open to Hadmor to argue that the union was liable for the tort of interfering with Hadmor's business by the unlawful means of threatening to induce breaches of Thames Television's employment contracts.

Section 219 only protects against liability *in tort* and only against liability for   3.6
the torts specified above. Accordingly, torts such as nuisance and torts based on breach of statutory duty are not protected. S.219 does not protect against *criminal* liability, so a campaign of industrial sabotage would not be protected. Nor does it protect against *contractual* liability. In the unlikely event that a

47

union concluded a collective agreement in the form of a legally enforceable contract, S.219 would provide no defence against a breach of that contract. It should be noted, however, that an act which is not actionable in itself by virtue of the statute cannot constitute the requisite 'unlawful means' for torts such as interfering with business by unlawful means or conspiracy to use unlawful means.

The Court of Session in Scotland has held that it is at least arguable that S.219 provides immunity for *trespass* – e.g. 'sit-ins' – where the only consequences which give rise to a claim are interferences with the trade or business of the complainer – see Plessey Co plc and anor v Wilson and ors 1982 IRLR 198, Ct Sess (Inner House) and Shell UK Ltd v McGillivray 1991 SLT 667, Ct Sess (Outer House). This view is unlikely to be adopted by the English courts, however, on the ground that trespass itself does not fall within the scope of the immunities. Common law liability of unions and individuals is discussed in further detail in Chapter 2.

3.7 Double liability

It is sometimes possible to classify what appears to be straightforward industrial action as an act that falls outside the scope of S.219. For example:

- **Prudential Assurance Co Ltd v Lorenz and ors** 1971 11 KIR 78, ChD: insurance agents were induced to break their contracts by not submitting accounts and returns to the employers. The High Court held that this was a breach of a fiduciary obligation of an agent to account to his principal. This obligation was implied by general law quite separately from any contractual obligation. This meant that the employers had a claim in *equity*, as well as in tort, and the statute only gave protection against the claim in tort.

In fact, this was straightforward primary industrial action in the context of a trade dispute and it was purely coincidental that it could be classified as breach of an equitable duty as well as a breach of contract. A similar point was considered by the House of Lords in Universe Tankships Inc of Monrovia v International Transport Workers' Federation and ors 1982 ICR 262, HL. The employer sought to recover a sum of money which had been paid to the union under economic duress (which was conceded by the union). Economic duress is not a tort, so S.219 did not apply. Their Lordships thought that the employer should not be allowed to circumvent S.219 simply by describing acts that would otherwise be rendered lawful by S.219 in a way that fell outside S.219. In the event, they decided (by a majority) that there was no trade dispute, so S.219 would not have applied in any case and the employer was entitled to recover the money.

48

Trade dispute

The meaning of 'trade dispute' is set out in S.244(1), which defines it as a 'dispute between workers and *their* employer which relates wholly or mainly to one or more' specified issues (our stress). The issues covered by S.244 are discussed below under 'Subject-matter of dispute'. 'Worker', in the context of a dispute with an employer, means a worker actually employed by that employer and 'employment' includes 'any relationship whereby one person personally does work or performs services for another'. It also covers a worker dismissed in connection with the dispute or a worker whose dismissal was one of the causes of the dispute – S.244(5).

In determining whether an employer was in a trade dispute with 'workers' for the purposes of S.244, the Court of Appeal in Transport and General Workers' Union v Associated British Ports Ltd 2001 EWCA Civ 2032, CA, also had regard to S.296(1) TULR(C)A, which further defines the term 'worker' as 'an individual who works, or normally works or seeks to work – (a) under a contract of employment, or (b) under any other contract whereby he undertakes to do or perform personally any work or services for another party to the contract who is not a professional client of his'. In that case a dispute arose between a group of ship pilots and the harbour authority for the Humber area, ABP. Under the Pilotage Act 1987 ABP was under a duty to provide pilotage services for ship owners and had the power to authorise individuals to work as ships' pilots. The pilots were self-employed and members of Humber Pilots Ltd (HP Ltd), which acted as their collective voice, but not as their employer. The pilots agreed with HP Ltd to provide their services in accordance with HP Ltd's rules and a written agreement between ABP and HP Ltd. The pilots became dissatisfied with their working conditions and HP Ltd notified ABP that it was terminating the written agreement. When attempts to negotiate a new arrangement failed, the pilots, in a ballot organised by their union, the TGWU, voted in favour of strike action. ABP was granted an interim injunction restraining the industrial action. Mr Justice Hunt, hearing the application in the High Court, held that the dispute was not between workers and their employer and that the TGWU would therefore not be protected under S.219 if it went ahead with the strike.

The Court of Appeal reversed this decision. In its view, the issue of whether **3.9** there was a contract between the individual pilots and ABP of a kind falling within S.296(1)(b) could not be determined solely by reference to the statutory provisions under which ABP operated, as statutory duties and powers could co-exist with contractual rights and obligations. Looking at the terms and conditions on which ABP granted authorisation to the pilots, the Court thought that the contractual language of the authorisation documents, the nature of the obligations undertaken by the pilots to ABP, and the extent of the ultimate control exercised by ABP over the activities of the pilots were all consistent with the existence of a contract between an authorised pilot and ABP. It was irrelevant to the characterisation of the contracts that the pilots were exclusive employees of the shipowner while they were on board performing pilotage services and that they also had a contractual relationship with their co-operative, HP Ltd. It therefore followed that the pilots were workers within the meaning of S.244(1) and that ABP was their employer within the meaning of that provision. The appeal was allowed and the interim injunction discharged.

Identifying the employer involved in the trade dispute will prove to be relatively straightforward in the majority of cases. Even if the employer alters his commercial identity during the dispute, the provisions will still apply. For example, in Examite Ltd v Whittaker and ors 1977 IRLR 312, CA, a new company, E Ltd, was formed to take over the business of BIS, which had been brought to a standstill by a strike. E Ltd engaged some of BIS's former workforce and started operating. The workers on strike continued their industrial action against E Ltd, which successfully sought an injunction restraining the workers on strike from intimidating people and procuring breaches of contract on the ground that it was not a party to the dispute – which was between the union and BIS. The injunction was discharged by the Court of Appeal on the basis that the reality of the situation was that the business was being carried on by the same people and that there was a continuation of the same dispute.

It has sometimes been argued that a dispute between workers and their employer is not necessarily the same as a dispute between the workers' union and the employer – i.e. that the union is pursuing a dispute of its own without reference to its members. Such an argument will be very difficult to sustain given that official industrial action must be supported by a ballot: a 'Yes' vote in an industrial action ballot will normally be taken as endorsement of the union's position by the workers.

3.10 In Associated British Ports and ors v Transport and General Workers' Union 1989 IRLR 291, ChD, negotiations between the union and the employers over a new national agreement to replace the National Dock Labour Scheme, which the Government proposed to repeal, broke down. The union called a strike, which was supported by a ballot. The employers argued that the dispute about a new national agreement was purely between the union and the employers and that the dockers themselves were engaged in a political (or non-trade) dispute about the abolition of the dock scheme. This argument failed in the High Court and was dropped on appeal. The Court held that the union was acting on behalf of the workers and that the affirmative strike vote amounted to an endorsement of the union's actions.

3.11 **Excluded disputes.** The requirement that a dispute must be between workers and their employer excludes a whole range of disputes from the protection of S.219. A dispute between two employers or between an employer and an employers' association is not a trade dispute, even if a union joins in on one side of the dispute. This is illustrated by:

- **Larkin and ors v Long** 1915 AC 814, HL: stevedoring employers formed an association with the object of obtaining higher rates from ship-owners (which would have the knock-on effect of improving the terms and conditions of employment of dockers). The union agreed with the employers' association that it would withdraw its members' labour from any non-member of the association. L, an employer, refused to join the association, and the union called a strike of his dock employees. The House of Lords held that there was no dispute between L and his employees. The only dispute was between an individual employer and the employers' association. The union did not change the character of the dispute by taking action to help one side. It followed that there was no *trade* dispute and that the union could not claim immunity for inducing L's employees to break their contracts of employment.

Similarly, a dispute between workers or rival trade unions is not a trade dispute. Two examples:

- **Cory Lighterage Ltd v Transport and General Workers' Union and ors** 1973 ICR 339, CA: S, a lighterman on the Thames, purposely let his union membership lapse at a time when there was a practice in the London docks of 100 per cent union membership. The employer suspended S on full pay, as his colleagues refused to work with him unless he paid his membership dues and S refused to do so. Unable to dismiss him, which (at the time) required the consent of the National Dock Labour Board, the employer sought an injunction restraining the union from instructing its members from withholding their labour. The Court of Appeal held that the dispute was between S and the union and its members, and that the employer, far from being or becoming a party to that dispute, had been wholly amenable to the union's requirement that S should be suspended and, if possible, dismissed. Such a dispute, being 'between workmen and workmen', was not a valid trade dispute for the purposes of the statutory immunities

- **JT Stratford and Son Ltd v Lindley and anor** 1965 AC 269, HL: the House of Lords granted an injunction restraining the union from 'blacking' the employer's business. The union's reason for taking action was to enhance its prestige after a rival trade union had succeeded in obtaining recognition from the employer. There was therefore no dispute between the workers and the employer: the real dispute was between the two unions, which fell outside the protection afforded by S.219. In reaching this conclusion, their Lordships thought it important that the union had not sought recognition from the employer. It therefore held that it was more a case of inter-union rivalry than one of a union taking action against the employer as a result of the employer recognising the other union.

3.12 Demarcation disputes are also excluded from the scope of S.219, as are disputes over a closed shop (which are unlawful anyway – see Chapter 4). The definition of trade dispute also excludes situations where an employer's own workers are not themselves involved in the dispute. For instance, an employer may be picketed by outside workers because he employs low-paid foreign workers who are themselves quite happy to accept low wages.

Action against the Government. Industrial action against the Government is not protected by the golden formula unless the Government is the workers' own employer. S.244(2) TULR(C)A does provide for two exceptions, however, which cover industrial disputes in the public sector. It provides that 'a dispute between a Minister of the Crown and any workers shall, notwithstanding that he is not the employer of those workers, be treated as a dispute between those workers and their employer if the dispute relates to matters which – (a) have been referred for consideration by a joint body on which, by virtue of provision made by or under any enactment, he is represented, or (b) cannot be settled without him exercising a power conferred on him by or under an enactment'.

For S.244(2) to apply, the dispute must still relate to one of the employment matters listed in S.244(1) (see below under 'Subject-matter of dispute'). Thus, protests against Government policy are not covered. In Wandsworth London Borough Council v National Association of Schoolmasters/Union of Women Teachers 1994 ICR 81, CA, the Court of Appeal had to grapple with the definition of a trade dispute in the context of a proposed boycott of assessment of pupils under the National Curriculum. The union argued successfully before the Court of Appeal that there was a trade dispute between the union and the Secretary of State for Education, which related wholly or mainly to the terms and conditions of its members, and that the dispute could not be settled without the Secretary of State exercising a power conferred on him by the Schoolteachers' Pay and Conditions Act 1991 or the Education Reform Act 1988.

3.13 ## Subject-matter of dispute
To qualify as a 'trade dispute' a dispute must relate *wholly or mainly* to one or more of the matters listed in S.244(1). These are:

'(a) terms and conditions of employment, or the physical conditions in which any workers are required to work;

(b) engagement or non-engagement, or termination or suspension of employment or the duties of employment, of one or more workers;

(c) allocation of work or the duties of employment between workers or groups of workers;

(d) matters of discipline;

(e) a worker's membership or non-membership of a trade union;

(f)   facilities for officials of trade unions; and

(g)   machinery for negotiation or consultation, and other procedures, relating to any of the above matters, including the recognition by employers or employers' associations of the right of a trade union to represent workers in such negotiation or consultation or in the carrying out of such procedures.'

Before considering some of these items in more detail, it is important to emphasise at the outset that, while the dispute has to relate to at least one subject matter listed in S.244(1)(a)–(g) in order to qualify as a 'trade dispute', there is no requirement that every worker must be affected by the matter that forms the basis of the dispute. This point was established by the High Court in British Telecommunications plc v Communication Workers Union 2004 IRLR 58, QBD. In that case, BT wanted to introduce a voluntary productivity scheme to certain of its operations. When attempts to introduce the scheme by collective agreement failed, it sought to introduce it on a voluntary basis. The CWU objected to this course of action and, following a ballot, gave notice to BT of a series of one-day strikes. BT took the view that the strike called by the union was outside the protection of S.219 and applied to the High Court for an injunction to restrain the proposed action. It argued, among other things, that the strike was not in furtherance of a 'trade dispute' within the meaning of S.244(1), as some of those balloted who might be called out on strike did not fall within the scope of the voluntary productivity scheme. They therefore had no trade dispute with BT about terms and conditions of employment.

The High Court rejected this argument. In the Court's view it involved reading **3.14** into S.244(1)(a) the word 'their' before 'employment'. To do so would be inconsistent with the words 'the physical conditions in which any workers are required to work', which indicated that a strike by some workers in relation to the physical conditions of other workers would fall within the definition of 'trade dispute'. Furthermore, such an interpretation would be inconsistent with S.244(1)(b), which refers, among other matters, to the 'termination... of employment, of one or more workers'. It was clear to the High Court that a strike resulting from the termination of employment of a worker is a strike by persons other than those whose contracts of employment have been terminated. Similarly, the Court considered that in S.244(1)(d) 'matters of discipline' must include disciplinary measures taken by an employer in relation to workers other than, or only in relation to some of those, who may be asked to take industrial action.

In reaching its decision on this point, the Court emphasised that 'the representative function of trade unions would be set at nought if it were the case that employees could not take industrial action in relation to an attempt to change terms and conditions of employment of some only of them' (sic). Nevertheless, the Court went on to grant BT the injunction sought on the

53

ground that the CWU failed to comply with the notice requirements under the TULR(C)A. This aspect of the decision is discussed in Chapter 5, 'Industrial action ballots'.

3.15 **Terms and conditions of employment.** The phrase 'terms and conditions of employment' in S.244(1)(a) was considered by the House of Lords in Universe Tankships Inc of Monrovia v International Transport Workers' Federation and ors 1982 ICR 262, HL. (At the time of the decision a dispute only had to be 'connected with' one or more of the items listed above in order to qualify as a trade dispute.) The question at issue was whether a demand that ship-owners contribute to a union welfare fund, which might be used for the benefit of crew members, was connected with terms and conditions of employment. The House of Lords made two main points:

- 'terms and conditions of employment' are not restricted to *contractual* terms. Their Lordships stated that the phrase includes terms that are applied by the parties in practice, even if not incorporated into contracts. They would extend to customary benefits and 'reasonable expectations' provided to employees by reason of their employment

- nevertheless, the expression is limited to terms that regulate the relationship between an employee and his or her employer. It does not extend to terms that regulate the relationship between an employer and a third party acting as principal rather than agent for the employee, such as the terms of a collective agreement which relate solely to the relationship between a trade union and employer.

Since any benefits to crew members from the union's welfare fund did not depend on the employer-employee relationship between ship-owners and crew, their Lordships (by a majority) concluded that the demand for a payment to the welfare fund was not connected with terms and conditions of employment. Lord Cross made the point that: 'A trade union cannot turn a dispute which in reality has no connection with terms and conditions of employment into a dispute connected with terms and conditions of employment by insisting that the employer inserts appropriate terms into the contracts of employment into which he enters.' Accordingly, inserting a clause into the employment contract of each crew member to the effect that the employer undertook to pay money into the fund would not have turned the dispute into a dispute connected with terms and conditions of employment.

3.16 The possibility of inserting a clause into employment contracts so as to link a dispute to terms and conditions of employment was previously mooted by Lord Denning MR in British Broadcasting Corporation v Hearn and ors 1977 ICR 685, CA – a case that involved employees refusing to work on television broadcasts to South Africa. In that case Lord Denning suggested that a contractual clause to the effect that members should not be required to take

54

part in broadcasts which were to be viewed in South Africa could be sufficient to link a dispute to an employee's terms and conditions.

In P (A Minor) v National Association of Schoolmasters/Union of Women Teachers 2003 ICR 386, HL, the claimant sought to rely on Lord Denning's remarks in an attempt to persuade the court that proposed strike action by a teachers' union fell outside the protection afforded by S.219. The case concerned teachers who refused to abide by a head teacher's instruction to take a disruptive pupil, P, back into their classrooms. When they voted overwhelmingly for strike action, P brought a claim under S.235A TULR(C)A (on the basis that the action would result in a reduction in the quality of services supplied to him) for an injunction restraining the action. P argued that any strike would be unlawful in that there was no 'trade dispute' within the meaning of S.244(1) in existence because the dispute did not relate to the teachers' terms and conditions of employment. P acknowledged that the teachers' contractual obligation to comply with the head teacher's direction was a rule governing their employment relationship. However, he submitted that a dispute about whether or not they should teach him was not a dispute about the rule (and, hence, about the terms and conditions of their employment), but about the *application* of the rule. Relying on BBC v Hearn, P said that if the teachers had claimed that the rule should be amended, they would have properly linked the dispute with their terms and conditions of employment. Their failure to do so meant that the dispute did not fall within S.244(1)(a).

The House of Lords rejected P's claim. In Lord Hoffmann's view, Parliament could not have intended the liability of the union to depend upon such fine distinctions. It was impossible to formulate a coherent distinction between a rule and the application of a rule. A dispute about what workers are obliged to do is a dispute about terms and conditions of employment. Furthermore, the decision in BBC v Hearn did not support the proposition that such a distinction should be drawn. In that case the employees had no complaint about any aspect of their work and Lord Denning MR had simply suggested a way in which they might have brought their situation within the definition of a trade dispute in S.244(1). In any event, Lord Cross, in the Universe Tankships case (above), had cautioned against taking Lord Denning's tentative observations too far. Lord Hoffmann also noted that in the BBC case the Court of Appeal had held that the use of the composite expression 'terms and conditions' demonstrated that Parliament intended it to be given a broad meaning. Accordingly, since the dispute was about the teachers' contractual obligation to teach P, the dispute not merely related to but was actually about terms and conditions, and therefore fell within S.244(1).

Future terms and conditions. For S.244(1)(a) to apply, the dispute must relate **3.17** to the employees' terms and conditions of employment with their *current* employer. In University College London Hospitals NHS Trust v UNISON 1999

55

ICR 204, CA, an NHS trust was in the process of negotiating with a private and unidentified consortium for the building and running of a new hospital. The trade union, UNISON, was against this method of financing the new hospital as a matter of principle and was also concerned to protect the rights of those of its members who would be transferred from the trust to the consortium. The union requested that the trust enter into a contractual agreement with the consortium whereby the consortium and 'its associates, sub-contractors and successors' would, for a period of up to 30 years, agree to provide terms and conditions equivalent to those provided by the trust. The employer refused the union's request, which led to a ballot in favour of industrial action.

The High Court granted the employer an interim injunction preventing the strikes from going ahead, which was upheld on appeal. The Court of Appeal pointed out that the sought-for guarantee was not restricted to the terms and conditions of existing employees of the trust. Given the 30-year length of the guarantee, it was inevitable that eventually the great majority of the consortium's staff would never have been employed by the trust. S.244 does not cover a dispute over terms and conditions of employees who have never been employed by the employer who is the subject of the strike action. Moreover, the dispute was not between 'workers and their employer' within the meaning of S.244 because the dispute was mainly concerned with different employment with an as yet unidentified employer.

3.18   That decision was then followed in London Underground Ltd v National Union of Rail, Maritime and Transport Workers, unreported 22.12.98, QBD, which concerned plans to transfer the running of parts of the London Underground from LU Ltd to three private sector companies. The union was concerned about the impact of these plans and demanded a number of guarantees for LU Ltd's employees, including the retention of travel facilities, no compulsory redundancies, no subcontracting, pensions to be made legally binding and new entrants being eligible to join, retention of existing terms and conditions of all staff and retention of the disciplinary procedure. The guarantees were to last for 30 years, which was the duration of the private companies' contract to run the underground. The High Court held that a strike called in support of the union's demands was not a 'trade dispute' within the meaning of S.244. The dispute was not concerned primarily with the terms and conditions of employment existing between the workers and LU Ltd, but with the terms and conditions of future workers who would be employed by the private companies. The Court rejected the union's attempt to distinguish the UNISON decision because in that case all the employees were to be transferred to the new employer whereas in the instant case the union was seeking the guarantees for all LU Ltd's 16,000 employees, only 5,500 of whom would be affected by the transfer to the private company. The RMT argued that this left a substantial number of employees who would be remaining with LU Ltd and about whom the RMT was concerned. The High Court held that it did not make any difference that some employees would remain employed by LU Ltd. The primary focus of the assurances sought by the union was on the employees who would be transferred from LU Ltd's employment to the infrastructure companies.

That did not conclude the matter, however. Dissatisfied with the Court of Appeal's decision in University College London Hospitals NHS Trust v UNISON (above), UNISON sought leave to appeal to the House of Lords. When this was refused, it took the case to the European Court of Human Rights (ECtHR), where it argued that the Court of Appeal's decision constituted an unlawful interference with the right to freedom of association guaranteed by Article 11 of the European Convention on Human Rights, and in particular the right of its members 'to form and join trade unions for the protection of [their] interests'. The UK Government, on the other hand, disputed that Article 11 came into play at all: the strike did not concern the occupational interests of the union's members, but the protection of as yet unidentified individuals to be employed by as yet unidentified transferee companies.

The ECtHR – in UNISON v United Kingdom 2002 IRLR 497, ECtHR – rejected the Government's argument that Article 11 was not engaged on the facts of this case. The approach taken by the domestic courts, that the dispute concerned the protection of unidentified individuals to be employed by unidentified transferee companies, was not a decisive consideration for the purposes of Article 11. Because the guarantees sought by the union would have provided its existing members with additional protection against any measures taken by a future transferee that might affect their pay and conditions, the ECtHR took the view that the strike was concerned with the occupational interests of its members in the sense covered by that Article.

3.19 Moreover, the Court was of the view that the prohibition of the strike action should be regarded as a restriction on the union's power to protect those interests and therefore amounted to a restriction on the right to freedom of association. However, it went on to hold that the restriction was a necessary and proportionate means of protecting the rights and freedoms of others – in this case, the employer's freedom to negotiate a contract with a potential transferee. In this context, the Court took account of the fact that the workers were not precluded from taking strike action against their new employer after the transfer, and so were not left defenceless against any future attempts to downgrade their pay and conditions. Furthermore, it thought that the United Kingdom had not exceeded the scope of the potential measures it could take in relation to restricting a trade union's right to take industrial action. UNISON's application was accordingly dismissed.

3.20 **Termination of employment.** The phrase 'termination of employment' in S.244(1)(b) can cover industrial action over impending or feared redundancies. Two illustrations:

- **Health Computing Ltd and anor v Meek and ors** 1981 ICR 24, ChD: a computer services company hoped to provide services for the NHS. NALGO considered that the contracting-out of computer work would have an adverse effect on the job security and prospects of NHS computer staff and therefore instructed its members to refuse to cooperate with the company. The High Court held that apprehensions about job security were connected with the termination of employment. It was unnecessary to show that these apprehensions were well-founded, only that they were sincerely held

- **Hadmor Productions Ltd and ors v Hamilton and anor** 1982 ICR 114, HL: union members were television technicians employed by Thames Television. The union threatened to 'black' programmes that were produced by an independent production company on the ground that the more work that was contracted out by Thames, the less there would be for its members who were employed by Thames and that redundancies might ensue as a result. A High Court judge refused to grant an interim injunction against the union, but the Court of Appeal overruled him on the ground that there was no trade dispute because the 'blacking' was simply to enforce a union policy against the use of independent production companies. The House of Lords held that on the facts the union was concerned about possible future redundancies. It followed that there *was* a trade dispute under S.244(1)(b). Their Lordships made the point that there is no need for dismissal notices to have been issued or threatened by the employer in order to trigger the subsection.

In the latter case the House of Lords thought that the dispute would arguably fall under S.244(1)(c) as well because it was connected with the allocation of work between groups of workers – i.e. between Thames employees and the employees of outside contractors. And as the union had claimed the right to be consulted about the use of programmes made by independent contractors, their Lordships thought that the dispute probably also fell under S.244(1)(g) since it was connected with 'machinery for negotiation or consultation'.

3.21 'Wholly or mainly'

In a number of the cases mentioned above, the courts were applying the old test of whether a dispute was 'connected with' one of the matters listed in S.244(1). The law was changed by the Employment Act 1982 and a dispute now only qualifies as a trade dispute if it relates *wholly or mainly* to one of the S.244(1) matters. Accordingly, a court will look at the *predominant* purpose of a dispute. Disputes that do not relate wholly or mainly to one or more of the matters listed in S.244(1) will fail to attract immunity.

In the majority of cases disputes are about matters such as pay, hours and holidays, which fall clearly within S.244(1)(a) as matters relating wholly or mainly to terms and conditions of employment. However, in other cases, particularly in the public sector where disputes can be at least partly fuelled by union hostility to Government policies, detecting the predominant purpose of the dispute may prove more difficult: such disputes will often be judged as having a political purpose and have no immunity. An example:

- **Mercury Communications Ltd v Scott-Garner and anor** 1984 ICR 74, CA: the Government proposed to privatise British Telecom and to open it up to (limited) competition from Mercury. The Post Office Engineering Union opposed both proposals and instructed its members not to interconnect Mercury with the British Telecom network. The union argued that there was a trade dispute about the fear of redundancies if the policies of privatisation and liberalisation went ahead. The Court of Appeal held that there was 'massive' evidence that the union was waging a campaign against the political decisions to liberalise the industry and to privatise British Telecom. Job security might be part of what the dispute was about, but it was not a major part. It followed that it was unlikely that the union could show that there was a trade dispute. In reaching its decision, the Court was particularly influenced by the fact that there was a Job Security Agreement which the union had not sought to invoke – a factor which indicated that the union was not really concerned about job security.

By contrast, the following two cases came to the opposite conclusion on what was the predominant purpose of the dispute in question:

- **Wandsworth London Borough Council v National Association of Schoolmasters/Union of Women Teachers** 1994 ICR 81, CA: NASUWT instructed its members to boycott proposed assessments of pupils under the national curriculum. The Court of Appeal held that the dispute related wholly or mainly to terms and conditions of employment and rejected the Council's argument that the dispute was principally concerned with the objections and reservations held by union members about the content of the work which they would be required to undertake. In reaching its conclusion, the Court had regard to the fact that since 1990 there had been increasing concern expressed by the union on behalf of its members with regard to working time. The Court also placed considerable emphasis on the wording of the ballot paper itself, which asked the members if they were willing to take action 'to protest against the excessive workload and unreasonable imposition made upon teachers, as a consequence of national curriculum assessment and testing'

- **Westminster City Council v UNISON** 2001 ICR 1046, CA: the Court of Appeal held that a dispute that ensued after the Council decided to transfer the functions of a housing unit to a private company was predominantly about a change of employer and therefore a 'trade dispute' within the meaning of S.244(1). The Court acknowledged that public policy issues

59

were of concern throughout the negotiations between the Council and the union and were the primary focus during the early stages. However, it was unsurprising that employees would be concerned with policy issues earlier on and with the implications of the transfer for their own futures when the change became imminent. By the time the ballot for industrial action took place, the main issue was clearly in relation to the change in the identity of the employer: the employees were primarily concerned with possible changes in their terms and conditions of employment.

3.22 What is crucial in determining whether there is a trade dispute is not the union's motives but the *subject-matter* of the dispute. If the Government imposes a wage freeze or statutory incomes policy, as different Governments did in the 1970s, a strike for a wage increase in excess of the Government's limit will be a trade dispute – because it is mainly concerned with terms and conditions of employment. It does not matter that such a strike could be described as 'political': if a dispute is wholly or mainly about wages it is a trade dispute.

Thus, in University College London Hospitals NHS Trust v UNISON 1999 ICR 204, CA (above), the fact that the union was opposed in principle to the privatisation of hospitals did not mean that the industrial action aimed at protecting the terms and conditions of employees who were to be transferred to the private consortium was not a trade dispute. The Court of Appeal observed that a union's policy of opposing a particular course of action may have a political objective. At the same time the union might have a more limited objective; namely, to alleviate the adverse consequences which it anticipates could flow from the more general policy. That more limited objective can be the reason for taking the strike action and can satisfy the requirements of S.244.

3.23 Overseas disputes

A trade dispute may relate to matters occurring outside the United Kingdom. Action taken in the United Kingdom in support of such a dispute will be treated as falling within the golden formula if the outcome of the dispute is likely to affect the participants in the United Kingdom in respect of one or more of the matters listed in S.244(1) – S.244(3).

On the face of it, this means that employees of a multinational corporation in the United Kingdom can take action in support of a dispute at the same multinational in, say, France, if they are likely to be affected by the outcome. But in almost all cases this will be *secondary* action because the UK employer will not be the employer who is party to the dispute. As such, the action is deprived of protection by Ss.219(4) and 224(1) and it will make no difference that the two employers are subsidiaries of the same parent company. As long as they are separate companies, action taken at one in support of a trade dispute at the other will be secondary action (see Chapter 4).

Acas conciliation

3.24

One of the functions of the Advisory, Conciliation and Arbitration Service (Acas) is to attempt to conciliate in trade disputes – Ss.209 and 210. *In this context only*, 'trade dispute' is defined in S.218(1) as meaning a 'dispute between employers and workers, or between workers and workers, which is connected with' one or more of the matters listed in S.244(1). This is the original definition of a trade dispute, which was narrowed by the Employment Act 1982 to that now found in S.244 (see above). There are two differences from the S.244 definition:

- a dispute may be between workers and workers, as well as between workers and their employer

- a dispute only needs to be 'connected with' one of the S.244(1) matters and does not have to relate 'wholly or mainly' to one of those matters.

'Worker' is defined, in relation to a dispute to which an employer is a party, as including any worker even if not employed by that employer – S.218(5).

The upshot of this wider definition for Acas purposes is that Acas is free to conciliate in virtually all cases where there is an actual or impending industrial dispute, including cases of inter-union disputes and secondary action. Acas will not be concerned with whether the action is likely to enjoy statutory immunity in tort or not. **3.25**

'In contemplation or furtherance'

3.26

The test of whether there is a trade dispute is an *objective* one – i.e. is there a dispute between workers and their employer that relates wholly or mainly to one or more of the matters listed in S.244(1)? But it is not enough to establish the existence of a trade dispute. A party claiming immunity must show that he or she is acting 'in contemplation or furtherance' of the dispute.

The House of Lords ruled in Express Newspapers Ltd v McShane and anor 1980 ICR 42, HL, that the test of whether an act is 'in furtherance' of a dispute is a *subjective* one. The test is satisfied where a party honestly and genuinely thinks that he or she is helping one side in a trade dispute which concerns one of the matters listed in S.244(1). It is unnecessary to consider whether the party is acting reasonably or, in particular, whether his or her actions are likely to, or did in fact, achieve their purpose.

An illustration: **3.27**

- **Duport Steels Ltd and ors v Sirs and ors** 1980 ICR 161, HL: the union called its members employed by the (then) nationalised British Steel Corporation out on strike over a pay dispute. That was unquestionably a trade dispute. About four weeks later the union called out all its members employed by

61

private sector steel companies (with whom there was no dispute) as well. The House of Lords held that calling out private sector members was an act taken with the genuine purpose of furthering the trade dispute with the British Steel Corporation. The union honestly believed that bringing about a national shortage of steel would put pressure on the Government to settle the public sector dispute.

(It should be noted that this case would now be caught by the ban on secondary industrial action that applies to many cases where there is doubt as to whether the action is in furtherance of a trade dispute: sympathy strikes, even if they are likely to further the original dispute, no longer enjoy immunity – see Chapter 4.)

Provided the party in question is supporting a dispute relating to one or more of the matters listed in S.244(1), the fact that the party may also have political (or other) motives will not prevent that party's actions from being deemed to be in furtherance or contemplation of a trade dispute. As Mr Justice Millett stated in Associated British Ports and ors v Transport and General Workers' Union 1989 IRLR 291, ChD: 'The presence of an improper motive is relevant only if it is so overriding that it negatives any genuine intention to promote or advance the dispute.' Similarly, in Norbrook Laboratories Ltd v King 1984 IRLR 200, NICA, the Northern Ireland Court of Appeal observed that in order to show that an act was done in contemplation or furtherance of a trade dispute, a person does not have to show that that was the exclusive intention; it is sufficient if it was one of the elements that induced that person to do the act in question.

3.28 Obviously, action cannot be in contemplation or furtherance of a trade dispute if there is in fact no trade dispute either existing or impending. The question of whether a dispute is existing or imminent is to be decided by an objective test – Express Newspapers Ltd v McShane and anor 1980 ICR 42, HL (above). It is a matter of fact and degree and each case will turn on its facts. Three illustrations:

- **Health Computing Ltd and anor v Meek and ors** 1981 ICR 24, ChD: NALGO sent out a circular to its members instructing them not to cooperate with a private computer firm because of fears over possible job losses affecting NHS computer staff. The High Court held that it was reasonable to foresee that NALGO's policy of banning the private firm from the NHS might lead to disputes with the employer health authorities and the circular had therefore been distributed in contemplation of those disputes

- **Conway v Wade** 1909 AC 506, HL: W told the employer that the union members of the workforce would withdraw their labour if C was not dismissed. It was found as a fact that this was untrue. The House of Lords held that it was not enough that W was thinking of stirring up trouble and causing a strike. There was no evidence that any dispute was likely to occur.

W could not be said to be acting in contemplation of a dispute, since the dispute was all in his mind

- **Bent's Brewery Co Ltd and ors v Hogan** 1945 2 All ER 570, Liverpool Spring Assizes: the employer sought an injunction to restrain the union from inducing members to disclose confidential information to the union in breach of their contracts of employment. The union had sent out a document to employees seeking information about wages and conditions. The court rejected an argument that the union was acting in contemplation of a trade dispute. There was no dispute or difference of opinion: the document was sent out to obtain information which, after consideration of the information obtained, might have led to a request which, if not granted, might have resulted in a dispute.

It is, however, possible to act in contemplation of a dispute which never occurs. It is expressly provided that an act which, if resisted, *would* have led to a trade dispute will be treated as being done in contemplation of a trade dispute notwithstanding that, because the other side submits, no dispute actually arises – S.244(4) (our stress). Thus, if a union threatens to call a strike and the employer immediately concedes, the union will be protected as having acted in contemplation of a trade dispute.

In Newham London Borough Council v National and Local Government Officers Association 1993 ICR 189, CA, the issue was whether a dispute was still ongoing or whether it had in fact ended. The Court of Appeal seemed to say that a dispute continues as long as one side honestly and genuinely believes that there is still a dispute. However, this appears to go against the House of Lords' ruling that the question of whether a trade dispute exists is to be decided on an objective test – see Express Newspapers Ltd v McShane and anor 1980 ICR 42, HL. It just so happens that in the Newham case the Court found that there was evidence of a 'real and live dispute' – a finding which reinforces the view that the test of whether there is a trade dispute is in fact an objective one.

4 Loss of immunity

Ballots and notice of industrial action

Secondary action

Dismissals during unofficial action

Unlawful picketing

Union-only and recognition clauses

Enforcing union membership

In Chapter 3 we discuss S.219 of the Trade Union and Labour Relations **4.1** (Consolidation) Act 1992 (TULR(C)A), which grants immunity from legal proceedings to persons who are legally responsible for the commission of any of the main industrial torts; namely, inducing a breach of contract or interference with contract, intimidation or conspiracy to do any of these torts (see Chapter 2 for an explanation of the industrial torts). In this chapter we outline the circumstances in which the immunity granted by S.219 is lost. This happens where:

- a union has taken official industrial action without the support of a secret ballot and/or where a union has not given the employer due notice of industrial action

- there is unlawful secondary action

- there is industrial action in support of workers dismissed while taking part in unofficial industrial action

- there is unlawful picketing

- a union has taken industrial action to impose union-only labour conditions or union recognition

- a union has taken action to impose union membership.

In each case, in order to determine whether industrial action is lawful, it is necessary to go through a three-stage process and ask the following questions:

- does the action concerned incur common law liability for one of the industrial torts? If there is no liability the action will be lawful, but almost invariably *effective* industrial action will incur tortious liability

- does S.219 provide immunity from that liability? If it does not, there is no need to consider the third question

65

- does anything in the TULR(C)A remove the S.219 defence and restore the original common law liability?

4.2 The first two stages are discussed in Chapter 2, 'Liability for industrial action', and Chapter 3, 'Trade union immunities'. This chapter addresses the third stage and explains the circumstances in which immunity for the industrial torts covered by S.219 will be lost. When considering this issue it is always useful to bear in mind who will actually be liable in tort if the S.219 immunity is removed. S.219 provides immunity to a *person* who acts in contemplation or furtherance of a trade dispute. This covers any legal person such as a trade union or individual union official or member. In reality, however, very few parties affected by industrial action take legal action against an individual. Legal proceedings are generally initiated against the relevant trade union provided the union is vicariously liable for that person's actions (see Chapter 2 under 'Union liability in tort').

4.3 Ballots and notice of industrial action

Briefly, a union will lose the immunity provided by S.219 if the complex balloting requirements contained in S.226 are not satisfied. A union will then be exposed to legal proceedings by any person affected by the industrial action. In addition, the union must ensure that certain pre-balloting information specified in S.226A is given to the employer. A union must also ensure that, where a ballot has resulted in a vote in favour of industrial action, the relevant employer has been given due notice of the union's intention to start or resume industrial action – S.234A. These balloting requirements are discussed in detail in Chapter 5, 'Industrial action ballots'.

4.4 Secondary action

Subject to the exception of lawful picketing (discussed under 'Lawful secondary action' below), secondary industrial action is rendered unlawful by S.224 TULR(C)A. Accordingly, unions that organise such action will lose immunity from legal proceedings brought under any of the industrial torts specified in S.219.

4.5 Definition of secondary action
Section 224(2) provides that:

'There is secondary action in relation to a trade dispute when, and only when, a person –

(a) induces another to break a contract of employment or interferes or induces another to interfere with its performance, or

(b) threatens that a contract of employment under which he or another is employed will be broken or its performance interfered with, or that he will induce another to break a contract of employment or to interfere with its performance,

and the employer under the contract of employment is not the employer party to the dispute.'

Primary action refers to acts done in contemplation or furtherance of a trade **4.6** dispute between workers and their own employer. A union organising primary action will normally be protected from liability by S.219, provided the action is supported by a ballot. Secondary action consists essentially of calling or threatening a strike or other industrial action by workers of an employer who is *not* a party to the primary dispute. Typically, this will involve inducing the workers of the secondary employer to suspend the supply of goods or services to the primary employer. (Note that the definition contained in S.224 does not cover the situation where a union which is in dispute with an employer *directly* persuades or induces a third party to breach a supply or other commercial contract with the target employer.)

In the context of secondary action the definition of 'contract of employment' includes not only a contract of service or apprenticeship but also the contract of a self-employed person who contracts personally to do work or perform services for another – S.224(6). This definition is deliberately wide and removes a loophole identified in Shipping Company Uniform Inc v International Transport Workers Federation and ors 1985 ICR 245, QBD. In that case the union had threatened to 'black' a ship by inducing pilots not to guide her out of harbour. The High Court held that this was not secondary action as defined in the Employment Act 1980 because the pilots were self-employed and did not work under contracts of employment. This action would now be caught by S.224(6) because the pilots worked under contracts to provide personal services.

Employer in dispute
4.7

Where more than one employer is in dispute with his workers, each dispute must be treated as a separate dispute – S.224(4). This would apply to a situation like the 1990 campaign for a shorter working week in the engineering industry where there was a series of parallel disputes with the same or similar subject-matter.

One employer cannot become a party to another employer's dispute – S.224(4). Accordingly, if Employer A (the primary employer) is involved in a trade dispute and Employer B offers to help out Employer A by, for example, delivering goods which are being held up by industrial action, a union might take the view that Employer B has become a party to the dispute. However, any argument along these lines would not succeed because Employer B is only a secondary employer in relation to the trade dispute. Accordingly, any instruction by the

67

union to its members at Employer B to break their contracts of employment by refusing to deal with Employer A would amount to the tort of inducing a person to break a contract of employment. The immunity contained in S.219 would not apply in this situation and Employer B could sue the union on the basis that the union had induced B's employees to break their contracts of employment. Employer A would also be able to sue the union for interference with its business by unlawful means and it might also be able to sue for interference by unlawful means of any contract it might have with B – the unlawful means being the union's instruction to Employer B's employees to break their contracts of employment.

4.8 There will be secondary action if action is artificially fomented or protracted at one company in order to bring pressure on another company. However, action which is primary action in relation to one genuine trade dispute may not be relied on as secondary action in relation to another dispute – S.224(5). Thus, if there are strikes arising out of trade disputes at both Company X and Company Y, and the strike at Company X results in the breach of a contract to supply goods to Company Y, Company Y cannot complain of secondary action by the organisers of the strike at Company X.

Secondary action aimed at an associated employer will not attract immunity. This is the case even if the manufacture or supply of goods and services has been diverted by the employer in dispute to an associated employer. It might be possible, however, for the workers of the associated employer to take primary action against their own employer on the basis that they object to the transfer of work from the employer involved in the dispute. However, any action would have to be sufficiently closely related to the matters listed in S.244(1) – which defines 'trade dispute' – to be protected (see Chapter 3 under 'Trade dispute' for details). The workers of the associated employer could possibly ensure this proximity by asking that a clause be inserted into their contracts of employment stating that they should not be required to handle such work. In this way the union might be able to argue that the dispute related to the terms and conditions of the workers' employment and that S.244(1)(a) was therefore satisfied. It would also be necessary to show that the action was taken to further the dispute with their own employer, and not to further the dispute with the employer that diverted the goods and services in the first place. (Note that two employers are treated as 'associated' for statutory purposes if one is a company of which the other (directly or indirectly) has control, or both are companies of which a third person (directly or indirectly) has control – S.297.)

There may be some integrated group structures where only one member of the group is the employer. This leaves open the possibility that several companies could be party to the same trade dispute. This might occur where a group of companies consisting of a parent company and a number of subsidiaries are interdependent, despite having quite different functions. For example, CPG Ltd is the parent company; CPG (Property) Ltd holds the title to the group's real estate; CPG (Manufacturing) Ltd operates the production of goods; and CPG (Services) Ltd supplies staff to other members of the group as and when required. In this situation none of the companies is independent of the others and it is therefore arguable that any trade dispute ought to be treated as a dispute with the group as a whole.

Lawful secondary action   4.9

As mentioned above, there is only one form of lawful secondary action that attracts the protection of the statutory immunities contained in S.219. This is where the action is *lawful picketing* – S.224(1). In order to attract immunity the requirements contained in Ss.220 and 224(3) must be satisfied. Lawful picketing is discussed at length in Chapter 6, 'Picketing'. Briefly, pickets must be picketing in contemplation or furtherance of a trade dispute; at or near their own workplace or former workplace; and be workers or former workers of the employer who is a party to the dispute (unless they are union officials representing and accompanying their members). Picketing must be limited to peacefully obtaining or communicating information, or peacefully persuading any person to work or abstain from working. Thus, it will be lawful to induce a supplier's lorry driver to break his or her contract of employment by not crossing a picket-line to supply goods or materials to the employer in dispute. But a union will have no immunity if it organises a picket at the supplier's premises.

Dismissals during unofficial action   4.10

Section 237(1) provides that: 'An employee has no right to complain of unfair dismissal if at the time of dismissal he was taking part in an unofficial strike or other unofficial industrial action.' One of the effects of this provision is that an employer can scapegoat employees by selectively dismissing union members involved in the action and avoid exposure to unfair dismissal claims.

Section 223 supplements this power to selectively dismiss by providing that a union will have no immunity from proceedings in tort in respect of industrial action (or the threat of such action) if the reason – or one of the reasons – for calling the action is the *fact or belief* that the employer has dismissed one or more employees in circumstances in which they have no right to complain of unfair dismissal because they were taking part in unofficial action at the time of dismissal. Thus, a union will not be able to enter into a lawful dispute in support of members dismissed while taking part in unofficial industrial action. This was held to be the case in British Railways Board v National Union of Rail, Maritime and Transport Workers, unreported 17.9.92, QBD.

Section 223 makes it clear that the fact or belief that a dismissal in connection 4.11 with unofficial action has taken place need only be *one* of the reasons for the action; it does not have to be the principal reason for the action. Unions must therefore tread very carefully in circumstances where dismissals in connection with unofficial action have taken place in the recent past and they subsequently decide to organise industrial action on an entirely separate matter. In such a situation a union would be well advised to dissociate this new action from the foregoing dismissals.

We deal with the dismissal provisions affecting employees taking unofficial action at greater length in Chapter 8, 'Industrial action dismissals'. However, it is worth noting here that S.237(2) states that a strike or other industrial action will be unofficial in relation to an employee unless (a) he or she is a member of a trade union and the action is *authorised or endorsed* by that union, or (b) he or she is not a member of a trade union but there are among those taking part in the industrial action members of a trade union by which the action has been authorised or endorsed. It is further provided that if none of those taking part in the action are union members, then it shall not be considered to be unofficial.

Under S.20(2) industrial action is deemed to be authorised or endorsed – i.e. it is *deemed to be official* action – if it is called by any person authorised to do so by the union's rule book or by the union leadership, or if it is in fact authorised or endorsed by any committee of the union or any other official of the union (whether employed by it or not). Action called by a person belonging to this third category only ceases to be deemed to be official – i.e. it becomes unofficial action as defined – when it has been repudiated by the principal executive committee, president or general secretary of the union – S.21(1).

4.12 Until the action is formally repudiated it will be treated as official. In this context, it should be noted that repudiation does not take effect until the end of the following working day – S.237(4). Accordingly, it follows that S.237(1) does not apply to employees if they are dismissed at a time when the industrial action has not been repudiated. In this situation, employees will be subject to the provisions on industrial action dismissals set out in Ss.238 and 238A – see Chapter 8. It also follows that industrial action taken in response to such dismissals will not lose immunity because the employees were dismissed at a time when they were deemed to be taking official action.

4.13 Unlawful picketing

As noted above under 'Secondary action', lawful picketing is the one form of secondary industrial action that retains immunity. Picketing which falls outside the strict requirements of S.220 will be unlawful. The consequences of unlawful picketing are discussed in greater detail in Chapter 6. Briefly, however, it is important to note that if unlawful picketing occurs the picket will lose the protection of S.219, leaving the picket (and possibly the union) open to legal proceedings – S.219(3).

Union-only and recognition clauses

Clauses in contracts for the supply of goods or services that require suppliers to employ union members only or to recognise or negotiate with unions are void. Ss.222(3) and 225(1) TULR(C)A remove immunity in tort from industrial action taken to impose union-only labour clauses or union recognition requirements.

Union-only clauses

Any term or condition in a contract for the supply of goods or services will be void if it requires that all or some of the work involved should be done by persons who are, or are not, members of trade unions or of a particular trade union – S.144 TULR(C)A.

It is also unlawful to refuse to *deal* with a supplier or prospective supplier of goods or services on union membership grounds – S.145. The circumstances in which a person will be held to have refused to deal with a supplier are spelled out in the section. The first occurs where a person maintains a list of approved suppliers, or suppliers from whom tenders may be invited, which leaves out a supplier 'on union membership grounds' – S.145(2). This means that a supplier must not be left off a list of approved suppliers on the ground that, if the supplier were awarded a contract, the work would be, or would be likely to be, done by persons who were, or who were not, members of trade unions or of a particular trade union.

Secondly, a person must not, in relation to a proposed contract for the supply of goods or services, exclude a supplier from the group of suppliers invited to submit tenders, or fail to permit a supplier to submit a tender, or otherwise determine not to enter into a contract with a supplier, on union membership or non-membership grounds – S.145(3). Finally, it is unlawful to terminate a contract for the supply of goods or services because of the union membership or non-membership of the workforce – S.145(4).

Industrial pressure to impose union-only clauses

An act loses immunity if it constitutes, or is one of a number of acts which together constitute, an inducement or attempted inducement of a person to incorporate in a contract with a supplier of goods or services a union (or non-union) labour-only clause – S.222(3)(a). It is also unlawful to apply pressure to induce, or attempt to induce, a person to avoid dealing with a supplier on the ground of union membership or non-membership – S.222(3)(b). Any trade dispute immunity is lost in these two circumstances. Note, however, that union pressure on an employer to impose a fair wages clause on a contractor would not be caught by these provisions.

'Inducement' need not involve industrial action, but may extend to a simple request not to deal with a particular contractor. In Messenger Newspapers Group Ltd v National Graphical Association (1982) 1984 IRLR 397, QBD, the union wrote to advertisers requesting them to cease advertising in local newspapers published by the Messenger Group. The union was trying to enforce acceptance of a closed shop by the Messenger Group. It was held that this was an infringement of S.222 – the union was inducing or attempting to induce advertisers to withdraw business because of the non-union composition of Messenger Group's workforce.

4.18 Action that is caught by S.222(3) may fall outside the definition of a 'trade dispute' in any event or, alternatively, may be viewed as secondary action and be unlawful as such. A trade dispute must be a dispute between workers and *their* employer – S.244(1). Industrial action against an employer aimed at inducing him not to deal with a supplier who employs non-union labour would be likely to be regarded as secondary action in furtherance of a dispute with the *supplier*, so immunity would not be provided by S.219 anyway.

4.19 **Union recognition clauses**

Any term or condition of a contract for the supply of goods or services will be void if it requires a party to the contract:

- to recognise one or more unions (whether or not named in the contract) for the purpose of negotiating on behalf of workers, or any class of worker, employed by him, or

- to negotiate or consult with, or with any official of, one or more unions (whether or not so named) – S.186.

It is also unlawful for a person to refuse to *deal* with a supplier or prospective supplier of goods and services where at least one of the grounds for not dealing with that supplier is that the supplier does not, or is not likely to, recognise, negotiate or consult with a union (or unions) – S.187(1).

4.20 Section 187(2) provides that a person refuses to deal with a person if:

- he or she excludes a supplier from an approved list of suppliers or of persons from whom tenders for the supply of goods or services may be invited, or

- he or she excludes that person from a group of persons from whom tenders for the supply of goods and services are invited, he or she fails to permit that person to submit such a tender or otherwise determines not to enter into a supply contract with that person, or

- he or she terminates a supply contract.

Industrial pressure to impose union recognition 4.21

Statutory immunity in tort is lost if a union induces or attempts to induce a person to incorporate a union recognition clause in a supply contract or otherwise to refuse to deal with a supplier who does not recognise trade unions – S.225(1). This covers the situation where the union is inducing one party to a supply contract to take action which will make the other party change its attitude to union recognition. (Note, however, that S.225 does not apply where workers take industrial action where their *own* employer refuses to recognise a union. In this situation, the action may attract statutory immunity under S.219 – see Chapter 3 under 'Trade dispute'.)

The union may also take direct action, typically by refusing to handle supplies from a contractor who does not recognise unions. This is caught by S.225(2)(a), which removes immunity from any act which interferes, or can reasonably be expected to interfere, with the supply of goods or services (whether or not under a contract). To establish liability in tort it is necessary to show that a person has (i) induced another to break a contract of employment or interfered or induced another to interfere with its performance, or (ii) threatened that a contract of employment under which he/she or another is employed will be broken or its performance interfered with, or that he/she will induce another to break a contract of employment or to interfere with its performance – S.225(2)(b). The supplier of the goods or services must be different from the employer under the contract of employment and one of the reasons for the action must be the fact or belief that the supplier does not, or might not, recognise, negotiate or consult with, or with an official of, one or more trade unions – S.225(2)(c).

Action caught by S.225 covers the situation where, for example, the employees 4.22 of A refuse to handle supplies from B, a contractor who does not recognise a particular union. Such action will usually amount to the industrial tort of interfering with B's business (or indirectly procuring a breach of B's commercial contract with A) by unlawful means and will – because of S.225(2) – be deprived of immunity. It may also be the case that the action will involve intimidation or conspiracy to interfere with B's business or commercial contract. Refusing to handle supplies from B will also, in practice, be deprived of immunity as being secondary action. In addition, A could argue that there is no legitimate trade dispute between himself and the union because the union's real dispute is with the supplier, so that immunity would not be provided by S.219 in the first place.

Enforcing union membership 4.23

There is no statutory immunity under S.219 where the reason – or one of the reasons – for the industrial action (or threat of such action) concerned is to enforce union membership. S.222(1) provides that immunity is removed where the reason – or one of the reasons – for the action complained of is the fact or belief that a particular employer:

73

- is employing, has employed or might employ a person who is not a union member, or who is not a member of a particular union or one of a number of particular unions, or

- is failing, has failed or might fail to discriminate against such a person.

Discrimination means treating workers or job applicants differently according to whether they are members of any or a particular trade union where the treatment accorded to union members is more favourable – S.222(2). Accordingly, a union will lose its immunity from liability in tort if it takes industrial action to enforce a demand that only union members be awarded a pay increase. However, industrial action in circumstances where an employer has offered more favourable treatment to non-union members would retain its immunity provided the union is only asking for equal treatment, as opposed to more favourable treatment, of its members.

4.24 The term 'an employer' in this context refers to the broad definition of an employer of workers, as opposed to just employees – S.222(4). And references to not being a member of a union are to not being a member of any union, of a particular union or one of a number of particular unions. Such references also cover not being a member of a particular branch or section of a trade union or of one of a number of particular branches or sections – S.222(5).

Section 222 has the broad effect of removing immunity from legal proceedings in respect of any of the industrial torts covered by S.219 which are committed as a result of action taken to enforce or impose a closed shop or to ensure that only members of one particular union are employed, either in general or on particular work (an 'in-house' dispute). It also removes immunity from any such tort committed in respect of an 'outside dispute' where, for example, a supplier or customer who employs non-union labour or who employs members of the 'wrong' union is boycotted. S.222 therefore recognises an individual's right to freedom of association as guaranteed by Article 11 of the European Convention on Human Rights, in that it reflects the negative right not to be compelled to join a union – see, for example, Sorenson v Denmark; Rasmussen v Denmark 2008 46 EHRR 29, ECtHR, where the European Court of Human Rights confirmed that Article 11 included both the right to join and also the right not to join a trade union.

5 Industrial action ballots

Preliminary considerations

Entitlement to vote

Separate workplace ballots

Ballot requirements

Period of effectiveness

An act done by a trade union to induce a person to take part, or continue to take **5.1** part, in industrial action is not protected by the statutory immunities contained in S.219 of the Trade Union and Labour Relations (Consolidation) Act 1992 (TULR(C)A) unless, among other things, the industrial action has the support of a ballot – S.226(1)(a). The requirement to hold a ballot prior to taking industrial action in order to render the action lawful was introduced by the Trade Union Act 1984. The relevant provisions, which have been substantially amended by succeeding Acts, are now contained in Part V of the TULR(C)A.

Some impression of the total incidence of trade union ballots can be obtained from data released by the Office for National Statistics for the period 2003 to 2007. The number of ballots calling for strike action steadily increased between 2003 and 2006, peaking at 1,290 in 2006 (of which 1,094 were in favour of a strike), before returning to the much lower figure of 713 in 2007 (of which 637 were in favour). By contrast, the number of ballots calling for industrial action short of a strike remained stable during the same four-year period. In 2007, for example, there was a total of 583 ballots calling for action short of a strike, 555 of which resulted in a vote in support of action.

The law does not make it obligatory as such to hold a ballot before calling industrial action and the courts have no power (as they did, briefly, under the Industrial Relations Act 1971) to order a ballot to be held. However, the effects of organising industrial action *without* the support of a properly conducted ballot (satisfying all the numerous statutory requirements) are threefold:

• industrial action authorised or endorsed by the union is deprived of statutory immunity in tort – S.226. The union will therefore be liable to court action by the *employer(s)* concerned. The industrial torts are discussed in Chapter 2, 'Liability for industrial action'

• *union members* have a statutory right to take court proceedings against their union for actual or prospective inducement to take part in industrial action which is unsupported by a ballot – S.62. This statutory right is in addition to any common law right a member may have when the union's action is

75

in breach of its rule book. (Members' rights are discussed in Chapter 7, 'Remedies for unlawful action')

- any *member of the public* who may, as a result of the industrial action, suffer a reduction in the quality of goods or services supplied or a prevention of, or a delay in, the supply of goods or services, can apply to the High Court or the Court of Session for an injunction to restrain the action – S.235A. This statutory right of action is discussed in Chapter 7.

5.2 But even where industrial action has the support of a ballot, immunity is not guaranteed. The following restrictions also apply:

- a single ballot of those expected to take part in industrial action will not normally be sufficient when separate workplaces are involved. As a general rule, separate ballots are required for each workplace, and the ballots must be secret postal ballots

- the ballot must comply strictly with a set of detailed statutory requirements. These were described by Lord Donaldson MR as 'a minefield in which it is all too easy to stray from the paths of safety and legality' – Post Office v Union of Communication Workers 1990 ICR 258, CA. In addition to prescribing conditions as to the content of the ballot paper, the conduct of the ballot and the role of independent scrutineers, the statutory requirements oblige the union to notify the employers affected of three separate matters: the fact of the ballot being held, the result of the ballot, and the proposed industrial action

- a ballot will not confer immunity on industrial action that is otherwise unlawful – for example, because it is secondary action or is in support of a closed shop or there is no genuine trade dispute

- ballots are only effective for a limited period – normally four weeks from the date of the ballot. However, this period may be extended to up to eight weeks by agreement between the union and the employer, and may be extended by order of the court if there are intervening legal proceedings.

The rules for industrial action ballots are notoriously complex. Key amendments to the law made by the Employment Relations Act 1999 (ERelA 1999) and the Employment Relations Act 2004 (ERelA 2004) went some way towards simplifying the legal requirements and explaining the technical intricacies involved. However, they did nothing to reduce the overall burden on unions to comply with detailed balloting provisions if they wished to retain the protection of S.219. The extent and complexity of the balloting provisions has led to the oft-mooted but rarely litigated question of whether they represent an unlawful restriction of Article 11 of the European Convention on Human Rights, which guarantees freedom of association with others, including the right to form and join trade unions. This question arose in Metrobus Ltd v Unite the Union 2010

ICR 173, CA, where the Court of Appeal was concerned with possible breaches by the union of the ballot and notice requirements. As part of its defence, the union argued that the restrictions imposed on trade unions by the TULR(C)A presented obstacles so numerous and so complex that errors by unions were almost inevitable, and that for this reason the rights under Article 11 were so constrained as not to be effectively exercisable in respect of industrial action. The Court rejected this argument, holding that, although the statutory ballot and notice requirements are detailed, they are not so onerous as to make the exercise of the right to freedom of association contained in Article 11 so restricted that the requirements are disproportionate. The rules were of a type permitted under Article 11(2), which allows for restrictions on the exercise of the right, and fell within the United Kingdom's 'margin of appreciation'. For further discussion of Article 11 rights, see Chapter 1.

In addition to the complex statutory provisions regulating industrial action **5.3** ballots, there is also a *Code of Practice on Industrial Action Ballots and Notice to Employers* ('the Code'), last revised in 2005. This was issued by the Secretary of State under powers conferred by Ss.203–208. Failure to observe provisions of the Code does not of itself render a union liable to any proceedings – S.207(1). However, the Code is admissible in evidence in any court proceedings and the court must take account of any provisions of the Code that appear to be relevant as indicating approved industrial practice – S.207(3).

Finally, it is worth mentioning that the costs of organising industrial action ballots can be significant. The Certification Officer used to have the power to refund certain costs incurred by trade unions in holding industrial action ballots. However, the provisions relating to public funds for industrial action ballots were repealed with effect from 1 April 1996.

Preliminary considerations   5.4

Any act for which a union is legally responsible (i.e. official union action) should be preceded by a ballot if the union wishes to avoid liability in tort for that act. The principles by which union liability is to be determined are examined in detail in Chapter 2, 'Liability for industrial action'. It is sufficient to note here that the actions of a wide range of persons, including shop stewards and other lay officials, will be deemed to have been authorised or endorsed by the union in question – S.20. Ballots must be held in respect of industrial action proposed to be taken by employees, by persons performing work or services personally for another (i.e. independent contractors and the self-employed) – S.235, and by persons holding an office or employment under the Crown – S.245.

Before an industrial action ballot is held, the union must:

• give notice of the ballot to the employer(s) in question

77

- provide a sample voting paper to the employer(s), and

- appoint an independent scrutineer to oversee the conduct of the ballot.

5.5 These requirements were introduced by the Trade Union Reform and Employment Rights Act 1993 (TURERA) and are considered separately below.

5.6 Notice of ballot to employer

The union must take such steps as are 'reasonably necessary' to ensure that every person 'who it is reasonable for the union to believe... will be the employer of persons who will be entitled to vote in the ballot' receives notice of the union's intention to hold an industrial action ballot, not later than *seven* days before the opening day of the ballot – S.226A(1)(a). The opening day of the ballot is defined as the first day when a voting paper is sent to any person entitled to vote – S.226A(4). The Code of Practice recommends that the union should allow sufficient time for delivery of the notice, use a suitable means of transmission (such as first-class post, courier, fax, e-mail or hand delivery) and consider obtaining confirmation that the employer has received the notice, e.g. by using recorded delivery (para 17).

The consequences of a union's failure to notify the employer before conducting a ballot are that the industrial action will not have the protection of the statutory immunities vis-à-vis *that* employer – S.226(1)(b). However, this does not prejudice the position in relation to other employers whose employees are participating in the industrial action, provided of course that the union has given them the necessary notice and information before conducting the ballot.

5.7 It is incumbent on the union to give notice of its intention to hold an industrial action ballot to *every* employer of those who will be entitled to vote. Whether the union has complied with this requirement is to be judged objectively and in the context of the negotiations that have taken place. In English, Welsh and Scottish Railway Ltd and anor v National Union of Rail, Maritime and Transport Workers 2004 EWCA Civ 1539, CA, the Court of Appeal held that a union's notice of intention to hold a ballot which was addressed to only one of two closely related companies involved in the dispute with the union was nevertheless effective. The case concerned two rail freight operating companies: EWS Ltd, which had 5,200 employees, and EWSI Ltd, which had only 273. Although they operated as part of a group, they were separate legal entities. However, the collective agreement that recognised the union for collective bargaining purposes referred to both companies as 'the company' in the singular, and the industrial relations of the two companies were conducted jointly by one person, S. When a dispute arose about working arrangements, the union negotiated with S and sent the subsequent notice of its intention to hold a ballot to him on the erroneous assumption that EWS Ltd employed all the employees who would be entitled to vote in the ballot. Attached to the notice was a sample of the voting form and a schedule containing a list of sites and numbers of employees at the sites whom the union believed would be entitled to vote in the ballot, including some sites that consisted exclusively or mainly of EWSI Ltd employees. When further negotiations broke down, the companies succeeded in obtaining a High Court injunction restraining the union from taking industrial action for, among other things, failing to comply with S.226A TULR(C)A. The union appealed to the Court of Appeal.

The Court of Appeal overturned the decision. Lord Justice Waller, giving the Court's judgment, emphasised that while it is very important that a union give an accurate notice to the right employer, he did not accept that because the notice had arrived on the desk of one company it followed that it had not arrived on the desk of the other. There were special circumstances in this case. Although the companies were two separate corporate entities, the former was considerably larger than the latter. In terms of their organisation, and in particular in so far as the collective agreement was concerned, they were dealt with as one negotiating entity. It was reasonably apparent from the documents before the Court that EWS Ltd had been treated as representing both companies in staff negotiations in the past. All previous disputes between the two companies and the union had been negotiated by S acting for both companies, and S was authorised to receive notices on behalf of both. In these circumstances, the Court held that, viewed objectively, the ballot notice would have been understood by a reasonable employer to be addressed to both companies, both because the words 'the company', viewed in context, were apt to cover both EWS Ltd and EWSI Ltd, and because of the schedule that was attached to the notice. Accordingly, the notice was valid and the injunction was discharged.

Content of the notice. The notice of the union's intention to hold a ballot must **5.8** be in writing, and must:

- state that the union intends to hold the ballot – S.226A(2)(a)

- specify the date which the union reasonably believes will be the opening day of the ballot – S.226A(2)(b) and

- contain:

  (i) a list of the categories of employee to which the employees concerned belong and a list of their workplaces; and figures for the total number of employees concerned and the number of employees for each category and workplace concerned, together with an explanation of how those figures were arrived at – S.226A(2)(c)(i), (2A) and (2B), or

  (ii) where some or all of the employees concerned are employees from whose wages the employer makes deductions representing payments to the union ('check-off'), either those lists and figures (with the explanation) mentioned in (i) above, or such information as will enable the employer readily to deduce: (a) the total number of employees concerned, (b) the categories to which they belong and the number of employees in those categories, and (c) the workplaces at which the employees concerned work and the number of employees who work at each of the workplaces – S.226A(2)(c)(ii) and (2C).

(Note that similar employee information must be provided to the employer under S.234A, which requires unions to give seven days' notice of any intended industrial action – see 'Ballot requirements' under 'Notice of industrial action to employer' below.)

5.9 The 'employees concerned' are those whom the union reasonably believes will be entitled to vote in the ballot – S.226A(2H). The workplace at which an employee works is the single set of premises at or from which he or she works or, in relation to any other employee, the premises with which his or her employment has the closest connection – S.226A(2I).

The lists, figures and information supplied must be as accurate as is reasonably practicable in the light of the information in the possession of the union at the relevant time – S.226A(2D). Information is in the possession of a union if it is held for union purposes in a document (either electronically or in any other form) and is in the possession or under the control of an officer or employee of the union – S.226A(2E).

5.10 **Level of detail necessary.** The third requirement in S.226A(2) – i.e. that governing the type of information the union must provide vis-à-vis the employees concerned – has been through various incarnations since it was first introduced. When originally inserted by TURERA, it provided that the notice must describe, *so as to enable the employer to readily ascertain them* (our stress), the employees who it was reasonable for the union to believe would be entitled to vote in the ballot. This was interpreted by the courts – most notably, in Blackpool and The Fylde College v National Association of Teachers in Further and Higher Education 1994 ICR 648, CA – as requiring the union in certain circumstances to supply the employer with the names of all those employees who would be balloted or called upon to take industrial action. The ERelA 1999 addressed this problem by inserting a new subsection to the effect that a union's failure to name employees in the notice would not be a ground for holding that it did not comply with the statutory requirements. This was subsequently reworded by the ERelA 2004 and now provides that nothing in S.226A requires a union to supply an employer with the names of the employees concerned – S.226A(2G). Thus, unions cannot be compelled to disclose the names of their members who may take part in strike action. That said, there is nothing to prevent a union from disclosing the names of its members if it wishes to do so.

The ERelA 1999 made further amendments to S.226A, stating that the notice must contain 'such information in the union's possession as would help the employer to make plans' and – ostensibly to simplify the law in this area – describing the type of information that must, at a minimum, be included as 'information as to the number, category or workplace of the employees concerned'. Lord Justice Robert Walker, commenting on these amendments in London Underground Ltd and ors v National Union of Rail, Maritime and Transport Workers 2001 ICR 647, CA, noted that the revised version did not alter the provision's legislative purpose, which was – and continued to be – 'to enable an employer to know which part or parts of its workforce were being invited to take industrial action, in order that the employer could (first) try to dissuade them and (secondly, and so far as unsuccessful in its first aim) make plans to avoid or minimise disruption and continue to communicate with the relevant part or parts of the workforce'. Nor was it intended to make compliance with preparing notices under S.226A (and S.234A) any easier. In fact, he proffered the view that, depending on the facts, a union's task of complying with the statutory notice requirements could be more onerous than under the pre-1999 version of the law on ballot notification.

In February 2003, the Department of Trade and Industry (now the Department **5.11** for Business, Innovation and Skills) conducted a general review of the changes to trade union law made by the ERelA 1999. While reaffirming its overall commitment to the essential features of industrial action law, it acknowledged that the introduction of the minimum information requirement in relation to ballot notices had made a union's tasks 'more arduous'. This, combined with the requirement to supply such information in the union's possession that 'would help the employer' faced with the threat of industrial action, had had the unintended effect of making the scope of the union's legal obligations under the Act even more 'uncertain'. The situation was summarised as follows: 'The courts have interpreted [S.226A] as requiring unions to attach detailed matrices to their notices identifying the number and grade of their members at each workplace involved in the dispute – a task which is exceptionally difficult to perform where membership turnover is high or where members are often re-deployed to different workplaces. The disclosure of such detailed information was not always necessary under the previous law… Unions have also complained that they are often required to supply detailed information – in addition to the matrices – to assist the employer "to make plans" [in accordance with S.226A(2)(c)], a phrase which is open to wide interpretation. In fact, unions do not know in advance what the notice requirements actually entail. This uncertainty is accentuated by the need for unions to provide information which might be held by lay officials, the precise extent of which will often be unknown to the union's full time officers (who are usually responsible for issuing notices)' (paras 3.26 and 3.27). The review concluded that 'in some ways, the attempt to simplify this law in the 1999 Act has made the law even more complex and burdensome. This was not the intention' (para 3.28).

In response to the findings of the review, the Government enacted the ERelA 2004, which introduced the current wording of S.226A (with effect from 1 October 2005). This, as we have seen, states that (except where the employer operates check-off – see below) the notice must contain a list of the categories of employee to which the employees concerned belong and the workplaces at which they work; and figures (together with an explanation of how they were arrived at) showing the total number of employees concerned, the number of them for each of the categories listed and the number of them that work at each of the workplaces listed – S.226A(2)(c)(i), (2A) and (2B). In addition, the 2004 Act clarified the meaning of information 'in the union's possession', restricting it to information that is held for union purposes in a document (either electronically or in any other form) in the possession or under the control of an officer or employee of the union – S.226A(2E). It follows that information held by shop stewards or other lay representatives is not information 'in the union's possession' for these purposes, although the Code of Practice unhelpfully states that these persons are 'probably' not covered (para 14). The requirement to provide information that would help the employer 'make plans' was removed altogether.

Categorisation of employees. When determining how to categorise a group of employees, the Code of Practice advises unions to choose a categorisation that relates to the nature of the work (para 15). Such categorisation, it continues, may be based on the occupation, grade or pay band of the employees concerned. In Westminster City Council v UNISON 2001 ICR 1046, CA, Lord Justice Buxton stated that 'category' means 'no more than a reference to the general type of workers'. In some cases, therefore, the requirement to provide 'a list of the categories of employee to which the employees concerned belong' in S.226A(2A) will be satisfied even if only a broad job description is provided. For example, referring to those to be balloted as teachers at a particular school may be entirely sufficient in some cases. However, in others, it will be incumbent on the union to provide more detailed information as to members' occupations to ensure that the employer knows which part or parts of the workforce will be asked to take part in industrial action and thus enable him to plan effectively for such an eventuality.

5.12 The Code states that the decision as to categorisation may be informed by the categorisations the employer uses in dealings with the union, and may be influenced by the type of data the union holds or has access to. The availability of data may therefore be a limiting factor in this regard. In Anglian Windows Ltd v GMB 2007 EWHC 917, QBD, for example, the GMB specified in the ballot notice the production units where it intended to ballot its members. One such unit was merely categorised as encompassing 'production workers'. The employer submitted that this description was inadequate because it failed to describe the functions of the employees in sufficient detail to enable it to plan a response to the strike. The employees in that particular unit included line workers, fitters, electricians, progress chasers and others. The GMB argued that it did not have the requisite information to identify the particular roles carried out by each of the members. The High Court found in the union's favour, holding that the evidence did not show that the GMB had information in its possession that would have enabled it to categorise its members better.

However, the opposite outcome was reached in EDF Energy Powerlink Ltd v National Union of Rail, Maritime and Transport Workers 2010 IRLR 114, QBD, which concerned employees working in EDF's installations that supply electrical power to the London Underground system. The RMT gave EDF notice of its intention to ballot 64 of its members 'employed by the company in the category of engineer/technician' at three different workplaces. EDF, which employed fitters, jointers, test room inspectors, day testers, shift testers and OLBI fitters within that job category, informed the union that it regarded the notice as deficient in that the information provided did not enable it to identify the affected employees at the three sites. EDF also referred to a notice of a ballot the RMT had given the previous year that had further particularised the affected employees as 'shift tester staff'. The union insisted that the notice met the requirements of S.226A, adding that its database did not contain any more detailed information. EDF subsequently sought an injunction restraining the union from taking industrial action.

The High Court granted the injunction. In its view, the employer was entitled to know who was being balloted in respect of the different trades: it would make a material difference to EDF whether it had to face the risk, for example, of a test room inspector withdrawing his or her labour as opposed to a fitter. Moreover, the union could not circumscribe the scope of its duty under S.226A by praying in aid the fact that it did not record this type of information. The Court noted that, by virtue of S.226A(2D), the information supplied must be as accurate as reasonably practicable in the light of the information in the union's possession (see 'Errors in the notice' below). While the information held by the union was therefore highly material when considering whether it had discharged its duty under S.226A, it was not, the Court thought, necessarily always decisive. Otherwise, it said 'there would be a temptation for... trade unions to record minimal information in their record-keeping of members in order to diminish the content of the duty to supply categories to the employer'. Furthermore, the Court found that it would have been practicable for the union to contact the shop stewards at the relevant workplaces and to discover the particular function in which the employees were engaged. Accordingly, the union had not given proper notice under S.226A.

In reaching this conclusion, it seems that the High Court may have been **5.13** influenced by the fact that a previous ballot notice given to EDF had contained specific reference to the job grade of the affected employees – information that had been obtained after the RMT had contacted the shop steward at the particular workplace directly. However, while it may have been entirely possible for the union to follow the same course of action in this case, it seems that the Court's decision that it was required to do so goes beyond the language of S.226A. The Court also expressed concern that a union might be able to comply with its notification duty simply by supplying minimal information to the employer as to the part(s) of the business affected. However, a union that deliberately keeps only, for instance, broad job descriptions of its members in order to avoid its obligations under S.226A will run the risk of losing its statutory protection to organise a lawful strike under the TULR(C)A. This should provide a powerful incentive to unions to keep records as detailed as reasonably practicable.

Finally, the Code recommends that when providing an explanation as to how the figures in the written notice were arrived at, unions should consider including a description of the sources of data used to compile the figures, e.g. membership lists held centrally or information held at regional offices, or data collected from surveys or other sources (para 16). However, unions are not legally obliged to provide this type of information.

'Check-off'. The ERelA 2004 added a new S.226A(2)(c)(ii) into the TULR(C)A, which provides that, where the employees concerned are employees from whose wages the employer makes deductions representing payments to the union – known as 'check-off' or 'DOCAS' (Deductions Of Contributions At Source) employees – the union has a choice as to the type of information it must give to the employer: it can supply either the lists and figures (with the explanation) required by S.226A(2)(c)(i), (2A) and (2B) as mentioned above or such information as will enable the employer readily to deduce that information for himself – S.226A(2)(c)(ii) and (2C). Accordingly, where all the employees whom the union believes will be induced to take part in industrial action are check-off employees, it can satisfy the information requirement of S.226A simply by giving the employer information relating to the check-off payments. The employer will then be able to check the payroll records to identify the employees concerned.

5.14 Although S.226A(2)(c)(ii) has somewhat eased the burden on unions to provide detailed information to employers where the members to be balloted are check-off employees, the wording initially gave rise to some confusion where the membership consisted of both check-off and non-check-off staff. The issue was whether, in these circumstances, S.226A(2)(c)(ii) – which applies where 'some or all' of the employees concerned are check-off employees – was satisfied where the union merely supplied information from which the employer could readily deduce the necessary information for himself without supplying the specific lists, figures and explanation required under S.226A(2)(c)(i). The Court of Appeal grappled with this question in Metrobus Ltd v Unite the Union 2010 ICR 173, CA. In that case, Unite, which represented bus drivers employed by

M Ltd, submitted a claim for improved pay and conditions in 2008. Dissatisfied with the response, it wrote to M Ltd, stating that it intended to hold an industrial action ballot. The ballot notice stated that the number of employees eligible to vote who were check-off employees was 776 and the number of non-check-off employees was 69, giving a total of 845 employees. A majority voted for strike action and subsequently went on strike. When this failed to resolve the dispute, Unite called another strike. In response, M Ltd successfully applied to the High Court for an injunction to prevent the strike action. The High Court judge held that Unite lost its immunity under S.219 TULR(C)A for various breaches of the notice and balloting requirements prior to taking industrial action, including a failure to supply M Ltd with an explanation as to how the figures were arrived at in accordance with S.226A(2)(c)(ii). Unite disputed that its ballot notice was invalid and appealed to the Court of Appeal, arguing that S.226A(2)(c)(ii) merely required it to provide information from which the employer could readily deduce the relevant information, including the explanation, himself.

The Court of Appeal was divided as to the correct interpretation of S.226A(2)(c)(ii). A majority (Lord Justice Lloyd and Sir Mark Potter, the President of the Family Division) took the view that, in the case of non-check-off employees, a union is obliged to provide a list of the number of employees, the number in each workplace and the number in each category, along with an explanation of how those figures were reached. Only in the case of check-off employees can a union simply provide such information as would allow the employer to readily deduce the totals discussed above, since in the case of other employees it will not be possible for the employer to readily deduce such information. In reaching this conclusion the majority took account of the Code of Practice, which states: 'Where only some of the employees concerned pay their union contributions by the "check off", the union's notice may include both types of information. That is, the lists, figures and explanations should be provided for those who do not pay their subscriptions through the check off whilst information relating to check-off payments may suffice for those who do' (para 14). Unite could have followed the Code's advice and provided lists, figures and an explanation for the non-check-off employees, while directing M Ltd to its payroll records for the others. It followed that the judge had correctly found that Unite, in not including an explanation, had erred, and that the notice was deficient in this respect.

Lord Justice Maurice Kay, dissenting on this issue, was of the view that where there are both check-off and non-check-off employees, the union has the choice of adopting the lists, figures and explanation model or adopting the 'readily deduce' approach. In support of this, he disputed the view expressed by the majority of the Court that it would not be possible to readily deduce the information about non-check-off employees. However, with the majority's view prevailing, the Court dismissed Unite's appeal.

85

5.15 *Examples.* Two examples of notices that satisfied the minimum information requirement in S.226A(2)(c):

- **Anglian Windows Ltd v GMB** 2007 EWHC 917, QBD: on 7 March 2007, the GMB gave AW Ltd notice of its intention to hold a ballot for industrial action and informed it that the first day of the ballot would be 15 March. The notice stated that 82 members were check-off employees. In addition, there were 187 members not on the check-off system. The notice continued: 'The information in GMB's possession relating to the categories to which the 187 employees concerned belong and the workplaces at which they work is as follows: all of these 187 direct debit/cash payment members are employed by you at Anglian Windows Ltd, Units 13, 14, 15, 17 and 19, PO Box 45, Anson Road, Norwich NR6 6EJ.' The categories of jobs were listed as follows: Unit 13: 91 production workers; Unit 14: 1 mechanic; Unit 15: 5 engineers; Unit 17: 3 production workers; Unit 19: 87 glass shop/production workers. The High Court held that this notice complied with the statutory requirements under S.226A(2)(c) and was therefore valid

- **Westminster City Council v UNISON** 2001 ICR 1046, CA: UNISON sent a ballot notice to the Council in response to the Council's decision to contract out the functions of its housing assessment and advice unit to a private company. The notice described the members to be balloted as 'those staff who pay their subscriptions via the [DOCAS system]. They work in the advice and assessment office at Harrow Road and they can be described as A&A workers. I believe there are 45 in total who will be balloted.' The Court of Appeal held that the notice was valid. Information was provided by reference to the DOCAS system, by which the individual identities of the employees concerned could easily be ascertained by the employer.

By contrast, the notice in RMT v London Underground (see above), detailing the members to be balloted as the union members employed by the employer 'in all categories at all workplaces... [of which] there are approximately 4938', fell far short of the statutory requirements. Similarly, the ballot notice in British Telecommunications plc v Communication Workers Union 2004 IRLR 58, QBD, was not detailed enough. The union stated in the notice that it intended to ballot 'all CWU Engineering members employed in BT Retail Customer Services Field Operations and in BT Northern Ireland (MEJ1, 4 and 5)', and that there were '14,001 such members'. The employer knew that 90 per cent of the employees in question were union members, but the High Court held that figures could vary greatly between different locations. Accordingly, the total number given in the notice should have been broken down to include the numbers employed in different categories. Only that information would have helped the employer to make plans in respect of the proposed strike.

5.16 **Errors in the notice.** Given the complexity of the statutory requirements and the far-reaching implications of getting things wrong, unions need to be extra vigilant when giving notice of any intended ballot to take industrial action. Nevertheless, where the union membership to be balloted runs into the hundreds or thousands, or even tens of thousands, errors will inevitably occur. The TULR(C)A provides no specific defence in these circumstances, however. In fact, the Government decided not to legislate to allow for small, accidental errors in this context to be disregarded. (This contrasts with the position in respect of, for example, inadvertent failures to accord members entitlement to vote in the ballot – see under 'Entitlement to vote' below.) That said, unions are afforded a degree of leniency in that S.226A(2D), inserted by the ERelA 2004, provides that the lists and figures or information supplied must be 'as accurate as is reasonably practicable' in the light of the information in the union's possession at the time when it complied with S.226A(1)(a). The Code acknowledges that it is unreasonable to expect union records to be perfectly accurate and to contain detailed information on all members, but goes on to advise that, if the union is aware of inaccuracies in its records, it is a 'desirable practice' for it to describe the main deficiencies in the notice (para 16).

However, if all the relevant information is in the union's possession and the errors in the notice are due to a failure by the union to verify its accuracy, it is unlikely that those errors will be ignored. In Willerby Holiday Homes Ltd v Union of Construction, Allied Trades and Technicians 2003 EWHC 2608, QBD, for example – a case decided before S.226A(2D) was introduced but unlikely to be decided any differently today – the union incorrectly stated in the ballot notice the number of employees entitled to vote. The High Court, hearing the employer's claim for damages covering the loss caused as a result of the subsequent industrial action, agreed that the notice failed to comply with S.226A. The incontrovertible fact was that the figure of 397 was wrong (the true number of members entitled to vote in the ballot being approximately 408). Moreover, the union had been aware at regional office level that the figure was wrong. Furthermore, the information regarding the new recruits was in the union's possession at the material time and the union also possessed information as to those employees who were paying their union subscriptions by direct debit or directly into the branch. In reaching its conclusion, the High Court rejected the union's contention that the company had obstructed its attempts to ascertain the true position. Nor did the court think it necessary to construe S.226(2)(c) as imposing on the employer an obligation to supply to the union information that was already in the union's possession, such as the employer's own list of check-off employees. Accordingly, the union was liable for any damages caused by the industrial action.

Similarly, in British Airways plc v Unite the Union 2009 EWHC 3541, QBD, **5.17** the union was unable to produce cogent evidence showing that it had taken all reasonably practicable steps to ascertain the correct number of its members entitled to vote in an industrial action ballot. The case involved a dispute between BA and Unite concerning staff reductions. On 6 November 2009,

87

Unite gave notice under S.226A that it intended to ballot its members – all 12,780 of them – on proposed strike action. An overwhelming majority voted in favour of a strike – due to take place over a 12-day period starting on 22 December – and BA sought an injunction to prevent the action going ahead.

BA submitted, among other things, that the S.226A notice was deficient because, by 6 November 2009, Unite knew that a substantial number of its members would have left BA's employment through voluntary redundancy by the time of the proposed strike, and that these members had therefore erroneously been included in the notice as being entitled to vote in the ballot. The union countered that it did all that was reasonably practicable to exclude those leaving on voluntary redundancy of whom it was aware, but that its attempts to discover more information were thwarted by a lack of cooperation and intransigence from BA. Accordingly, it should be entitled to rely on S.226A(2D) to excuse any errors in the ballot notice.

Mrs Justice Cox, hearing the application, rejected the union's contention that it had done everything reasonably practicable to ensure the accuracy of the information provided to BA. In light of the information in Unite's possession at the time of the notice, it was aware, or ought to have been aware, that the figures contained therein included a substantial number of members who were shortly to leave on voluntary redundancy. The notice therefore included those who the union could not reasonably have believed would be entitled to vote in the ballot. The union could have taken steps – as, indeed, it had done on a previous occasion – to enquire who among its members would be leaving and when. It also failed to issue clear instructions to its membership, informing them that if they were leaving in November and December they were not entitled to vote and must not vote in the ballot. The union had a number of opportunities to do this (via various documents, bulletins and website postings), but failed to do so. Furthermore, an advice hotline that members could call was primarily intended to ensure that members entitled to vote received their ballot papers – not to inform those taking voluntary redundancy that they should not vote. Nor was there evidence indicating that any of the inaccuracies in the information provided by the union was due to intransigence or lack of cooperation on the part of BA. Accordingly, Unite could not rely on S.226A(2D) to excuse any errors in the ballot notice and the company was granted an interim injunction to restrain the proposed unlawful industrial action. (This case is also discussed under 'Entitlement to vote – determining the balloting constituency' and 'Ballot requirements – notice of industrial action to employer' below.)

5.18 Note that the Code states that it would be in the interests of good industrial relations practice for an employer who believes that the notice he has received does not contain sufficient information to comply with the statutory requirements to raise this with the union promptly before pursuing the matter in the courts. The Code also advises unions to check that an employer who has been sent a notice accepts that the information provided complies with the requirements of S.226A (para 18).

Sample voting paper 5.19

In addition to giving the employer notice of the ballot, the union must take such steps as are reasonably necessary to ensure that, not later than three days before the opening day of the ballot, the employer receives a sample ballot paper – S.226A(1)(b). The opening day of the ballot is defined as the first day when a voting paper is sent to any person entitled to vote – S.226A(4). Where there is more than one employer involved, then all those involved must receive a sample ballot paper.

The sample ballot paper must be a sample of the actual voting paper to be sent to the employees, or, where more than one form will be used, a sample of all the forms to be sent to the employees – S.226A(2F). References to 'employees' in S.226A(2F) are to those employees of the employer whom the union reasonably believes will be entitled to vote in the ballot – S.226A(2H). Thus, where more than one employer is involved and different forms of voting paper are used, unions need ensure only that each employer receives the sample voting paper (or papers) that is (are) to be sent to his employees. In other words, unions are not required to send employers sample voting papers that are to be sent only to the employees of other employers.

The Code of Practice recommends that, if the sample voting paper is available 5.20 in time, the union may wish to include it with the notice of intention to ballot. In any event, the union should allow sufficient time, using appropriate means of transmission, for sending the voting paper and should, if possible, obtain confirmation of receipt (para 20). Where, after sending the sample voting paper, the union makes any changes to it, it must send a sample of the revised version to the employer. In these circumstances, the union must ensure that the opening date of the ballot can still be adhered to or, if this is no longer possible, stipulate a new date.

A union's failure to provide a sample voting paper to an employer before conducting a ballot will mean that the industrial action will not have the protection of the statutory immunities vis-à-vis *that* employer – S.226(1)(b). However, this does not prejudice the position in relation to other employers whose employees are participating in the industrial action, provided, of course, that the union gives them the sample voting paper before conducting the ballot.

Independent scrutineer 5.21

A trade union must appoint an independent scrutineer before holding an industrial action ballot – S.226B. This obligation does not apply to ballots where the total number of members entitled to vote – or the aggregate number

89

of members if separate workplace ballots are held – is 50 or less – S.226C. However, the Code of Practice recommends that unions should consider the benefit of appointing a scrutineer in *all* industrial action ballots, as this will enable it to demonstrate compliance with the statutory requirements more easily (para 13). It also recommends that the scrutineer be appointed before steps are taken to satisfy any other legal requirements (para 11).

Only those persons specified as 'qualified persons' in regulations issued by the Secretary of State are entitled to act as scrutineers for this purpose – S.226B(2)(a). There are six bodies specified by name: Electoral Reform Services Ltd, Association of Electoral Administrators, DRS Data Services Ltd, Opt2vote Ltd, Election.com Ltd, Popularis Ltd and the Involvement and Participation Association – Article 7 of the Trade Union Ballots and Elections (Independent Scrutineer Qualifications) Order 1993 SI 1993/1909 (as amended). Solicitors with current practising certificates and chartered and certified accountants who are qualified as auditors may also act as scrutineers, although they may be ineligible depending on their union connections and previous activities – S.226B(2)(a) and Articles 3–6 Trade Union Ballots and Elections (Independent Scrutineer Qualifications) Order 1993 SI 1993/1909. The union may appoint the scrutineer of its choice from among those qualified, provided that the union has no grounds for believing that the scrutineer will not carry out his or her functions competently or that his or her independence in relation to the union or in relation to the ballot might reasonably be called into question – S.226B(2)(b). The name of the scrutineer appointed must appear on the ballot paper – S.229(1A)(a). Unlike the provisions governing the scrutiny of other union ballots (election of officers, for example), the scrutineer of an industrial action ballot has no power to check the union's membership register.

5.22   The scrutineer's function is to make a report to the union on the conduct of the ballot as soon as is reasonably practicable after the date of the ballot and, in any event, not more than four weeks after that date – S.226B(1)(b). The 'date of the ballot' means, in the case of a ballot in which votes may be cast on more than one day, the last of those days – S.246. The scrutineer must take such steps as appear to be appropriate for the purpose of enabling the report to be made – S.226B(1)(a). Unions must ensure that the scrutineer carries out his or her statutory functions and that there is no interference with the carrying out of those functions by either the union or any of its members, officials or employees – S.226B(3). Unions are also obliged to comply with all reasonable requests made by the scrutineer in connection with the carrying out of his or her functions – S.226B(4). The Code of Practice states that the union may entrust the scrutineer to carry out additional tasks on its behalf, such as supervising the production and distribution of voting papers, being the nominated person to whom voting papers should be returned and retaining custody of all returned voting papers for a set period after the ballot, where this would be helpful as a means of ensuring adequate standards for the conduct of the ballot or simplifying the balloting process (para 12).

The scrutineer's report on the ballot must state whether he or she is satisfied that:

- there are no reasonable grounds for believing that there was any contravention of any requirement imposed in relation to the ballot

- the arrangements for the handling of the voting papers throughout the conduct of the ballot – including the counting of the votes – included all such security arrangements as were reasonably practicable for the purpose of minimising the risk that any unfairness or malpractice might occur, and

- he or she has been able to carry out the functions of a scrutineer without interference from the union or any of its members, officials or employees – S.231B(1).

If the scrutineer is not satisfied as to any of those matters, then the report must give the reasons for that dissatisfaction – S.231B(1). The mere fact of a critical scrutineer's report will not by itself invalidate the ballot, but it will provide grounds on which an individual union member or an employer can argue that the action is not protected by the statutory immunities and accordingly seek an injunction and/or damages. S.226(2) states that industrial action shall be regarded as having the support of a ballot only if, among other things, the requirements of S.226B (so far as applicable before and during the holding of a ballot) are satisfied, and the requirements of S.226B (so far as applicable after the holding of the ballot) and S.231B have been satisfied at the time legal proceedings are commenced. In order to reduce the risk of challenge to the ballot's validity, the Code of Practice recommends unions to delay any call for industrial action until they have obtained the scrutineer's report on the ballot (para 49). However, as industrial action ballots are only effective for a limited period (see below under 'Period of effectiveness'), it is commonly the case that the industrial action will have commenced prior to the union's receipt of the scrutineer's report and consequently employers or union members may, assuming the scrutineer's report provides grounds for doing so, sue for an injunction to restrain any further action and sue for damages in relation to the (arguably unlawful) action already carried out.

The union must provide a copy of the scrutineer's report as soon as practicable **5.23** (either free of charge or on payment of a reasonable fee) to anyone entitled to vote in the ballot or to the employer of any such person, provided the request is made within six months of the date of the ballot – S.231B(2).

Finally, there is no provision enabling a union to replace an inadequate or incompetent scrutineer following his or her appointment. It is unclear what consequences would flow if a union attempted to replace an unsatisfactory scrutineer midway through the balloting process. Although the matter has not been tested, an employer in these circumstances might be able to argue that the union had not complied with the obligation to appoint a scrutineer before holding a ballot.

5.24 Entitlement to vote

All union members who it is reasonable at the time of the ballot for the union to believe will be induced by the union to take part, or continue to take part, in the industrial action must be given an equal entitlement to vote – S.227(1). This includes *self-employed* members who personally do work or provide services for another – S.235. No other union members must be balloted – S.227(1).

Unions are not allowed to inflate support for industrial action by obtaining sympathy votes from members who will not be involved in the action. Thus, if a union is planning to call a strike of bus drivers only, it must not include bus conductors in the ballot. To do so would render the ballot invalid – S.226(2)(a)(ii). It is not, however, a prerequisite that the members accorded an entitlement to vote must be directly affected by the matters in dispute – British Telecommunications plc v Communication Workers Union 2004 IRLR 58, QBD. This case is discussed in Chapter 3, 'Trade union immunities', under 'Trade dispute'. The key question is always whether the member will be induced to take part in the proposed industrial action. For example, in Anglian Windows Ltd v GMB 2007 EWHC 917, QBD, a dispute arose over the pay rate at one of the employer's production units. The union gave notice of its intention to ballot its members for industrial action in that production unit as well as four others. The employer argued that the notice was invalid, as the ballot should be restricted to those members in the production unit affected by the pay issue. The High Court disagreed, stating that determination of those entitled to vote was not dependent on whether an employee was involved in the dispute but on whether the union believes that the employee will be induced to take part in the dispute.

5.25 Every person who is entitled to vote in the ballot must, *so far as is reasonably practicable*, have a voting paper sent to his or her home address and be given a convenient opportunity to vote by post – S.230(2). This is discussed below in the section on 'Ballot requirements' under 'Conduct of the ballot'.

5.26 Determining the balloting constituency

In determining which members must be given an entitlement to vote under S.227(1), the union should ask itself the following two questions in respect of each member:

- will it induce the member to take part (or continue to take part) in the industrial action?

- is it reasonable at the time of the ballot for it to believe that the member will be induced to take part (or continue to take part) in the industrial action?

Both answers will invariably depend on the information the union holds about the member, such as their profession, grade or place of work – see further under 'Denial of entitlement to vote' below.

Inducement must come from union. Section 227(1) states that entitlement to **5.27** vote in an industrial action ballot must be accorded to all members who it is reasonable for the union to believe will be induced *by the union* to take part in the industrial action in question. The words in italics were added by the ERelA 2004 after the case of National Union of Rail, Maritime and Transport Workers v Midland Mainline Ltd 2001 IRLR 813, CA, revealed that without them there was a lack of clarity as to which members should be given an entitlement to vote. In that case, the RMT was in dispute with MM Ltd over the safety responsibilities of operational train crew. It balloted 91 union members, a majority of whom voted for strike action. However, the union then discovered that there were an additional 25 union members who worked as operational train crew who had not received ballot papers and had consequently not been given the opportunity to vote. Nor had they received a written instruction from the union to take part in the strike. There were several reasons for this, including that some members had fallen into arrears with their membership contributions and that others had failed to have their union records updated when they became operational train crew.

MM Ltd obtained a High Court injunction restraining the RMT from taking strike action. The Court of Appeal upheld the injunction. On the question of whether the unballoted union members should have been given an entitlement to vote, the Court noted that the version of S.227(1) in force at the time required the union to ballot members who, at the time of the ballot, it believed would be induced to take part in the industrial action. In the Court's view, it was 'overwhelmingly probable' that if there were unballoted members in the designated class, there would be some who would be induced to take industrial action because they thought it was appropriate, and there would be some who would have voted against the strike, given the chance, but who would nonetheless be induced to take part in the knowledge that many of their colleagues would expect them to do so. The Court rejected the union's argument that unless the union or one of its staff intended to ask a specific member to take part in industrial action, the union could not believe that he or she would be so induced by the union's actions. As a result, the Court held that it was not reasonable for the union to believe that all operational train crew members who had not been balloted would not take part in the strike, and it followed that those unballoted members should have been accorded an entitlement to vote.

5.28 The words 'by the union' inserted into S.227(1) by the ERelA 2004 now make it clear that a union does not have to give an entitlement to vote to members who might take part in the industrial action even though they were not induced to do so by the union. Arguably, this has made life a little easier for unions. However, the root of the problem remains; namely, the difficulty in identifying all members of the relevant class who may be entitled to vote, particularly in circumstances where neither party is willing to cooperate in sharing information. In RMT v Midland Mainline Ltd (see above) the Court of Appeal commented that this problem may at least be partially resolved by the involvement of Acas, which can carry out membership checks without disclosing confidential information to either party. However, employers may not have much incentive to help unions comply with their pre-strike procedures.

5.29 **'At the time of the ballot'.** Under S.227(1), the union is required to ballot any member who it is reasonable *at the time of the ballot* for the union to believe will be induced by it to take part in the industrial action. Unfortunately, the TULR(C)A sheds no further light on what is meant by this phrase. However, this issue was considered by the House of Lords in P (A Minor) v National Association of Schoolmasters/Union of Women Teachers 2003 ICR 386, HL. There Lord Walker proffered the view that the fact that Parliament had not used the more precise expression of the 'date of the ballot' (which is defined in S.246) suggested that the period of the whole ballot process, as opposed to a single date, was the intended meaning. Lord Hoffmann agreed, adding that, in any event, he did not think it mattered what particular time is meant by 'the time of the ballot' in S.227(1). The question is whether, looking at the balloting process as a whole, any members were not accorded entitlement to vote.

5.30 **Reasonable belief.** Under S.227(1), the union must ballot only those union members whom it reasonably believes, at the time of the ballot, will be induced by it to take part in the planned industrial action. The validity of the ballot will accordingly be compromised if any other union member is balloted. In determining the correct balloting constituency, the union is therefore required to ask itself the following question: is it reasonable, at the time of the ballot, to believe that a particular member will actually take part in the proposed industrial action? If, for example, the union is aware that a member will have left the employer's employment by the time the industrial action is due to take place, it would not be reasonable for the union to believe that he or she will take part in that action. As a result, that member is not entitled to vote and must not be included in the ballot. If the union fails to exclude such a member from the ballot, the ballot will be invalid and the union will lose statutory immunity in respect of any torts committed by it if the strike goes ahead.

This situation arose in British Airways plc v Unite the Union 2009 EWHC 3541, QBD, which concerned a dispute between BA and Unite over the company's decision to reduce the number of cabin crew on flights out of

Heathrow. Unite argued that this change amounted to a breach of their members' contracts of employment and conducted a ballot of the 12,700 members affected, asking them if they wanted to take industrial action over the issue. An overwhelming majority voted in favour of a strike, which was due to take place over a 12-day period starting on 22 December 2009. In response, BA applied to the High Court for an interim injunction to prevent the strike taking place.

In the High Court, BA submitted that Unite had failed to comply with S.227(1) **5.31** because it had included in the ballot several hundred cabin crew who were in the process of taking voluntary redundancy. It had not been reasonable for the union to believe at the time of the ballot that these members would take part in the industrial action, as it knew that they would have already left the company's employment by the time of the strike. Furthermore, BA argued, Unite had failed to take reasonable steps to ensure that these members did not cast a vote. As a result, the notice informing BA of the union's intention to ballot its members and the notice of the proposed industrial action were deficient in that they contained inaccurate figures as to the number of employees involved. Unite countered that any failure to comply with the statutory requirements was accidental and therefore fell within the 'small accidental failures' provision in S.232B (see 'Small accidental failures' below).

Mrs Justice Cox, hearing the application, accepted the company's arguments and granted the injunction on the ground that any proposed industrial action was unlawful. In her view, Unite failed to establish that it held a reasonable belief in the entitlement to vote of *all* its members: it was in possession of information concerning employees who had volunteered for redundancy and was therefore aware, or should have been aware, that the figures provided to BA included those who had opted for voluntary redundancy and were not entitled to vote. It also followed from this that the union could not rely on S.232B, as its failure to exclude the redundancy leavers could not be classified as 'accidental'.

This case serves as a stark reminder to unions of the legal pitfalls involved in the balloting process. In order to comply with the law it may not be sufficient for the union simply to consider which of its members is likely to take part in strike action. It may also need to ascertain whether any members are due to leave before the strike takes place. However, it is worth remembering that the union's obligations in this regard are not absolute. Provided it conducts reasonable inquiries into whether any redundancies – compulsory or otherwise – are taking place or whether someone is under notice of termination of their employment, the union is likely to have complied with S.227(1). It may, however, be advisable for the union to issue instructions to members about not voting in the ballot if they will be leaving employment by a particular date – something Unite failed to do in the above case. (This case is also discussed

95

under 'Preliminary considerations – notice of ballot to employer' above and 'Ballot requirements – notice of industrial action to employer' below.)

5.32 Denial of entitlement to vote

Section 232A TULR(C)A provides that industrial action will *not* be regarded as having the support of a ballot if the following conditions apply in the case of any person:

- he or she was a member of the trade union at the time when the ballot was held

- it was reasonable at that time for the union to believe that he or she would be induced to take part (or to continue to take part) in the industrial action

- he or she was not accorded entitlement to vote in the ballot, and

- he or she was induced by the union to take part (or to continue to take part) in the industrial action. (An inducement is still an inducement if it is or would be ineffective, either because of a union member's known unwillingness to be influenced by it or for any other reason – S.226(4).)

It follows that *deliberately* denying the right of even one member to vote and then calling on that person to participate in the strike action will invalidate a ballot, with the result that statutory immunity will be lost – S.226(2)(bb). But that does not mean that all members must vote for a ballot to be effective, since in any ballot with a sizeable voting constituency a number of potential voters will not exercise their right to vote, whether through deliberate choice or through apathy.

5.33 In British Railways Board v National Union of Railwaymen 1989 ICR 678, CA – a case decided before the introduction of the 'small accidental errors' exception in S.232B TULR(C)A (see below) – the NUR issued 63,700 ballot papers, of which 51,600 were returned. After eliminating spoiled or blank ballot papers there was a majority of 9,300 in favour of strike action. British Rail argued that the ballot was invalid because about 200 NUR members had not had an opportunity of voting; and there were about 70,000 members in the categories the NUR was seeking to ballot but only 63,700 ballot papers were issued. The Court of Appeal held that there is a profound difference between denying someone's entitlement to vote and inadvertently failing to give someone an opportunity to vote. It was inevitable in a balloting operation of this size, involving a very large number of sites, that some members would be accidentally omitted from the ballot. On the evidence, the NUR had given everybody entitled to vote an opportunity to do so so far as was reasonably practicable, and trifling errors should not be allowed to invalidate the ballot. The Court added that one would not expect the total number of ballot papers issued to be the same as the total number of people entitled to vote because a number of people will not bother to pick up a ballot paper.

The House of Lords applied a similar reasoning in the case of P (A Minor) v National Association of Schoolmasters/Union of Women Teachers 2003 ICR 386, HL. The case concerned a disruptive pupil, P, who had been excluded from the school but then reinstated. The head teacher instructed the teachers to take him back into their classrooms. Following further incidents of disruption by P, the NASUWT, the union representing the teachers, balloted members over taking industrial action in response to the head teacher's direction that they teach P. Two teachers at the school who were union members did not receive a ballot paper because they had recently joined from other schools and had failed to notify the NASUWT of their change of employment. Following the ballot, the NASUWT wrote to all its members at the school, including the two teachers who had not been balloted, instructing them to take industrial action. In response, P brought a claim under S.235A TULR(C)A, seeking an injunction requiring the NASUWT to call off the industrial action. He failed before the High Court and the Court of Appeal and appealed to the House of Lords.

The key question their Lordships had to decide was whether the industrial action should be regarded as not having had the support of a ballot by virtue of S.232A because two members of the union not included in the ballot had nevertheless been induced to take part in the industrial action. Lord Walker held that, in his view, it was doubtful whether the fact that the two teachers had not been included in the ballot meant that they had been denied entitlement to vote. The union's inaccurate printout of its members at the school was the source of the error in the distribution of ballot papers. But there was nothing in the statutory provisions, or in the way in which the union's head office had acted, to indicate that the printout was intended to be definitive. Had either of the teachers rung up the head office to protest at the non-receipt of a ballot paper, the answer might have been, 'It is too late to do anything about it', but it would not have been, 'You are not entitled to vote'. The printout was not an electoral roll, which is a definitive record of entitlement to vote in parliamentary or local government elections. Accordingly, it was possible to distinguish entitlement to vote from opportunity to vote. The failure to include the two teachers in the ballot meant that they had been denied an opportunity to vote, but did not amount to a denial of their entitlement to vote under S.227(1) or S.232A(c).

In Lord Hoffmann's view, the key question was whether condition (c) of S.232A **5.34** was satisfied – i.e. whether the teachers had been denied entitlement to vote in the ballot. He first considered what amounted to entitlement to vote under S.232A(c), and concluded that it meant nothing different from the meaning of entitlement to vote in S.227(1), which provides that a member will not have been denied entitlement to vote in the ballot where it is not reasonable for the union at the time of the ballot to believe that that member will be induced to take part in the industrial action. His Lordship concluded that it was not reasonable for the union to hold such a belief in respect of the two teachers since they had failed to inform their union of their change of employment. Therefore,

97

the union's failure to include the two teachers in the ballot did not mean that those teachers had been denied entitlement to vote under S.227(1) or S.232A(c).

5.35 'Small accidental failures'

An inadvertent failure to comply with the strict balloting provisions will not necessarily result in a loss of statutory immunity. S.232B TULR(C)A provides that a failure (or failures) to accord union members entitlement to vote in accordance with S.227(1) (entitlement to vote in a ballot), S.230(2) (conduct of a ballot) or S.230(2B) (conduct of a ballot in relation to merchant seamen and women) shall be disregarded if it is (or if they, taken together, are) 'accidental and on a scale which is unlikely to affect the result of the ballot'.

This 'small accidental failures' exception applies 'for all purposes (including, in particular, those of S.232A(c)', with the effect that small accidental failures to accord union members entitlement to vote will not invalidate a ballot and can be ignored. So, in P (A Minor) v National Association of Schoolmasters/Union of Women Teachers (above) the House of Lords held that, while the union's failure to send the two teachers a ballot paper amounted to a breach of S.230(2), the mistake fell within the small errors exception under S.232B. As a result, the mistake was to be disregarded and the ballot was valid for the purposes of the union's industrial action.

5.36

Although S.232B gives statutory force to the proposition that accidental errors should not be allowed to invalidate the balloting process, such errors can only be disregarded if they are *on a scale which is unlikely to affect the outcome of the ballot*. So, if there is a majority of 100 workers in favour of strike action and the union has inadvertently failed to send out 50 ballot papers, that failure should be disregarded. However, if 100 or more potential voters are missed out this could have an effect on the outcome of the ballot and it will be open to a court to declare the ballot invalid. For instance, in RMT v Midland Mainline (above) the union balloted 91 union members about proposed industrial action. Of those, 25 voted in favour of strike action, 17 voted against and 49 abstained. It was subsequently discovered that an additional 25 members had not received ballot papers and had consequently not been given an opportunity to vote. The Court of Appeal thought that, even if four of these could be disregarded under the 'small accidental failures' exception in S.232B, the remaining 21 were too significant in number to be disregarded. The Court accordingly upheld an injunction restraining the industrial action.

5.37 New union members

Another potential difficulty in determining the balloting constituency concerns the position of new union members. If, during a prolonged industrial campaign, a number of employees (possibly new to the organisation) join the trade union and are induced to participate in the industrial action, will that invalidate the earlier ballot? In London Underground Ltd v National Union of Rail, Maritime and Transport Workers 1996 ICR 170, CA, the RMT managed to recruit a substantial number of new members during an industrial action campaign who had not been included in the original ballot. The Court of Appeal noted that S.227(1) 'requires the union to ballot all those *of its members* who it is reasonable *at the time of the ballot* for the union to believe will be called upon to take part in the industrial action proposed and no others'. According to the Court, this means that new members who have joined since the service of the ballot notice (but before the ballot takes place), *must* be included in the ballot (although we would add the proviso that it must be reasonably practicable to include them in the ballot at this stage – see S.230(2), discussed below under 'Ballot requirements'), while non-members *must not* be balloted. In the Court's opinion, there was nothing in the legislation that prevented the union from calling out new members who were not balloted to take industrial action – and who could not be lawfully included in the ballot – because they were not members of the union at the relevant time.

The Court noted that this interpretation was contrary to the view of Lord **5.38** Donaldson MR in Post Office v Union of Communication Workers 1990 ICR 258, CA, where he said that the call for industrial action should be limited to those who were employed by the employer and given an opportunity of voting at the time of the ballot. In the Court's view, Lord Donaldson's conclusions were unsustainable in relation to changes in union membership. A union cannot identify future members and, even if it could, it cannot ballot them because only existing union members can be included in the ballot.

For further discussion on the meaning of 'at the time of the ballot', see under 'Determining the balloting constituency' above.

Existing members – new jobs   5.39
In London Underground Ltd v National Union of Rail, Maritime and Transport Workers (above) the Court of Appeal held that individuals who were not union members at the time of the ballot, but who subsequently joined the union, could be called upon to take industrial action. But what happens if a person who *was* a member of the relevant union at the time of the ballot, but who was not balloted because he or she did not belong to the group of workers in dispute, subsequently changes jobs and joins that group of workers? Can that individual be called upon to take industrial action? The unequivocal answer to this question is 'yes'. S.232A provides that, for statutory immunity to be lost, it must have been reasonable *at the time of the ballot* for the trade union to believe that the person who was denied entitlement to vote would be induced to take part in the industrial action. In the majority of cases where a member changes jobs *after* the ballot has taken place, it will not be reasonable for the union to believe, at the time of the ballot, that he or she will be called upon to take action.

99

5.40 Separate workplace ballots

The Employment Act 1988 introduced a further requirement where the union members likely to take part in industrial action have different places of work. As a general rule, a separate ballot must be held for each workplace (rather than a single ballot covering all members at the different workplaces) – S.228(1) and (3) TULR(C)A. It is unlawful to organise industrial action at a particular workplace unless a majority in favour has been obtained *at that workplace* – S.226(3). The rationale of this provision is that a militant majority at one particular workplace should not be allowed to override non-militant majorities elsewhere.

'Workplace' means, in relation to a person who is employed, the single set of premises at or from which the person works – S.228(4)(a). If there are several such sets of premises or no premises at all, the workplace is the premises with which the person's employment has the closest connection – S.228(4)(b). This definition was put to the test in Anglian Windows Ltd v GMB 2007 EWHC 917, QBD, which concerned a manufacturer of double-glazed windows, doors and conservatories whose principal place of business was at the Airport Industrial Estate in Norwich, where it operated six production units. Each unit was entirely separate and self-contained. Another fabrication factory was located in Rochdale. A pay dispute ensued at the Norwich site and the GMB gave notice to AW Ltd of its intention to hold a ballot among its members in a total of five production units. A majority voted for strike action and AW Ltd sought an injunction restraining the GMB from going ahead. One of the company's arguments was that the GMB had erroneously held a single ballot covering all five production units when, on a proper reading of S.228, a single ballot was required in relation to each, as these were separate workplaces for the purposes of the section.

5.41 The High Court judge thought that this argument was not without merit. In particular, he noted that employees were assigned to a particular unit; their pay slips indicated the unit at which they worked; each unit carried out different activities; and each unit had its own car park and shop steward. However, he was ultimately of the view that the union's arguments on this issue were to be preferred. AW Ltd conducted its business at two sites, one in Norwich and the other in Rochdale. It would be natural for any employees who worked at any of the units at the Airport Industrial Estate to regard their workplace as the Estate in Norwich. In fact, the contract of employment referred to the place of work as 'Norwich'. As a result, the judge held that the GMB had been entitled to hold a single ballot covering the five production units.

The judge's reasoning in this case would seem to accord with the definition of 'workplace' in S.228(4), which focuses on the 'premises' at or from which a person works. The use of the word 'premises' suggests that S.228 is wide

100

enough to encompass different units or departments contained in the same building or situated at the same location.

There are important exceptions to the general rule that a separate ballot must be held for each workplace. These apply where:

- the union has a reasonable belief that all the members balloted have the same workplace

- different workplaces have a specific factor in common that makes it desirable to hold a combined ballot, or

- overseas members are involved.

However, even if an exception applies, it remains open to the union to decide **5.42** to hold a single (and separate) ballot at each workplace. Where the union is entitled to hold a single ballot across a number of workplaces and the majority is in favour of industrial action, it is lawful for the union to organise industrial action at any such workplace. Thus, the fact that a majority of employees at a particular workplace have voted against taking industrial action will not matter if a majority overall are in favour of the action. This was confirmed by the High Court in University of Central England and anor v National and Local Government Officers' Association 1993 IRLR 81, QBD.

Reasonable belief in single workplace 5.43
The requirement for separate workplace ballots does not apply where the union reasonably believes that the members accorded entitlement to vote do in fact have the same workplace – S.228(2). This exception is likely to be of limited application, since it would not normally be reasonable for a union not to know where its members work. It might apply where a small group of members works at an isolated site or where a few members have been transferred just before the ballot is held. What matters is whether the union's belief in a single workplace is reasonable.

'Common factor' across different workplaces 5.44
The second exception covers three specific sets of circumstances where it makes sense to hold an aggregate ballot across different workplaces because of a factor that all workplaces have in common – S.228A(1). These circumstances are explained below. Note that S.228A(1) provides that an aggregate ballot may be held in place of 'some or all of the separate ballots'. In theory, it is therefore open to the union to aggregate only some of the single ballots. For example, if it wants to ballot members across six different workplaces, it could hold an aggregate ballot covering four of them and hold two separate ballots in the remaining two.

Common interest. Unions can hold an aggregate ballot if at each of the **5.45** workplaces covered by the ballot there is at least one of its members affected by

101

the dispute – S.228A(2). Members are 'affected by the dispute' if the dispute relates (wholly or partly) to a decision the union reasonably believes the employer has made or will make concerning:

- the terms and conditions of employment, or the physical conditions in which they are required to work

- the engagement or non-engagement, or termination or suspension of employment or the duties of employment of one or more workers, or

- the allocation of work or the duties of employment between workers or groups of workers

and the members are directly affected by that decision – S.228A(5)(a). So if, for example, the dispute concerned Sunday working, and such working occurred at workplaces A and B but not workplace C, the union could hold an aggregate ballot across workplaces A and B, but would have to hold a separate ballot at workplace C (assuming it wished to ballot its members at workplace C).

5.46 Union members are also affected by a dispute where:

- the dispute relates to a matter of discipline and the matter directly affects them – S.228A(5)(b)

- the dispute relates to their membership or non-membership of the union – S.228A(5)(c)

- the dispute relates to facilities for trade union officials and the members are officials who have used or would use the facilities concerned – S.228A(5)(d).

It is worth repeating that this exception in S.228A(2) applies even where only one member at each of the workplaces is so affected. The rationale behind this was explained by Lord McIntosh, speaking at the time the provision was tabled in the House of Lords, as follows: 'Where one or more workers are directly involved, it will normally be the case that others at the same workplace, sometimes many others, will rightly feel themselves to be indirectly involved by an employer's handling of an issue; for example, the way the employer handles a matter may set a precedent for the handling of similar matters in relation to other workers.' (House of Lords Debate 15 July 1999, Vol 604, col 576.)

5.47 **Common occupation(s) and employer(s).** An aggregate ballot may also take place where entitlement to vote is accorded to, and limited to, all members of the union who the union reasonably believes have an occupation of a particular kind (or kinds) and who are employed by one or more of the employers with whom the union is in dispute – S.228A(3). Thus, a voting unit could be described as 'drivers' or 'conductors' or 'fitters', these being occupational descriptions. The union can, in the same ballot, ballot all drivers, conductors and fitters.

102

Common employer(s). Section 228A(4) provides that an aggregate ballot can **5.48** be held where entitlement to vote is accorded to, and limited to, *all* union members who are employed by one or more of the employers with whom the union is in dispute.

The second and third exceptions only apply where the union ballots *all* its members with the factor in common across the different workplaces. So, if it decides to ballot, say, drivers at two workplaces but not all of the workplaces where drivers work, single ballots will have to be held at each workplace.

Difficulties can arise in those industries or sectors where the union and/or **5.49** members wish to ensure that emergency cover is available during the strike or other industrial action (the nursing profession, for example). The union must only ballot those whom it intends to induce to take part in the action, and it must not induce anyone who has been denied the opportunity to vote in the ballot. Rather than exclude the members it is anticipated will provide emergency cover (in which case the union will be unable to aggregate the ballot), the most sensible course would probably be to ballot all the relevant members, who can then rotate emergency cover among themselves.

Overseas members
5.50
Where the union has overseas members, it can elect whether or not to accord any of those members entitlement to vote in a ballot and nothing in Ss.226B to 230 and 231B applies in relation to an overseas member or a vote cast by such a member – S.232(1). Ss.226B to 230 and 231B cover the appointment of a scrutineer and the scrutineer's report; the exclusion of small ballots; entitlement to vote in a ballot; separate workplace ballots; aggregate ballots; voting papers; and the conduct of ballots. Where overseas members have voted in a ballot, references in Ss.231 and 231A (which govern the information unions are required to give as to the result of the ballot) to persons entitled to vote do not include overseas members and should be read as requiring the information to distinguish between overseas members and other members – S.232(2).

'Overseas member' means a union member, other than a merchant seaman/ woman or offshore worker, who is outside Great Britain during the period of the ballot – S.232(3). 'Merchant seaman/woman' is defined as a person whose employment, or the greater part of it, is carried out on board sea-going ships; and an 'offshore worker' is a person in offshore employment, except where the employment is in an area where the law of Northern Ireland applies. 'Great Britain' means England, Wales and Scotland; it does not include Northern Ireland, the Channel Islands or the Isle of Man.

Although a union is not obliged to ballot its overseas members and may ignore **5.51** them altogether in the arrangements for an industrial action ballot, there are two sets of circumstances in which a union member who is in *Northern Ireland* at the time of a ballot is *not* to be treated as an overseas member:

103

- if separate workplace ballots are being carried out or if a single ballot is being held where it is reasonable for the union to believe that all members accorded an entitlement to vote have the same workplace and, in either case, the member's workplace is in Great Britain. This means that members who are temporarily seconded to Northern Ireland must be included in a ballot – S.232(4)(a), and

- if a general ballot is being carried out *and* it relates to industrial action involving members both in Great Britain and in Northern Ireland – S.232(4)(b).

Failure to accord entitlement to vote to members in Northern Ireland in the above circumstances will render a ballot invalid.

5.52 Ballot requirements

The detailed balloting requirements relate to the following:

- content of the voting paper

- conduct of the ballot

- information to be given to the employer as to the result of the ballot

- notice of industrial action to be given to the employer

- calling industrial action.

Each of these requirements will be considered separately.

5.53 Content of the voting paper

There are a number of mandatory requirements for ballot papers, failure to comply with which will invalidate the ballot. An example of a voting paper that complies with the statutory requirements can be found in Annex 2 to the Code of Practice.

5.54 Details to be included. The voting paper must:

- state the name of the independent scrutineer

- clearly specify the address to which, and the date by which, it is to be returned

- be given one of a series of consecutive whole numbers, every one of which is used in giving a different number in that series to each voting paper printed or otherwise produced for the purposes of the ballot

- be marked with its number – S.229(1A).

5.55 Person authorised to call action. The voting paper must specify *who* – in the event of a vote in favour of industrial action – is authorised to call on union

members to take part or continue to take part in the action – S.229(3). Only the person so specified may take the decision to call the industrial action, otherwise the action will be unlawful – S.233(1).

This requirement was considered by the Court of Appeal in Tanks and Drums Ltd v Transport and General Workers' Union 1992 ICR 1, CA, where it held that the person named in the ballot paper as being authorised to take the decision to call industrial action could not delegate that authority to another. There, the ballot paper specified that the general secretary was the person authorised to call industrial action. The general secretary was informed by the regional secretary of the result of the ballot and that there was a substantial majority in favour of industrial action, and was asked by the regional secretary for permission to call industrial action if a meeting with the employer the following day did not result in a settlement. The general secretary gave his permission, and a strike was called after a breakdown of negotiations. The employer obtained an ex parte injunction to restrain the action on the basis that it had been unlawfully called. The union successfully appealed against the grant of the injunction, and the Court of Appeal dismissed the employer's appeal.

The Court stated that it was not prepared to engage in 'hair-splitting' **5.56** distinctions: what mattered was not the identity of the individual who actually called for the strike on the ground, but whether the person specified as authorised to call for the action had delegated his or her decision-making authority. This would be a question of fact and degree in each case. The Court of Appeal stated that there must be a close link in time between the call for the action and the action itself. Thus, had the general secretary, at the start of a series of negotiations, said to the regional secretary, 'You have my permission to call strike action if after some time the negotiations are not going well', that form of 'blanket authority' would be an unlawful delegation of the authority to call the action. Equally, the Court recognised that 'some matters must be left for the judgment of those on the ground who have to decide how and when as a matter of common sense the call for action is to be put into operation'.

The voting paper does not have to specify the name of an individual, but may specify a description of persons authorised to call industrial action – e.g. one or more members of the principal executive committee of the union or a specified category of union official. In complying with this requirement the union may ignore its rule book: the person or persons specified need not be authorised by the union's rules to call industrial action. But he, she or they must fall within one of the following categories:

- persons who are in fact empowered by the rules to authorise or endorse industrial action, or

- the principal executive committee, president or general secretary, or

105

- any other committee of the union or any other official of the union (whether or not employed by the union) – Ss.229(3) and 20(2).

A committee of the union is any group of persons constituted in accordance with the rules of the union. Officials, as defined, include shop stewards.

5.57 **Mandatory statement.** The following statement must appear on every voting paper:

> 'If you take part in a strike or other industrial action, you may be in breach of your contract of employment. However, if you are dismissed for taking part in strike or other industrial action which is called officially and is otherwise lawful, the dismissal will be unfair if it takes place fewer than twelve weeks after you started taking part in the action, and depending on the circumstances may be unfair if it takes place later' – S.229(4).

(The provisions on industrial action dismissals are discussed in detail in Chapter 8, 'Industrial action dismissals'.)

This mandatory statement must not be qualified or commented on by anything else on the voting paper. So, for example, a union running a ballot on industrial action to take the form of refusing to work voluntary overtime is not allowed to express its view, even if it is correct, that such action would not be in breach of employment contracts.

5.58 **Appropriate questions.** The voting paper must contain at least one of the two following questions:

- are you prepared to take part (or to continue to take part) in a strike?

- are you prepared to take part (or to continue to take part) in industrial action short of a strike? – S.229(2).

The union may frame the question as it wishes, as long as it does not qualify or comment on the mandatory statement above and provided that it can be answered by a simple 'Yes' or 'No'.

5.59 It is common for unions to include both questions on the voting paper on the basis that if it appears that there is not a majority in favour of a strike there may nevertheless be a majority in favour of taking lesser action. Although there is no requirement to give members a choice – see, for example, British Telecommunications plc v Communication Workers Union 2004 IRLR 58, QBD, where a choice is given separate questions must be asked. In Post Office v Union of Communication Workers 1990 ICR 258, CA, the union balloted its members with a single question asking whether they were 'willing to take industrial action up to and including strike action'. A majority voted in favour of the question as framed and the union called a series of one-day strikes. The Court of Appeal ruled that this 'rolled-up' question was not an 'appropriate question' as defined in the legislation and that the union's call for strike action did not have the support of a ballot. The union should have asked two separate questions. It could not be argued that a majority vote for strike action would automatically authorise industrial action short of a strike.

Section 229(2A) TULR(C)A goes on to clarify that for the purposes of the balloting provisions in S.229(2) an overtime ban and a call-out ban both constitute industrial action short of a strike. This provision was inserted by the ERelA 1999 to reverse the decision in Connex South Eastern Ltd v National Union of Rail, Maritime and Transport Workers 1999 IRLR 249, CA. In that case the RMT balloted train conductors on taking industrial action in the form of a ban on overtime and rest-day working. The ballot paper asked the conductors to vote 'Yes' or 'No' to strike action, making no mention of industrial action short of a strike. Having obtained a majority 'Yes' vote, the RMT gave the employer notice of the proposed action. The employer alleged that the action planned was, in fact, industrial action short of a strike, for which the union had no lawful mandate. The Court of Appeal took as its starting point S.246 TULR(C)A, which defines a 'strike' as 'any concerted stoppage of work'. The Court held that this definition was broad enough to cover any mutually planned refusal to work, including a ban on overtime and rest-day working. It followed that the union had asked its members the correct question in the ballot.

Although the union in the Connex case benefited from a wide definition of the term 'strike', in many cases it was the unions that had the most to fear from the decision. This is because it is generally easier to obtain a vote in favour of action short of a strike than strike action. S.229(2A) now clarifies the status of overtime bans and call-out bans by defining both as 'industrial action short of a strike' for the purposes of framing the question on the ballot paper. The definition of 'strike' in S.246 TULR(C)A was similarly amended so as not to apply to S.229(2). For further details, see Chapter 1, 'Overview', in the section on 'Strikes'. However, the wide definition of a strike in S.246 as 'any concerted stoppage of work' has remained unchanged, with the result that other forms of limited industrial action involving a stoppage of work – including, oddly, bans on rest-day working – will presumably still constitute 'strike' action for balloting purposes.

Matters in dispute. It seems that a voting paper should not refer to matters **5.60** which do not constitute a current trade dispute with the employer. In London Underground Ltd v National Union of Railwaymen 1989 IRLR 341, QBD, the union balloted its members with a single question which read: 'Do you agree to support the executive committee in their fight to maintain the current agreement on seniority and to resist the imposition of organisational changes, [unsatisfactory attendance procedures and competitive tendering] by taking strike action?' A majority voted in favour of strike action. There was a dispute between the parties about the agreement on seniority: the employer wished to introduce a system of promotion by merit to replace promotion by seniority and the union objected to this. However, the employer argued that there was no current dispute between the parties over the other three issues mentioned in the ballot paper. Mr Justice Simon Brown accepted this and ruled that the ballot was invalid because it asked if union members were prepared to strike by reference to issues which were not trade disputes. As the voting paper was worded, a majority of the voters might have supported strike action over issues that were not in fact trade disputes, but been against striking over the only issue that actually did amount to a trade dispute.

In Associated British Ports and ors v Transport and General Workers' Union 1989 IRLR 291, ChD, it was argued that a strike ballot inadequately defined the issues with which the dispute was concerned. Mr Justice Millett said that there was no requirement to define every issue with which a dispute was concerned. What was necessary was for the union to establish that a strike had the support of a ballot. This might make it necessary to identify a strike which was called with a strike which had been voted for, but this would be a matter of evidence. In the case under consideration – the 1989 docks strike – there was not the slightest difficulty in identifying the dispute and that the strike called would be in furtherance of that dispute.

5.61 Conduct of the ballot

All industrial action ballots must be secret postal ballots. Apart from merchant seamen or women, every person who is entitled to vote in the ballot must, so far as is reasonably practicable, have a voting paper sent to him or her by post at home or at such other address as has been requested in writing, and be given a convenient opportunity to vote by post – S.230(2). The method of voting must be the marking of a voting paper by the person voting – S.229(1).

The Code of Practice recommends that unions allow sufficient time for the voting papers to be distributed and returned as well as for members to consider their vote (para 27). The appropriate period in this context may vary according to the geographical dispersion of the workforce, their familiarity with the issues in the dispute, the class of post used and whether the ballot is being held at a time of year when members are more than usually likely to be away from home or the workplace, e.g. during the summer holidays. The Code considers that, as a general rule, seven days should be the minimum period where voting papers are sent out and returned by first-class post and 14 days where second-class post is used. In very exceptional circumstances, it may be possible to have shorter periods for ballots with very small, concentrated constituencies who can be expected to be familiar with the terms of the dispute. Certificates of posting should be obtained to confirm when and how many voting papers were sent out – para 28.

A ballot must be conducted so as to secure that, so far as is reasonably **5.62** practicable, those voting do so in secret – S.230(4)(a). Accordingly, the name (or any other identifying mark) of the person voting should not appear on the voting paper. The ballot must also be conducted so as to ensure that the votes cast are fairly and accurately counted, although any inaccuracy may be disregarded if it is accidental and on a scale which could not affect the result of the ballot – S.230(4). Although, unlike other union ballots, there is no statutory requirement that votes be counted by the independent scrutineer, the scrutineer must state in his or her report that the arrangements for the counting of the votes included such security arrangements as were reasonably practicable for the purpose of minimising the risk that any unfairness or malpractice might occur – S.231B(1)(b).

All those voting in the ballot must be allowed to vote without interference from, or constraint imposed by, the union or any of its members, officials or employees – S.230(1)(a). However, this does not mean that the union is not entitled to be partisan and campaign vigorously for a 'Yes' vote – see Newham London Borough Council v National and Local Government Officers Association 1993 ICR 189, CA. What the union presumably must not do is intimidate sections of the membership, by either physical or verbal threats, in order to pressure them into approving the industrial action.

Those voting should also be enabled to do so, so far as is reasonably practicable, without incurring any direct cost – S.230(1)(b). Accordingly, the union should supply pre-paid reply envelopes to all the members who are entitled to vote.

Although these requirements are expressed as mandatory they are not absolute, **5.63** in the sense that the union's duty is to comply with its statutory obligations *in so far as is reasonably practicable*. This is a reflection of the industrial realities within which unions operate in that it is inevitable, especially in the case of large ballots conducted over many different areas, that unintentional clerical errors or other accidents may occur and deprive a certain number of members of their opportunity to vote. As Lord Donaldson MR explained in British Railways Board v National Union of Railwaymen 1989 ICR 678, CA, where over 63,000 ballot papers were issued: 'It seems inevitable where you have a balloting operation of this size conducted in an industrial context that there will be a few people whose names ought to be on a list but which are not on a list, perhaps because they have changed jobs; there will be a few people who have not notified changes of address or whose ballot papers, if sent by post, may go astray; there will be a number of things which inevitably will go wrong. Indeed, if... the union claimed to produce evidence that every one of the entitled members had received a ballot paper and returned it, I think that the court would have been justified in looking very carefully at that evidence to see whether something had not been fiddled. It just does not happen like that in

109

real life, and that, of course, was recognised by Parliament when it used the words "so far as... reasonably practicable".'

In National Union of Rail, Maritime and Transport Workers v Midland Mainline Ltd 2001 IRLR 813, CA, the Court of Appeal suggested that a union was unlikely to fall foul of S.230(2) (provision of voting papers and opportunity to vote) where it has a system in place for reminding members of the need to notify it of a change of address. Where a member fails to do so, the union cannot be blamed for the subsequent failure to send the voting paper to the correct address. Conversely, if the union fails to properly record changes of address notified to it, it cannot be said that it has done all that was reasonably practicable to ensure that a voting paper was sent to that particular member. And in P (A Minor) v National Association of Schoolmasters/Union of Women Teachers 2003 ICR 386, HL, the House of Lords held that the fact that the union had failed to include two members in the ballot because they had failed to inform the union of their change of employment clearly fell within the reasonable practicability proviso under S.230(2).

Furthermore, S.232B TULR(C)A specifically excuses inadvertent failures that do not affect the end result of the ballot by providing that a failure (or failures) to comply with S.227(1) (entitlement to vote in the ballot) or S.230(2) (provision of voting papers and opportunity to vote) or S.230(2B) (provision of voting papers and opportunity to vote in relation to merchant seamen and women) shall be disregarded if it is (or if they, taken together, are) 'accidental and on a scale which is unlikely to affect the result of the ballot'. For further details see 'Entitlement to vote – "small accidental failures"' above.

5.64 **Ballot result.** The result of the ballot must be made public. As soon as is reasonably practicable, the union must inform all those voting in the ballot of the total number of votes cast, the numbers of 'Yes' and 'No' votes and the number of spoiled voting papers – S.231. If overseas members have voted in the ballot, their votes must be shown separately under each category – S.232(2)(b). The union is not obliged to inform the overseas members of the result, however – S.232(2)(a).

Industrial action will have the support of a ballot for the purposes of S.226(1) (requirement of ballot before action by trade union) if 'the majority voting in the ballot answered "Yes" to the question applicable' – S.226(2)(a)(iii). In West Midlands Travel Ltd v Transport and General Workers' Union 1994 IRLR 578, CA, the Court of Appeal held that 'majority' in this context meant the majority of those who had actually answered the particular question, even if they did not constitute a majority of all those who returned the ballot papers. There, the union had conducted an industrial action ballot with two questions on the ballot paper, one for strike action and one for action short of a strike. In response to the first question, 1,265 members answered 'Yes', 1,225 answered 'No' and 147 left the question blank. In response to the second question, 1,059 answered 'Yes', 1,156 answered 'No' and 427 did not answer the question. Excluding 22 spoiled ballot papers, it was agreed that 2,642 members had voted on at least one of the questions. The employer argued that subsequent industrial action was unlawful because in order for there to be a majority in favour of strike action at least 1,321 affirmative votes were needed. The Court of Appeal rejected the employer's argument, holding that each question had to be treated as a separate ballot and that, since a majority of those who answered the part of the ballot concerned with strike action had voted in favour of such action, the subsequent strike was lawful.

Merchant seamen/women. The TULR(C)A contains specific provisions **5.65** covering the balloting of merchant seamen and women, i.e. those whose employment, or the greater part of it, is carried out on board sea-going ships – S.230(2C). Where the union reasonably believes that the seaman/woman will be employed on a ship either at sea or at a place outside Great Britain at some time during the ballot and that it will be convenient for him or her to receive the voting paper and to vote on the ship or the foreign port where the ship is, the union must, if it is reasonably practicable, make the voting paper available to him or her at that place and give him or her an opportunity to vote – S.230(2A) and (2B).

These provisions are an exception to the general rule that voting papers must be sent to members' home addresses, which may be difficult in the case of merchant seamen and women who are often away from home for long periods. The provisions apply where the merchant seamen and women are at sea or at a foreign port for just part of the balloting period. In deciding whether to send the ballot paper to the ship or to a foreign port where the ship is, the union must judge whether it would be convenient for the member to receive the ballot paper in this way. In practice, this judgment should not pose difficulties for unions. If in doubt, they can always ask their members in advance of any ballot what their movements are expected to be.

Informing employer of ballot result   5.66
A union's obligation to notify the employer(s) of its intention to hold an industrial action ballot and the information it must at that stage supply to all relevant employers has been considered above (see 'Preliminary considerations'). The union must also notify and provide information to the employer(s) on two further occasions – after the ballot has been held and prior to the calling of any industrial action. The requirements of the strike notice are discussed below under 'Notice of industrial action to employer'.

As soon as is reasonably practicable after the holding of the ballot, the trade union must take such steps as are reasonably necessary to ensure that every relevant employer is informed of the result of the ballot, giving the same information as it is required to give under S.231 to the persons entitled to vote

111

in the ballot (i.e. the total number of votes cast, the numbers of 'Yes' and 'No' votes and the number of spoiled voting papers) – S.231A(1) TULR(C)A. 'Relevant employer' means any employer who it is reasonable for the union to believe was the employer of any persons entitled to vote at the time of the ballot – S.231A(2). In cases where a union ballots members employed by different employers, the union must supply the information to each of the employers concerned. Where a union fails to comply with S.231A in relation to an employer, the industrial action will not be regarded as having the support of a ballot vis-à-vis that employer – S.226(3A). It is therefore lawful for a union to call on its members to take action where the employer of those members was informed of the result, even if other employers were not informed.

5.67 Although the union is afforded some latitude when it comes to informing the employer of the result of the ballot, any unnecessary delay is likely to be at its own peril. In Metrobus Ltd v Unite the Union 2010 ICR 173, CA, Unite balloted bus drivers involved in a pay dispute with M Ltd. On 1 September 2008 the independent scrutineer, ERS Ltd, faxed the ballot result to Unite, but the fax was not received until 2 September. It was not until 3 September that Unite's regional organiser, G, received the approval of the general secretary for strike action. G wrote to M Ltd that day and informed it that the members had voted in favour of industrial action. The strike went ahead and, when the dispute continued, Unite planned a second strike. M Ltd obtained an injunction from the High Court preventing this. The judge found that Unite had committed various breaches of the law on industrial action ballots, among them a breach of S.231A by not informing M Ltd of the result of the ballot until 3 September. Unite appealed to the Court of Appeal.

Lord Justice Lloyd, who gave the leading judgment, confirmed that the obligation in S.231A to inform the employer of the result 'as soon as reasonably practicable' applies regardless of whether the union decides to take industrial action. Although the initial delay in this case was attributable to the late arrival of a fax, Lloyd LJ took the view that, having not heard from ERS Ltd on the morning of 1 September, it would have been 'proper and reasonable' for Unite to contact ERS Ltd that afternoon. Even if the union could have properly waited until the result was received on the afternoon of 2 September, it could and should have passed the result on by the end of the day. The delay of a further day (from 2 to 3 September) meant that the union had not informed the employer as soon as reasonably practicable. The injunction was accordingly upheld.

5.68 **Notice of industrial action to employer**
Trade unions must take such steps as are reasonably necessary to ensure that any affected employer 'receives within the appropriate period a relevant notice' covering the proposed industrial action – S.234A(1). The 'appropriate period' is the period beginning with the day when the union informed every relevant employer of the result of the ballot and ending with the *seventh* day before the

day, or the first of the days, specified in the notice for industrial action to commence – S.234A(4). The Code of Practice recommends that the union should allow sufficient time for delivery of the notice, use a suitable means of transmission (such as first-class post, courier, fax, e-mail or hand delivery) and consider obtaining confirmation that the employer has received the notice, e.g. by using recorded delivery (paras 17 and 51).

The notice must be received by any employer who it is reasonable for the union to believe, at the latest time when steps could be taken to ensure that he receives such a notice, is the employer of an affected employee – S.234A(2). Whether the union has properly notified any relevant employer is to be judged objectively and in the context of the negotiations that have taken place – English, Welsh and Scottish Railway Ltd and anor v National Union of Rail, Maritime and Transport Workers 2004 EWCA Civ 1539, CA. (This case is discussed under 'Preliminary considerations – notice of ballot to employer' above.) As with the requirements to notify employers of the fact that a ballot is to be held and of the ballot result, where there is more than one employer involved, a failure to comply with S.234A in respect of a particular employer results in loss of immunity vis-à-vis that employer only – S.234A(1).

A 'relevant notice' is a notice in writing which: **5.69**

- contains –

    (i)   a list of the categories of employee to which the affected employees belong and their workplaces; and figures for the total number of affected employees, the number of affected employees for each category and workplace, together with an explanation of how those figures were arrived at – S.234A(3)(a)(i), (3A) and (3B), or

    (ii) where some or all of the affected employees are employees from whose wages the employer makes deductions representing payments to the union ('check-off'), either those lists and figures (with the explanation) mentioned in (i) above, or such information as will enable the employer readily to deduce: (a) the total number of affected employees, (b) the categories to which they belong and the number of employees in those categories, and (c) the workplaces at which the affected employees work and the number of them who work at each of those workplaces – S.234A(3)(a)(ii) and (3C), *and*

- states whether industrial action is intended to be continuous or discontinuous and specifies –

    (i)   where it is to be continuous, the intended date for any of the affected employees to begin to take part in the action,

    (ii) where it is to be discontinuous, the intended dates for any of the affected employees to take part in the action – S.234A(3)(b).

113

The 'affected employees' are those employees of the employer who the union reasonably believes will be induced, or have already been induced, by it to take part or continue to take part in the industrial action – S.234A(5C). The workplace at which an employee works is the single set of premises at or from which the person works or, in relation to any other employee, the premises with which the person's employment has the closest connection – S.234A(5D).

Both these requirements are considered separately below.

5.70 **Employee information required.** The information that must, at a minimum, be included in the notice to the employer under S.234A largely mirrors the information that the union has already provided to the employer in the notice of industrial action ballot that must be given prior to the ballot going ahead in accordance with S.226A – see 'Preliminary considerations' above. As we discussed in that section, both provisions have undergone various changes over the years and their – somewhat formulaic – wording reflects the need to strike a balance between ensuring that union members' identities remain confidential while at the same time giving employers sufficient information to know which part(s) of their business will be affected by the proposed industrial action and prepare for it accordingly.

Since 1 October 2005, the notice under S.234A must contain a list of the categories to which the affected employees belong and a list of the workplaces at which they work, together with figures showing the total number of the affected employees, the number of them in each category and the number of them that work at each workplace. However, the union is not required to supply the employer with the names of the affected employees – S.234A(3F), although if it wants to disclose the names, it is free to do so.

5.71 The Code of Practice recommends that, when providing an explanation as to how the figures in the written notice were arrived at, unions include a description of the source of data used to compile the figures, e.g. membership lists held centrally or information held at regional offices, or data collected from surveys or other sources (paras 16 and 51). However, this goes beyond what is required by the legislation.

In any event, the union cannot give information that is not in its possession. Information is 'in the possession of the union' if it is held for union purposes in a document (either in electronic or in other form) and is in the possession or under the control of an officer or employee of the union – S.234A(3E). Information held only by branch officials or other lay representatives of the union is not in the union's possession. (Note, however, that the Code of Practice unhelpfully states that these persons will 'probably' not be covered – para 50.)

Generally speaking, the 'category' to which an employee belongs is 'no more than a reference to the general type of workers' – Westminster City Council v UNISON 2001 ICR 1046, CA. In some cases, therefore, the information requirement will be satisfied even if only a broad job description is provided. For example, referring to the affected employees as teachers at a particular school may be entirely sufficient. However, in other circumstances it may be incumbent on the union to provide more detailed information as to members' occupations to ensure that the employer knows which part or parts of the workforce will take part in industrial action and can prepare contingency plans accordingly.

The Code of Practice advises unions to choose a categorisation that relates to **5.72** the nature of the work (paras 15 and 51). Such categorisation, it continues, may be based on the occupation, grade or pay band of the employees concerned. The decision may also be informed by the categorisations the employer uses in dealings with the union or be influenced by the type of data available to the union. The data the union holds or has access to may thus be a limiting factor in respect of the amount of detail it can be expected to give. For example, in Anglian Windows Ltd v GMB 2007 EWHC 917, QBD, a case that arose under S.226A, the union was able to resist the employer's argument that it had inadequately particularised the category of employees to be balloted (by failing to describe the functions of the employees in sufficient detail) on the ground that this information was not in its possession. This case is discussed above under 'Preliminary considerations'. Generally speaking, the category (or categories) to which the affected employees belong will match those given in the ballot notice under S.226A.

Although we have stressed the similarities between the notices required under Ss.226A and 234A, there is one notable difference. Under S.226A, the ballot notice must specify the 'employees concerned', who, by virtue of S.226A(2H), are those who the union reasonably believes will be entitled to vote in the ballot. S.234A, on the other hand, requires notice to be given in respect of the 'affected employees', who are those whom the union reasonably believes will be induced to take part in the industrial action. Therefore, it is entirely possible that a greater number of employees will need to be included under the S.234A notice than under the S.226A notice, as there may well be employees who will be induced to take part in the strike who were not entitled to vote or who are not even union members.

Section 234A(3)(a)(ii) allows unions to meet their obligations under S.234A by referring in the notice to affected employees from whose wages the employer makes deductions from pay representing payments to the union (a practice known as 'check-off'). Information provided in this way must enable the employer readily to deduce the total number of the affected employees, the categories of employee to which the affected employees belong and the number of the affected employees in each of those categories, and the workplaces at which the affected employees work and the number of them who work at each of these workplaces.

115

5.73 In Metrobus Ltd v Unite the Union 2010 ICR 173, CA, the Court of Appeal considered the application of S.234A(3)(a)(ii) where the affected employees consist of a mixture of check-off and non-check-off staff. The question that arose was whether, in these circumstances, the requirements in S.234A(3) were satisfied where the union did not supply separate lists and figures, together with the necessary explanation, but merely gave the company information from which it could readily deduce that information itself. The Court of Appeal, albeit by a majority, held that, in the case of non-check-off employees, a union is obliged to provide a list of the number of employees, the number in each workplace and the number in each category, along with an explanation of how the figures were worked out. Only in the case of check-off employees can a union simply provide such information as would allow the employer to readily deduce the totals discussed above, since in the case of other employees it will not be possible for the employer to readily deduce such information. As the union had failed to supply the employer with an explanation as to how the figures were arrived at in accordance with S.234A(3), the S.234A notice was invalid. An injunction was accordingly upheld.

The lists and figures or information supplied under S.234A must be 'as accurate as is reasonably practicable' in the light of the information in the union's possession at the time when it complied with its obligation to provide the notice of industrial action – S.234A(3D). For example, in Metrobus Ltd v Unite the Union (see above) the Court of Appeal held that a numerical error in the strike notice did not vitiate the notice: the notice understated the number of check-off employees by ten, which was, in the context of a workforce of about 850, 'trivial and insignificant' and could have 'no impact on the employer's response to the strike notice or its preparations to cope with the strike'. Furthermore, an error in a figure which the union did not have to provide, having provided the information from which the employer could deduce the correct details in accordance with S.234A(3)(a)(ii), was not a fatal defect. (Note that there is no equivalent provision to S.232B that allows small, accidental errors in S.234A notices to be disregarded. This defence is discussed under 'Entitlement to vote – "small accidental failures"' above.)

By contrast, in British Airways plc v Unite the Union 2009 EWHC 3541, QBD, a strike notice that erroneously included several hundred union members who would have left BA's employment by the time of the proposed strike – and who the union could therefore not have reasonably believed would have been induced by it to take part in the strike – could not be saved by S.234A(3D). Mrs Justice Cox, hearing the company's application for an interim injunction, rejected the union's claim that it had done everything reasonably practicable to discover the identity of members who would have already left by the time of the strike. In particular, she found that, prior to the union giving notice of the intended strike action under S.234A, BA had written to Unite querying the accuracy of the numbers provided in the notice and asking whether voluntary redundancy leavers had in fact been included. Unite had failed to respond, thereby undermining its argument that it had done its best to ensure that the numbers provided were accurate and that those taking voluntary redundancy had been removed from the list of those entitled to vote. If, as the union contended, its attempts to discover who was leaving were thwarted by the company, this would have been the perfect opportunity to raise its concern with the company. The injunction to prevent the strike was accordingly granted. (This case is also discussed under 'Preliminary considerations – notice of ballot to employer' and 'Entitlement to vote – determining the balloting constituency' above.)

The Code advises that where the employer receives a notice which he believes **5.74** does not contain sufficient information to comply with the statutory requirements, he should raise this with the union 'promptly' before pursuing the matter in the court (paras 18 and 51). This is exactly what BA did in the above case. It may also be beneficial to the union to ascertain whether the employer accepts the validity of the S.234A notice before calling the industrial action.

Nature of industrial action. The second requirement in S.234A(3) is that the **5.75** notice of industrial action must state whether the action is intended to be continuous or discontinuous and specify the intended date on which employees are to take part in it – S.234A(3)(b). Industrial action is taken to be discontinuous if a union intends it to take place only on some days on which there is an opportunity to take the action – S.234A(6)(a). Action is continuous if a union intends it not to be so restricted – S.234A(6)(b). Since each date on which action is to take place must be covered by seven days' notice, the union will either have to specify a full list of days at the outset or, alternatively, give a separate seven days' notice of each stoppage. Either way, the element of surprise – one of the major advantages to a union of calling discontinuous action – will be lost.

A notice of industrial action will not be valid – and consequently the union will not be protected in tort – if any employees covered by it, and falling within a notified category of employee and a notified workplace, are induced to take part in action either before the notified start date of the action or, if the action is discontinuous, on a day which has not been specified in the notice – S.234A(5). A 'notified category of employee' and a 'notified workplace' mean a category of employee or workplace respectively that is listed in the notice or, where S.234A(3)(a)(ii) applies, such category or workplace as the employer, at the time he receives the notice, can readily deduce from information provided to him – S.234A(5B).

Where continuous action which has been authorised or endorsed by a union **5.76** ceases to be so authorised or endorsed, but is later authorised or endorsed again by the union wishing to restart the action – either on a continuous or discontinuous basis – the original seven days' notice cannot be relied upon. A new notice must be given – S.234A(7). The effect of this provision is to

117

discourage unions from suspending industrial action and attempting to settle the dispute since, if the negotiations fail, a new notice will have to be issued at least seven days before action is resumed. However, S.234A(7B) allows the union and the employer to suspend industrial action by *joint agreement* while negotiations are in progress without the need for the union to issue a fresh notice before action is resumed. S.234A(7B) provides that a new notice need not be issued where:

- a union agrees with an employer, before industrial action ceases to be authorised or endorsed, that it will cease to be authorised or endorsed with effect from a date specified in the agreement (the suspension date) and that it may again be authorised or endorsed with effect from a date not earlier than a date specified in the agreement (the resumption date)

- the action ceases to be authorised or endorsed with effect from the suspension date, and

- the action is again authorised or endorsed with effect from a date which is not earlier than the resumption date or such later date as may be agreed between the union and the employer.

A further exception to the requirement that seven days' notice of the resumption of industrial action must be given arises where the action ceases to be authorised or endorsed in order to enable the union to comply with a court order or an undertaking given to the court, and is later resumed – S.234A(7A).

As the Code of Practice notes, for these exceptions to apply the resumed industrial action must be 'of the same kind as covered in the original notice' – para 52. If, for example, the later action is taken by different or additional descriptions of workers, then a new notice must be given.

5.77 Calling industrial action

Industrial action will not be regarded as having the support of a ballot unless it is called by the specified person and the specified conditions are satisfied – S.233(1). A 'specified person' is a person specified (or of a description specified) in the voting paper in accordance with S.229(3) – S.233(2) (see 'Content of the voting paper' above). The specified conditions are that:

- there must have been no call by the union to take part or continue to take part in industrial action to which the ballot relates before the date of the ballot. There must also have been no authorisation or endorsement by the union of any such unballoted action – S.233(3)(a)

- the industrial action must begin before the ballot ceases to be effective – S.233(3)(b). This condition is discussed below under 'Period of effectiveness'.

The first of these conditions means that if a union calls, authorises or endorses industrial action to which a ballot relates before a ballot is held, it cannot

118

subsequently validate that action by conducting a ballot, even if the ballot complies with all the other legislative requirements. The action will continue to be regarded as being without the support of a ballot and therefore unlawful. However, it will be a question of fact in each case as to whether the union has called, authorised or endorsed industrial action prior to a ballot. An example:

- **Newham London Borough Council v National and Local Government Officers Association** 1993 ICR 189, CA: the employer made three employees redundant, following which their colleagues in the same section took strike action which was not preceded by a ballot. Two further limited strikes occurred which were preceded by ballots. The union then decided to escalate the action by conducting a branch-wide ballot of its members and sent letters to the Council and members to that effect on June 19. The ballot resulted in a majority in favour of strike action and a branch-wide strike began. The employer successfully applied to the High Court for an injunction on the basis that there was a serious issue to be tried as to whether the union, by sending the letters, was calling, authorising or endorsing action to which the ballot related. The Court of Appeal allowed the union's appeal against the grant of the injunction. In the Court's view, the union was merely communicating its decision to authorise a ballot of its members with a view to more extensive industrial action being taken and indicating the manner in which the ballot was going to be carried out. Although the union clearly wanted industrial action to be extended to other members in addition to those who were already on strike, it was perfectly entitled to be partisan provided the legislative requirements were complied with. The two strikes following the first one were lawful (having been preceded by a ballot); they did not require the support of a further ballot and the subsequent ballot did not relate and was not intended to relate to the industrial action already being taken. The fact that the earlier action would be subsumed in the later industrial action did not mean that the later action was in any way concerned with the earlier action.

The Code of Practice recommends that a union should consider delaying any **5.78** call for industrial action until the scrutineer's report has been obtained (para 49). Whether this is a practical option will depend on the particular circumstances and, in particular, on the fact that any industrial action supported by the ballot must take place within four weeks of the date of the ballot (see below).

Period of effectiveness   5.79

The general rule is that a ballot ceases to be effective at the end of the period of *four* weeks starting with the date of the ballot – S.234(1)(a). However, this may be extended to up to *eight* weeks from the date of the ballot by agreement between the union and the employer – S.234(1)(b). Where the workers of two

119

or more employers are balloted, the option of agreeing an extension will operate separately in relation to each employer. The purpose behind allowing an extension is to avoid the situation in which a union feels obliged to organise industrial action within four weeks of the ballot, even though the parties are attempting to negotiate a settlement of the dispute. Where votes are cast on more than one day, the 'date of the ballot' is the last of those days – S.246.

If industrial action first takes place after the period specified in S.234(1), it will not be treated as having the support of a ballot. In RJB Mining (UK) Ltd v National Union of Mineworkers 1995 IRLR 556, CA, voting in the strike ballot closed at 10 am on 16 May. The ballot ceased to be effective four weeks later, at midnight on 12 June. Acting under erroneous legal advice, the NUM called the action for the start of the day shift on 13 June. The union tried to argue that the action was in effect due to commence at midnight and that midnight was included in both days, so that a strike commencing at midnight on 12/13 June commenced on 12 June. The Court of Appeal held that, although the word 'midnight' is used to describe the end of one day and the beginning of another, there is no moment in time which belongs to both days. Even if the strike did start at midnight, the date on which it commenced was 13 June. Accordingly, an injunction was granted restraining the proposed action.

5.80 Industrial action started within the four-week period, or within a longer agreed period of up to eight weeks, may continue afterwards – provided that it is the same industrial action. It is necessary, therefore, to distinguish between continuing industrial action that has been suspended and starting new industrial action, which requires a fresh ballot. (Note, however, that if the action is merely suspended for a period so that there is no need to hold a fresh ballot, the union will still have to give the employer seven days' notice that action is to be resumed, unless the action has been suspended by agreement in accordance with S.234A(7B) – see 'Ballot requirements – notice of industrial action to employer' above.)

In the following case the Court of Appeal held that the union had resumed the same industrial action following a short suspension:

- **Monsanto plc v Transport and General Workers' Union** 1987 ICR 269, CA: industrial action took place after a ballot in favour. The action was later suspended for two weeks while negotiations between the union and the employer took place, but the negotiations broke down and the union reimposed industrial action – more than four weeks after the original ballot. The Court of Appeal held that the industrial action followed unsuccessful attempts to settle the original dispute. It was, accordingly, still part of the original dispute and a fresh ballot was unnecessary.

In the following cases, however, it was held that the unions had started new industrial action and that a fresh ballot was required:

- **Post Office v Union of Communication Workers** 1990 ICR 258, CA: following a ballot the union called a series of one-day strikes between September and December 1988. The union then discontinued industrial action in favour of a public relations campaign. Nine months later, in September 1989, it called for a fresh strike in purported reliance on the original ballot. The Court of Appeal held that it was clear that the industrial action had come to an end in December 1988 and had been followed by a complete change of tactics. The reversion to a policy of industrial action in September 1989 represented entirely new and disconnected action which needed the support of a fresh ballot

- **London Underground Ltd v National Union of Rail, Maritime and Transport Workers**, unreported 22.12.98, QBD: in March 1998 the Government announced plans for a public/private partnership to run London Underground. The RMT was concerned at this prospect and in May 1998 it obtained a substantial majority in favour of strike action in a ballot. A 48-hour strike took place in June and a 24-hour strike was held in July. Following consultation on the Government's plans, it was proposed that three private sector companies should be set up to run the infrastructure and that there should be one operating company, which would remain in the public sector. On 15 December 1998 the RMT gave notice that it intended to resume industrial action in reliance on the ballot held in May 1998. The High Court held that the RMT could not rely on the May 1998 ballot to cover the proposed strike action. Five months had elapsed since the last strike action in July 1998 and the protection of the original ballot had been exhausted. The Court rejected the argument that the original action had merely been suspended. The Court also held that the May 1998 ballot gave protection for a particular dispute and that the nature of the dispute had changed. In April 1998 the RMT's primary objective was that all employees should remain employed by London Underground Ltd. But by November 1998 the union's objective was to obtain the best possible deal for those employees who were to be transferred to the privately owned infrastructure companies. The Court concluded that a new ballot was required and granted an interim injunction to restrain the proposed action.

Intervening legal proceedings 5.81

The limit on the effectiveness of a ballot came into prominence in connection with the 1989 docks strike. The Government introduced legislation, which became the Dock Work Act 1989, to abolish the National Dock Labour Scheme. The TGWU balloted its members in the docks and obtained a substantial majority in favour of strike action. The port employers then launched legal proceedings for an injunction to stop the strike. They lost in the High Court, succeeded in the Court of Appeal, and ultimately lost in the House of Lords (see Associated British Ports and anor v Transport and General

121

Workers' Union and anor 1989 ICR 557, HL). By that time, however, the original four-week period had expired and the TGWU had to reballot its members. This put them at a severe tactical disadvantage, particularly as the Act had by then come into force, and this was clearly one of the employers' aims in resorting to the courts in the first place.

This kind of situation is now dealt with by S.234(2) TULR(C)A, which provides that industrial action ballots will *not* automatically cease to be effective after four weeks (or after the longer agreed period of up to eight weeks) if there are intervening legal proceedings. Instead, the period of effectiveness may be extended to a maximum of *12 weeks* if certain conditions are met. These provide that:

- if there is a ballot in favour of industrial action, and

- during all or part of the period during which the ballot is effective, calling industrial action is prohibited by a court order or because of an undertaking given by the union to the court, and

- the court order subsequently lapses or is set aside or the union ceases to be bound by its undertaking

then the union may apply to the court for an order that the period during which industrial action was prohibited shall not count towards the period of effectiveness of the ballot. This will typically cover the case where an injunction is granted against a union and then set aside on appeal – e.g. the situation that arose in the 1989 docks strike.

5.82 The union's application must be made 'forthwith' on the prohibition ceasing to have effect to the court that set aside the prohibition – S.234(3)(a). In the less likely event of a temporary order or undertaking lapsing without the decision of a court, the application must be made forthwith to the original court where the temporary order was made or the undertaking was given – S.234(3)(b). In any event, no application can be made after a period of *eight weeks starting with the date of the ballot*. If the prohibition remains in force beyond the eight-week period, the union will have to hold a fresh ballot whatever happens.

Extension of the period of effectiveness of a ballot under S.234 is not automatic, however. The court must *not* make an order if it appears to the judge(s) that:

- the result of the ballot no longer represents the views of the union members concerned, *or*

- an event is likely to occur as a result of which a fresh ballot would result in a vote against industrial action – S.234(4).

5.83 It would appear to be for the employer to produce evidence to support these propositions – e.g. by indicating an improved offer which would be likely to settle the dispute. There is no appeal from a court's decision to make or refuse an order extending the period of effectiveness of a ballot – S.234(5).

The period between making an application to extend the currency of a ballot and the court's decision to grant or refuse an extension does not count towards the period of effectiveness. But this is subject to an overriding proviso that no ballot can be regarded as effective after the period of 12 weeks beginning with the date of the ballot – S.234(6).

The application of S.234(2) is best illustrated by a practical example. In Transport and General Workers' Union v Associated British Ports Ltd 2001 EWCA Civ 2032, CA, a dispute arose between ABP, which managed harbours in the Humber area, and ship pilots who were authorised by it to provide pilotage services. When negotiations failed, a ballot for strike action was held on 16 October 2001 by the pilots' union, the TGWU. The pilots voted for strike action, which was due to start on 6 November 2001 and last until 4 December 2001. ABP applied to the High Court for an interim injunction to restrain the strike until the matter could be heard in full by a court. The High Court granted the injunction, prohibiting the calling of industrial action between 1 and 12 November 2001. The Court of Appeal, in a judgment given on 3 December 2001, overturned the decision and discharged the interim injunction on the basis that the TGWU was entitled to statutory immunity under S.219 TULR(C)A from the claims by ABP.

The TGWU then asked the Court of Appeal to extend the period of effectiveness **5.84** of the original strike ballot that had been held on 16 October 2001. The Court noted that a notice of strike action had been given for the period of 6 November to 4 December and that, in the absence of any exercise of discretion by the Court under S.234(2), strike action under the existing ballot could therefore only take place on 3 and 4 December 2001 (given that the Court was giving judgment on 3 December) and that thereafter it would be necessary to hold a fresh ballot. The injunction prohibited the calling of industrial action between 1 and 12 November 2001 – a 12-day period. The TGWU was therefore entitled to apply to the Court for an order that the 12-day period should not count towards the period of effectiveness of the ballot, with the result that the TGWU would have a further 12 days after December 4 in which it would be at liberty to give notice of strike action.

After hearing arguments from both parties, the Court concluded that the 12-day period should not count towards the duration of the effectiveness of the ballot. There had been no culpable delay on the part of the TGWU when lodging its appeal with the Court as it had been waiting for written reasons for the High Court's judgment, as well as preparing – at the request of the Court of Appeal – a skeleton argument to submit to the Court along with the appeal. In addition, it was unlikely that members of the TGWU would vote against industrial action if another ballot were to be held. For these reasons the period of effectiveness of the original ballot was extended by 12 days.

123

6 Picketing

Statutory protection for picketing

Loss of protection

Civil liability

Criminal liability

Protection from Harassment Act 1997

Secondary picketing

Picketing is not a form of 'industrial action' in the traditional sense, but rather **6.1** a means by which some forms of industrial action – especially strikes – are made more effective. The term 'picketing' has never been legally defined, but is usually taken to cover the various activities of workers designed to persuade others to join their strike or to desist from delivering goods or services to their employer.

Picketing will be lawful provided it falls within the narrow confines of S.220 of the Trade Union and Labour Relations (Consolidation) Act 1992 (TULR(C)A), which permits peaceful picketing in contemplation or furtherance of a trade dispute at or near the pickets' place of work. If pickets lose this limited statutory protection, they expose themselves and potentially their trade union to liability for a number of industrial and other torts that may be committed during picketing. A picket is also at risk of committing a number of criminal offences under, for example, the Public Order Act 1986.

In addition, the police have a duty to prevent a breach of the peace and this duty overrides any 'right' employees may have to picket. Thus, in exercising their duty to keep the peace, the police have a considerable discretion to regulate the activities and numbers of pickets. As a consequence, pickets are often arrested during the course of industrial disputes.

These matters are discussed fully below. There is a 'Code of Practice on **6.2** Picketing' ('the Code of Practice'), issued by the Government in 1992, to which we make reference where appropriate. The Code is not binding on any court of law but is admissible in evidence and has often been relied on for guidance by judges – S.207 TULR(C)A.

Finally, a thorough examination of the law on picketing would not be complete without reference to the Human Rights Act 1998 and the obligation, by virtue of S.3 of that Act, on courts and tribunals to have regard to the rights guaranteed by the European Convention on Human Rights when interpreting domestic legislation. Article 11(1) of the Convention states that everyone has the right to

125

freedom of peaceful assembly. In Djavit An v Turkey 2005 40 EHRR 45, ECtHR, the European Court of Human Rights observed that this 'is a fundamental right in a democratic society and, like the right to freedom of expression [which is guaranteed by Article 10(1)], is one of the foundations of such a society. Thus, it should not be interpreted restrictively.' Nevertheless, it must be remembered that both these rights are qualified and any interference with them can be justified in the interests of public safety, the protection of public order or the protection of the rights and freedoms of others. (For a general discussion of the impact of the Convention rights on industrial action law, see Chapter 1.)

6.3 Statutory protection for picketing

The statutory immunity for picketing is contained in S.220(1) TULR(C)A, which states: 'It is lawful for a person in contemplation or furtherance of a trade dispute to attend – (a) at or near his own place of work… for the purpose only of peacefully obtaining or communicating information, or peacefully persuading any person to work or abstain from working.'

The essential elements of the so-called 'right to picket' are explained below. In addition, the Code of Practice contains practical guidance on how to organise a picket-line and stay within the protection afforded by S.220. In particular, it outlines the functions of the picket organiser and recommends that essential supplies and services (for example, the police, fire, ambulance, medical and nursing services) should not be interrupted while picketing is taking place (paras 54–64).

6.4 'In contemplation or furtherance of a trade dispute'

For S.220 to apply, the picketing must be 'in contemplation or furtherance of a trade dispute'. The meaning of this phrase is dealt with in Chapter 3, 'Trade union immunities'. But note that, for picketing to be 'in furtherance of a trade dispute', it must be targeted at the pickets' employer:

- **J and R Kenny Cleaning Services v Transport and General Workers' Union,** unreported 8.6.89, CA: ICC was a contract cleaning company that employed a team of cleaners at British Rail's 'Rail House' in Liverpool. However, British Rail became dissatisfied with the cleaning work and replaced ICC with another cleaning firm, KCS. As a result, ICC dismissed the cleaners, who then set up a picket outside the Rail House. KCS sought an injunction to restrain the picketing. The Court of Appeal held that the picketing was not 'in furtherance of a trade dispute' because the pickets' purpose was not to persuade their employer – in this case their former employer, ICC – to reapply for the cleaning contract or to re-employ the pickets or, indeed, to take any action whatsoever. Rather, the picket was designed to compel KCS to employ the dismissed workers.

Purpose of picket   6.5

Picketing is only lawful under S.220 for the purposes stated – i.e. for peacefully obtaining or communicating information or persuading people to work or not to work. If pickets attend at or near their place of work with such purposes in mind, their *attendance* will be lawful – so long as their good intentions are translated into practice. But note that this is a right to attend with intention to persuade only; it does not legalise any of the activities of the pickets in the course of that attendance. Thus the right to attend is *not* tantamount to a right to persuade, nor does it give pickets the right to stop those whom they seek to persuade and oblige them to listen:

- **Broome v Director of Public Prosecutions** 1974 ICR 84, HL: during a national building strike, B, a picket, tried to dissuade a driver from entering a building site. After failing to convince the driver to turn back, B stood in front of the lorry and continued to try to persuade him. B was asked first by the driver and then by a police officer to get out of the way. When he refused he was arrested. The magistrates refused to convict B for obstruction of the highway on the ground that the statutory right to persuade peacefully is meaningless unless the picket is able to force the person whom he wishes to persuade to stop and listen for a reasonable length of time. The House of Lords, however, disagreed. It held that picketing is lawful only if attendance is for the purpose of peacefully persuading or communicating information. If attendance is for any other purpose, such as preventing free passage on the highway, the picketing is unlawful. There could not be implied into the wording of the statute any right to compel others to stop and listen.

In deciding the nature of the pickets' purpose, the courts will apply an objective test, taking into account all the relevant circumstances – Piddington v Bates 1960 3 All ER 660, Div Ct. This means that a mere protestation of peaceful intent on the part of the pickets will not be enough and what they actually do during the course of the picket will be of great relevance in ascertaining their purpose.

The wording of S.220 suggests that the protection afforded by that section will 6.6
only be available where the picket's purpose is exclusively to peacefully persuade or communicate information. Para 25 of the Code of Practice corroborates this. This implies that if a picket does anything that threatens or causes a breach of the peace, it will be taken as an indication that his or her purpose in attending was not peaceful. However, in Gate Gourmet London Ltd v Transport and General Workers' Union and ors 2005 IRLR 881, QBD, the High Court adopted a more liberal interpretation of S.220. In that case, a large number of dismissed employees picketed outside GGL Ltd's premises. The company

127

complained that the pickets' activities went beyond peaceful protest and sought a number of injunctions. Considering the nature of the pickets' purpose, Mr Justice Fulford noted that there was a 'substantial amount of shouting and chanting from the pickets', but went on to state that this 'may well come within the parameters of lawful and peaceful assembly'. In his view, noisy picketing was not necessarily synonymous with unlawful picketing, as a distinction had to be drawn between 'chanting and calling out on the one hand and shouting abuse and threats on the other'. However, in this case, the problem was that 'a largely lawful and peaceful (if somewhat noisy) picket' was having its proper activities compromised by repeated incidents that were occurring away from, but nonetheless still close to, the picket-lines. For example, pickets stood in the road and interrupted traffic, threatened and verbally abused some employees who were going into work and deliberately blocked access to the employer's premises. In view of this, Fulford J decided to grant a more limited injunction to restore lawful picketing and good public order by prohibiting all unlawful behaviour and confining the activities of the pickets to no more than peaceful attempts at communicating with employees coming to and from work.

6.7 Place of picket

An employee can only picket 'at or near his or her place of work'. Unlike the balloting provisions, there is no definition of 'place of work'. The Code of Practice provides a definition of sorts when it states that it is lawful to attend 'at, or near, an entrance to or exit from the factory, site or office at which the picket works', but that it is not lawful to picket 'at an entrance to, or exit from, any place of work other than his own... even, for example, if those working at the other place of work are employed by the same employer, or are covered by the same collective bargaining arrangements' (paras 17 and 18).

Where an employee does not have a central or single workplace, or where the workplace is such that it is 'impracticable' to picket there, S.220(2) allows him or her to picket at *any* of the employer's premises from which he or she works or from which his or her work is administered. This affects mobile workers such as lorry drivers and salespersons and also workers on oil-rigs and other such sites where picketing would be impossible.

6.8 Exceptions. There are two exceptions to the rule that a picket can only picket his or her own place of work. These cover union officials and former employees.

Union officials. Section 220(1)(b) states that a union official may join a picket-line other than at his or her place of work if he or she is accompanying a member he or she represents (provided, of course, that the picket-line is at the member's place of work). The term 'official' includes both lay and salaried officials and covers shop stewards elected in accordance with the union's rules – S.119. A national union officer is taken to represent all members of the union and may therefore accompany any of them on the picket-line. But a district or regional official or a convenor of shop stewards in a multi-union plant must take care to ensure that the pickets whom he or she accompanies are ones he or she actually represents – S.220(4). And once there, if all the official's members leave the picket-line or are replaced, he or she must leave too.

Former employees. The second exception relates to ex-employees. A person **6.9** sacked in connection with a trade dispute, or whose termination of employment was one of the circumstances giving rise to the trade dispute, may picket his or her former workplace – S.220(3). But the ex-employee may only do so for as long as he or she remains unemployed. Once the ex-employee obtains new employment, he or she is no longer allowed to join the picket-line. It seems to follow from this that, where someone has two jobs and is sacked from one in connection with a trade dispute, that person – not being 'a worker not in employment' within the meaning of S.220(3) – cannot picket at all.

A problem arises where an employer sacks an employee and then closes down the workplace, as this often leaves the dismissed employee with nowhere to picket. Two examples:

- **Union Traffic Ltd v Transport and General Workers' Union and ors** 1989 ICR 98, CA: UT Ltd operated several trading divisions, including a transport/ road haulage division and a container repairs division. The transport/road haulage division carried on business at a number of depots throughout the country, including GD and Son, which was based in Liverpool. At Widnes there was another GD and Son depot. The container repairs were operated under the name of CE, also in Liverpool. When UT Ltd decided to close down the Liverpool road haulage depot, the dismissed workers picketed the Widnes depot and the premises of CE. The employer sought an injunction restraining the picketing as it was not at the pickets' place of work. The employees argued that these sites, being premises which they visited in the course of their employment, were places from which they worked. The Court of Appeal held that the pickets had clearly worked from the closed Liverpool depot, with the other depots being no more than occasional ports of call. The pickets were not, therefore, picketing their own place of work. Underlying the pickets' arguments, said the Court, was the premise that everyone involved in a legitimate trade dispute must have somewhere to picket effectively, but that was not so. The picketing in this case was not at the pickets' place of work and therefore did not fall within S.220

- **News Group Newspapers Ltd and ors v Society of Graphical and Allied Trades '82 and ors (No.2)** 1987 ICR 181, QBD: the employer was a newspaper publisher originally based in Fleet Street. The workforce went on strike and was dismissed. Immediately thereafter, the employer closed down the Fleet Street plant and transferred the whole operation to a new plant in Wapping. The sacked employees organised a picket outside the

Wapping plant. The employer sought an injunction restraining the activities of the pickets on the grounds that, among other things, their attendance was not lawful under S.220 because the Wapping plant was not the sacked employees' former place of work. The employees argued, on the other hand, that since the work they used to do had been moved to Wapping, the latter site was in effect their former place of work. Mr Justice Stuart-Smith was of the view that 'place of work' in S.220 referred to a geographical location and, since the employees had never worked at the Wapping plant, it could not be described as their place of work. The picketing was therefore not lawful under S.220.

In cases like those described above, it may be possible to argue that it was *impracticable* for the employees to picket their former place of work – because there was no one there – so that under S.220(2)(b) they should be entitled to picket the place from which their work was administered. However, a court might reject such an argument on the grounds that S.220(2) is concerned solely with cases of *physical* impracticability, such as an oil-rig, and that it is not in this strict sense impracticable for employees to picket a workplace that has closed down – merely futile.

6.10 **Picketing on private property.** Section 220 does not render it lawful to picket without permission on or inside any part of the premises that is private property and persons who do so will be liable to trespass. The leading case is:

- **British Airports Authority v Ashton and ors** 1983 ICR 696, QBD: A was a BAA employee. He anticipated an industrial dispute and, in accordance with normal practice, an agreement was reached on the number and location of pickets allowed at Heathrow Airport (which is owned and operated by BAA). As a result of the agreement, pickets were not permitted at the control posts, but employees were allowed to have a presence there as long as armbands were not worn and vehicles were not stopped. Some time later, A and a number of others picketed at a control post and proceeded to stop vehicles. These pickets refused a police request to leave and were arrested and charged with infringements of the airport bye-laws. The justices refused to convict on the ground that the pickets' activities were protected by S.220. On appeal, however, the High Court held that S.220 gives no right to attend on land against the will of its owner, nor does it affect the operation of any bye-laws by which the use and operation of that land is regulated.

Pickets may therefore find it difficult to picket 'at or near' their workplace where that workplace is surrounded by private property which they are not permitted to enter. All may depend upon the courts' willingness to adopt a liberal construction of the phrase 'at or near' the place of work, as is illustrated by the following case:

130

- **Rayware Ltd and anor v Transport and General Workers' Union and anor** 1989 ICR 457, CA: R Ltd carried on business on a private trading estate where 20 other concerns also leased sites. The only means of access to any of the premises was by a service road belonging to the owners of the trading park. When an industrial dispute arose between R Ltd and its employees, a number of employees set up a picket-line at the gate to the trading estate. R Ltd's premises were 0.7 miles distant from this gate and several other factory premises lay between those premises and the picketing point. The employer argued that a picket-line over half a mile away was not 'at or near' the pickets' workplace and therefore fell outside S.220. At first instance the High Court agreed. The Court of Appeal, however, overruled that decision. Lord Justice May stated that the question was one of fact and degree in each case. He accepted that the phrase 'at or near' had to be considered in a geographical sense but, bearing in mind the intent and purpose of the legislation, and its context, he felt that common sense had to play a large part. Since the picket-line in this case was at the nearest point at which the workers could stand without trespassing, it was 'at or near' the employees' workplace for the purposes of S.220.

Similarly, in Gate Gourmet London Ltd v Transport and General Workers' Union and ors (above), the judge accepted that a picket-line located about 500 metres from the entrance to the employer's premises, which had been designated as a 'permitted' site for lawful industrial action by the owner of the land, came within the protection afforded by S.220. As this case illustrates, obtaining prior permission by the landowner where the entrance to the employer's premises is surrounded by private property is advisable, not least to ensure that the picket-line is located as close as possible to the employees' (former) place of work. **6.11**

Number of pickets
6.12

Section 220 makes no reference to the maximum number of people allowed to form a picket-line. However, the fact that the picket must be for peaceful purposes inevitably places a limit on how many can attend. Mass picketing is likely to intimidate or otherwise threaten a breach of the peace. Similarly, if pickets turn up in large numbers a court is likely to infer that the intention was to obstruct the highway. In reality, therefore, large numbers will almost invariably cause the picketing to fall outside the scope of S.220.

In deciding what is a reasonable number of pickets, the courts have allowed themselves to be guided by the Code of Practice, which recommends that 'pickets and their organisers should ensure that in general the number of pickets does not exceed six at any entrance to, or exit from, a workplace; frequently a smaller number will be appropriate' (para 51). The attitude of the courts in respect of this guidance was summed up by Mr Justice Scott in Thomas and ors v National Union of Mineworkers (South Wales Area) and ors 1985 ICR 886, ChD, when he said: 'Paragraph 31 [now 51] does not make it a criminal offence

131

or tortious to have more than six persons on a picket-line. Nor is less than six any guarantee of lawfulness. The paragraph simply provides a guide as to a sensible number for a picket-line in order that the weight of numbers should not intimidate those who wish to go to work. I am directed by S.3(8) of the Act of 1980 [now S.207 TULR(C)A] to take this guidance into account.' The result is that courts will usually seek to limit the numbers on a picket-line to a maximum of six. It must be emphasised, however, that this is not a hard-and-fast rule and there may be circumstances where a larger number will be considered perfectly reasonable.

6.13 It comes as no surprise that Article 11(1) of the European Convention on Human Rights, which states that *everyone* has the right to freedom of peaceful assembly, has had an impact on the question of when it is reasonable to limit the size of a picket. This point is aptly demonstrated by the High Court's decision in Gate Gourmet London Ltd v Transport and General Workers' Union and ors 2005 IRLR 881, QBD. GGL Ltd supplies in-flight catering to airlines. When employees at its Heathrow South premises took unofficial strike action following a dispute about changes to working practices, the company dismissed approximately 622 employees. The dismissed employees set up a number of picket-lines at or near their former workplace: a picket of between six and 20 people occupied site A on the side of the road opposite GGL Ltd's premises; over 200 people attended a picket at site B about 500 metres from the entrance to the premises; and another picket of about 12 people was located at two nearby bus stops.

GGL Ltd sought a number of injunctions in the High Court, alleging that the pickets' intimidatory and threatening behaviour towards its employees was escalating and having a detrimental effect on its business: sickness absence levels had increased dramatically and, during the course of one week, ten employees had resigned. In particular, GGL Ltd sought to limit the number of pickets at sites A and B to ten.

Mr Justice Fulford accepted that unlawful activities were indeed taking place. Considering the role, if any, the numbers of pickets present played in this respect, he noted that, as a general rule, the relatively large numbers (around 200 people) at site B meant that there was an increased risk that any unlawful activity would recur in future. However, he rejected GGL Ltd's argument that the sheer weight of numbers present meant that the situation would necessarily 'get out of control' or that workers were being prevented from carrying out their duties because this constituted mass picketing. Moreover, regard had to be had to the right to peaceful assembly, as guaranteed by Article 11 of the Convention, as well as the right to freedom of expression contained in Article 10. In his view, the right to peaceful assembly, both under the common law and the Convention, 'has a long and important history in our democratic system of government and a court will be slow to deny those who seek it the opportunity, within the law, to express their opposition to some event that concerns their lives'. Limiting the number entitled to attend at either site A or B would mean that many who had not in any way breached the law would be denied an opportunity to express their point of view and concerns in this public way. In determining whether to limit the size of a picket, the court had to carefully balance the curtailment of the rights of those gathered against what was necessary in a democratic society for the prevention of crime.

Applying these principles to the facts of the case, Fulford J concluded that, **6.14** given that the unlawful activities were occurring away from the picket-line, it would be premature to limit the number of pickets at this stage in relation to site B. Instead, it was appropriate to grant an injunction to restore lawful picketing and good public order by prohibiting all unlawful behaviour, including that occurring away from the site. Furthermore, the pickets would not be allowed to approach, and engage in conversation, employees who were en route to or from their place of work. He fully appreciated that this restricted one of the customary lawful activities of picketing (i.e. the opportunity to persuade others to abstain from working) but considered this necessary for the prevention of crime. In the event that this injunction failed to curtail the unlawful behaviour, he would then have no choice but to put a limit on the number of pickets that could lawfully be present at site B.

Turning to site A, Fulford J made it clear that the same considerations applied. However, due to the recent level of intimidation that had taken place at that site, he decided to limit the number of pickets there to six. Furthermore, he held that pickets should no longer be positioned at or near the bus stops, as this had also given rise to interference with employees going to and from the premises. (It is interesting to note here that the judge limited the number of pickets at site A to six rather than ten, as had been requested by the employer. He may have been influenced by the maximum number recommended by the Code of Practice.)

Pickets, marches and demonstrations 6.15

It is not always easy to distinguish between those who are picketing and those who are simply marching or demonstrating. A court will often need to define which groups are 'pickets' and which are not when deciding which categories of demonstrators to grant injunctions against.

This was one of the issues which arose in News Group Newspapers Ltd and ors v Society of Graphical and Allied Trades '82 and ors (No.2) 1987 ICR 181, QBD (see above), where the union's large-scale protests at Wapping involved thousands of people on a weekly basis. The union sought to argue that only the six official pickets wearing armbands were picketing. The 50–200 people who held demonstrations and rallies each day, and the 700–6,000 others who marched to the plant every Wednesday and Saturday, were, according to the union, simply exercising their civil rights to march and demonstrate. The

133

employer, on the other hand, claimed that those attending near the plant should also be regarded as engaged in picketing. The High Court, after noting that 'picketing' had not been defined by statute, held that the activities of both the official pickets and the daily demonstrators came within the term. Their intention was to persuade others not to work, and that was 'picketing' as commonly understood. However, those taking part in peaceful marches and rallies along the highway into the adjacent square were not pickets – unless they broke rank and began obstructing the highway and threatening or abusing employees in order to dissuade them from working.

6.16 Loss of protection

Picketing which satisfies the S.220 conditions will be lawful under both criminal and civil law. In particular, such 'lawful' picketing will attract the immunity from liability for the industrial torts conferred by S.219 (see Chapter 3, 'Trade union immunities'). This is particularly important for trade unions. which may be liable for the acts of the pickets.

Picketing which does not satisfy S.220, however, suffers in a number of ways. For instance, the pickets will lose the statutory protection for attendance on the public highway with intent to persuade, and accordingly may be liable in the tort of trespass to the highway. However, the real significance of the loss of S.220 protection is that it necessarily entails the further loss of the S.219 immunity from liability for the industrial torts – see S.219(3). This is important because picketing invariably involves the kind of inducement of breach of, or interference with, contracts that constitutes the industrial torts. In Union Traffic Ltd v Transport and General Workers' Union and ors 1989 ICR 98, CA, for example, the Court of Appeal held that the mere presence of pickets was capable of constituting the tort of inducing breach of contract, even where there is no question of obstruction, intimidation, threats, violence or harassment. As a result, employers will usually be able to gain an injunction to restrain picketing that falls outside the protection afforded by S.220.

6.17 It must be stressed, though, that there is no tort or crime of 'unlawful picketing' as such and picketing which does not secure the protection of S.220 is not in itself unlawful. Rather, any unlawfulness depends upon whether a tort or crime has occurred in the course of picketing. So pickets who picket elsewhere than at their place of work, or who go beyond the prescribed lawful purposes, must rely on their rights as ordinary citizens to free speech, assembly and demonstration. But these rights, although arguably wider in scope since the introduction of Articles 10 and 11 of the European Convention on Human Rights, are seldom compatible with the rights of employers and of other employees who wish to work, and all pickets therefore run the risk of committing a wide range of torts and crimes during the course of picketing. The most important of these are discussed below – with the exception of the industrial torts, which are dealt with in Chapter 2, 'Liability for industrial action'. We note at this juncture, however, that the trend of 'modern-day' picketing is towards boycotting and leafleting campaigns which may not constitute any of the industrial torts – see, for example, Middlebrook Mushrooms Ltd v Transport and General Workers' Union and ors 1993 ICR 612, CA, which is also discussed in Chapter 2.

Civil liability   6.18

The civil liability of picketers includes trespass to the highway and private nuisance. Picketers may also be liable in the tort of public nuisance if an individual can show that he or she has suffered greater loss than the public at large. However, public nuisance is primarily a criminal offence at common law and will be considered below under 'Criminal liability'.

Trespass to the highway   6.19
Section 220 permits attendance on the public highway provided the conditions mentioned in that section are fulfilled. If S.220 immunity is lost, however, the presence of pickets on the public highway may constitute the tort of trespass.

The public have a right of way over the public highway, but this right must be used in a reasonable manner. Traditionally, the common law allowed members of the public to pass over and along the public highway for the purpose of getting from one place to another, and to even stop for purposes reasonably incidental to that passage. Thus activities such as queuing for a bus and window-shopping would be reasonable, as would a peaceful and orderly march or procession through a street, since the marchers would still be essentially exercising their right to pass along the highway from one place to another. Clearly a picket – the whole purpose of which is to stand still and guard a certain property – was likely to be considered an abuse of the right of passage and therefore a trespass. Nor would the pickets be able to avoid a claim of trespass simply by the device of keeping on the move. In Tynan v Balmer 1966 2 WLR 1181, Div Ct, pickets walked in a continuous circle in front of the factory gate, thereby blocking the entrance. This was held to be a trespass.

However, in Director of Public Prosecutions v Jones and anor 1999 2 AC 240, **6.20** HL, the House of Lords took a somewhat more liberal view of the public's right to use the highway. Their Lordships held, by a majority, that the public's use is not limited to that which is incidental or ancillary to the primary right of passage along the highway. Rather, the House of Lords restated the right as being the right to enjoy the *use* of the highway for any reasonable activities that are consistent with (i.e. do not impede) the primary use of the highway for passage and repassage along it.

Although a picket which obstructs the highway will clearly still be unlawful following this decision, the majority did come to the conclusion that a peaceful non-obstructive assembly on the highway constituted a reasonable use of the highway. However, in the opinion of Lord Clyde, the use of the highway must be for a reasonable period only. Any permanent picket will therefore fall outside the scope of this right. (The Jones case is primarily concerned with the offence of trespassory assembly and is discussed in the section on 'Criminal liability' below.)

These cases were decided before S.3 of the Human Rights Act 1998, which requires courts and tribunals to have regard to the rights guaranteed by the European Convention on Human Rights when interpreting domestic legislation, came into effect. As Article 11 of the Convention confers a right to freedom of peaceful assembly, it is arguable that the public's right to use the highway should now be given a broad application; although to our knowledge there have been no reported cases that have grappled with this issue. However, it should be noted that Article 11 is subject to any restrictions that may be imposed by Member States. The question of when pickets who use the highway commit a tort is therefore far from clear. This uncertainty may present little difficulty in practice, however. This is because trespass will be committed against the owner of the soil under the highway, and it is only the owner who will be able to bring a claim. In the absence of any contrary evidence, the owner of land abutting onto the highway will be deemed to own it up to the mid-point. But in most cases nowadays the owner will be the highway authority, which may be unlikely to take court action seeking an injunction or damages (which, in any event, would only be nominal).

6.21 Private nuisance

Where someone unreasonably interferes with another's enjoyment or use of his or her land (which includes buildings and business premises), that person commits the tort of private nuisance. The claimant must show a proprietary interest either in the land on which the nuisance occurs or on land adjacent to it. Possession (as opposed to ownership) is sufficient.

Peaceful picketing is not in itself a nuisance, so even if it does not come within the protection of S.220, it may still not constitute a tort. Picketing will become a nuisance, however, if it is accompanied by any element of unreasonable behaviour such as violence, by excessive numbers, or by attempts to obstruct, intimidate, molest or mount a blockade – Ward Lock and Co Ltd v Operative Printers' Assistants' Society and anor 1906 22 TLR 327, CA. Clearly, unreasonable interference with the rights of access to a property of workers, suppliers or customers will amount to a nuisance against the owner of that property. An example:

- **Norbrook Laboratories Ltd v King** 1984 IRLR 200, NICA: in the course of a trade dispute at the employer's laboratories, a picket-line was organised by K, a branch secretary of the TGWU. The picket-line obstructed the access to the laboratories both by force of numbers and by the deliberate parking of cars so as to prevent lorries from entering the premises. On at least two occasions up to 30 pickets surrounded a car seeking access to the premises and drummed on the roof, bonnet and windscreen. Shop stewards on one occasion also stood in front of a lorry to prevent it from entering. The Northern Ireland Court of Appeal held that these activities constituted the tort of nuisance and had caused damage to the employer by preventing deliveries to and from its premises.

In Mersey Dock and Harbour Company v Verrinder and ors 1982 IRLR 152, **6.22** ChD, the High Court attempted to extend the application of private nuisance to peaceful pickets merely by reference to an intention on the part of the pickets to achieve a particular industrial result. Although accepting on the evidence that there was no violence or intimidation on the part of the pickets, the High Court nevertheless held that their actions were tortious because their intention and purpose was to attempt to coerce the claimants into employing only those haulage contractors preferred by the pickets. This decision runs contrary to the well-established principle that, to amount to a nuisance, picketing must be accompanied by some element of violence, harassment or similar acts. Although the fact that the pickets have an ulterior purpose to achieve an industrial result may arguably take the picketing outside S.220 (though even this is doubtful), that purpose should, on accepted principle, be irrelevant as to whether or not the picketing amounts to a private nuisance. Otherwise every picket-line would be a private nuisance because every picket-line has an industrial agenda.

In any event, the approach taken in the Verrinder case has not always been adopted by other judges. In Thomas and ors v National Union of Mineworkers (South Wales Area) and ors 1985 ICR 886, ChD, for instance, Mr Justice Scott considered that picketing (on business premises, at least) was not of itself tortious – it only became so if it was carried out in an unreasonable manner.

In the Thomas case it was not the employer but the non-striking workers who brought a claim of nuisance against the pickets. These workers suffered abuse and threats from some 60–70 picketing miners at the colliery gates as they tried to go in to work. Scott J held that this form of harassment, which unreasonably interfered with the claimants' right to use the public highway in order to get to work, was actionable as a private nuisance, although he added that 'the label for the tort does not, in my view, matter'. The suggestion that the activities of the pickets could constitute a private nuisance might seem somewhat bizarre, since the claimants in this case did not have the necessary proprietary interest in the land upon or adjacent to which the nuisance occurred. What Scott J was in

137

effect doing was taking the highly unorthodox step of creating a new common law tort of 'harassment' or 'interference with the right to use the public highway'.

6.23 However, in Hunter v Canary Wharf Ltd 1997 2 All ER 426, HL, the House of Lords reaffirmed the traditional view that only those with a proprietary interest in the land in question can sue in private nuisance and that no *common law* tort of intentional harassment exists. (Note, however, that the Protection from Harassment Act 1997 has now created a *statutory* tort of harassment – see under 'Protection from Harassment Act 1997' below.)

It was established in Thomas and ors v National Union of Mineworkers (South Wales Area) and ors (above) that the picketing of a person's home will always be a nuisance, however peaceful and however few pickets are involved. This principle seems sound enough, although there could be problems in cases where the employer lives 'above the shop'.

6.24 Union liability

The liability of a union for the tortious acts of its members on the picket-line falls into two categories. Liability for the industrial torts committed by its members is governed by S.20 TULR(C)A, which makes unions liable for acts that have been 'authorised or endorsed' by the union. The liability of a union for other torts – such as nuisance and trespass – that are committed by its members on the picket-line is governed by common law principles, which provide that a union will be liable for persons acting with its express or implied authority. Both S.20 and the common law are discussed in Chapter 2 under 'Union liability in tort'.

6.25 Criminal liability

There is a wide array of criminal offences that picketers might commit, including public nuisance, obstruction of the highway, offences under S.241 TULR(C)A, public order offences and breaches of the peace.

6.26 Public nuisance

A nuisance becomes a 'public' one if it takes the form of a wrongful act or omission that materially affects the comfort and convenience of a member of the public. As such it is primarily a criminal offence for the police to act on. As noted above under 'Civil liability', where a private individual (such as an employer, a customer or supplier, or an employee prevented from working) can show that he or she has suffered particular damage beyond the general inconvenience or injury suffered by the public at large, that person has a right to sue in tort as well – he or she does not have to show a proprietary interest to succeed. Furthermore, a claimant in public nuisance (as opposed to private nuisance) may recover damages for any personal injury suffered – see In re Corby Group Litigation 2009 QB 335, CA.

Any unreasonable and wrongful use of the highway which prevents free and safe passage along it will be a public nuisance. Clearly, any picketing which falls outside the protection of S.220 may well constitute this offence. It should be noted that the public have a right to pass over every part of the highway, so it will not be enough for pickets causing an obstruction to say that people could have crossed the road or otherwise continued their journey despite the obstruction. The primary consideration in each case will be whether the obstruction was *reasonable*. Mass picketing will almost inevitably be unreasonable but peaceful picketing in small numbers may well not be. An example:

- **News Group Newspapers Ltd and ors v Society of Graphical and Allied Trades '82 and ors (No.2)** 1987 ICR 181, QBD: the workers at Wapping who passed the pickets (officially six) and demonstrators (sometimes numbering several thousand) were subjected to abuse and threats and sometimes violence. The High Court held that the activity at Wapping was, among other things, an unreasonable obstruction of the highway affecting the public at large and was therefore a public nuisance. The Court further held that, because the claimants had incurred the expense of busing employees to work and had lost journalists because of the activities of the pickets and demonstrators, they had suffered special damage and were entitled to bring a civil action for public nuisance.

Much of the conduct that amounts to a public nuisance in a picketing context **6.27** is also covered by S.137 of the Highways Act 1980, which makes it an offence without lawful authority or excuse to wilfully obstruct free passage along the highway (see below). For example, a picket hindering someone from entering his or her workplace will not only commit a public nuisance but also the statutory offence of obstructing the highway. Because of this overlap, reliance on the common law tort is likely to diminish as a result of the House of Lords' decision in R v Rimmington; R v Goldstein 2006 1 AC 459, HL, where it was held that where there is a choice between charging a person under the common law offence of causing a public nuisance or under an express statutory provision, it is always good practice that the offence should be prosecuted under the relevant statutory provision unless there is good reason for doing otherwise.

Obstruction of the highway   6.28
It is an offence for a person without lawful authority or excuse to wilfully obstruct free passage along the highway – S.137 Highways Act 1980. As with public nuisance, this offence will only be committed if the obstruction is *unreasonable* – and this will depend on all the circumstances, including the length of time the obstruction continues, the place where it occurs and its purpose – Nagy v Weston 1965 1 All ER 78, Div Ct. A person's honest belief that he or she has lawful authority to obstruct the highway will not be a defence if that belief is mistaken – Arrowsmith v Jenkins 1963 2 QB 561, Div Ct.

As far as obstructions caused by picketing are concerned, much will depend on whether there is lawful authority or excuse for the obstruction. If the picketing confines itself both to the location and to the purposes set out in S.220 TULR(C)A, it will have the lawful excuse provided by that section. But if the purpose of the picket is not merely to persuade or communicate information but also to obstruct, it is likely to amount to the offence. Thus, in Broome v Director of Public Prosecutions 1974 ICR 84, HL, a picket who stood in front of a lorry to prevent the driver entering the premises was convicted of obstructing the highway.

6.29 In Hirst and Agu v Chief Constable of the West Yorkshire Police 1987 85 Cr App Rep 143, Div Ct, Lord Justice Glidewell stated that acts done with 'lawful authority' included activities done under express permits – for example, street trading and charity collecting. 'Lawful excuse', on the other hand, embraced activities which were inherently lawful in themselves and which would only constitute an unlawful obstruction if the particular activity was an *unreasonable* use of the highway. In Glidewell LJ's view, 'an obstruction of the highway caused by *unlawful picketing* in pursuance of a trade dispute cannot be said to be an activity for which there is a lawful excuse' (our stress). Presumably the reference to 'unlawful picketing' in this context was to picketing that involved some civil or criminal wrong rather than to picketing which merely fell outside S.220, since picketing is not necessarily unlawful simply because it loses that statutory protection.

6.30 Offences under S.241 TULR(C)A
Section 241 TULR(C)A contains a set of criminal offences formerly found in S.7 of the Conspiracy and Protection of Property Act 1875 that are highly relevant to the activities of pickets. For many years these offences were thought to be virtually obsolete, but they were revived during the miners' strike of 1984 when some 650 charges were brought under the section.

Section 241 outlines five acts which, if done 'with a view to compelling another person to abstain from doing or to do any act which that person has a legal right to do or abstain from doing', will constitute an offence. The acts in question must be wrongful and without legal authority. That is, the conduct must amount at least to a civil wrong – such as trespass or nuisance – before it is caught by the section. The effect of the section is, in the words of Lord Justice Moulton in Ward Lock and Co Ltd v Operative Printers' Assistants' Society and anor 1906 22 TLR 327, CA, 'to visit certain selected classes of acts which were previously wrongful, i.e. were at least civil torts, with penal consequences capable of being summarily inflicted'. According to the High Court of Justiciary in Galt (Procurator Fiscal) v Philp and ors 1984 IRLR 156, High Court of Justiciary, such acts include those protected by S.219 immunity since that section only covers proceedings in tort. (S.219 immunity is discussed in Chapter 3.)

The wrongful acts contained in S.241 are: **6.31**

- using violence to or intimidating the other person or his or her spouse or civil partner or children or injuring his or her property – S.241(1)(a). (Civil partners are two people of the same sex who have entered into a civil partnership – S.1 Civil Partnership Act 2004.) Intimidation is not restricted to threats of violence to the person, but means simply 'the using of language which causes another man to fear' – Judge v Bennett 1887 4 TLR 75, Div Ct

- persistently following the other person about from place to place – S.241(1)(b). In Elsey v Smith (Procurator Fiscal) 1983 IRLR 292, High Court of Justiciary, E was on strike and sought to persuade two non-striking workers, M and R, to stop working. Wherever M and R drove, E and others followed in three cars. In particular, when M and R were on the motorway they would overtake and then rapidly slow down, thus impeding M and R's progress. The High Court of Justiciary held that this amounted to persistent following and was an offence under the Act

- hiding any tools, clothes or other property owned or used by the other person, or depriving him or her of, or hindering him or her in, the use thereof – S.241(1)(c). Note that the deprivation or hindering must be wrongful, so that if the accused in fact owned the tools he or she is probably entitled to do what he or she likes with them and will not have committed this offence

- watching or besetting the house or other place where the other person resides, or works, or carries on business or happens to be, or the approach to such house or place – S.241(1)(d). Neither 'watching' nor 'besetting' is defined in the Act. However, it must be remembered that the acts must be wrongful (i.e. must amount at least to a nuisance, trespass or other civil wrong). Peaceful picketing under S.220 would not constitute the offence of besetting because 'attendance' within the meaning of that section is 'lawfully authorised'. On the other hand, Scott J's statement in Thomas and ors v National Union of Mineworkers (South Wales Area) and ors 1985 ICR 886, ChD, to the effect that any picket of a person's home will be a nuisance is clearly of relevance to this offence. In Galt (Procurator Fiscal) v Philp and ors (above) the High Court of Justiciary held that 'besetting' does not need to be from the outside of premises but can include an internal occupation such as a sit-in. The watching and besetting can be for a short time only and does not have to be at a place habitually frequented by the worker, such as his or her place of work or his or her home

- following such other person with two or more other persons in a disorderly manner in or through any street or road – S.241(1)(e). See Elsey v Smith (Procurator Fiscal) (above).

It should be emphasised that the above acts need to be taken 'with a view to **6.32** *compelling*' the other person (our stress). In other words, their purpose must

141

not be merely to persuade but to force the other to comply whether he or she is willing or not – Director of Public Prosecutions v Fidler and anor 1992 1 WLR 91, Div Ct.

Finally, it should be noted that these offences extend to the situation where a person does one of the specified acts to another person with a view to compelling not that person but a *third party* to do something or abstain from doing something. For example, the offence will be committed if A does one of the acts to B with a view to compelling C to do something which he or she has a legal right to abstain from doing. Thus in J Lyons and Sons v Wilkins (No.2) 1899 1 Ch 255, CA, the accused committed the offence when he wrongfully watched and beset the employer's property with a view to compelling workers not to work.

A person guilty of an offence under S.241 is liable on summary conviction to imprisonment for a term not exceeding six months and/or a fine – S.241(2).

6.33 Aggravated trespass

Section 68 of the Criminal Justice and Public Order Act 1994 created an offence of 'aggravated trespass'. It provides that a person commits an offence if he or she trespasses on land (including buildings) and, in relation to any lawful activity which persons are engaging in or are about to engage in on that or adjoining land, does there anything which he or she intends to have the effect of: (a) intimidating those persons or any of them so as to deter them from engaging in that activity; (b) obstructing that activity; or (c) disrupting that activity. A person guilty of this offence is liable to not more than three months' imprisonment and/or a fine. 'Land' does not include the highways and roads. S.69 gives a 'senior police officer' present at the scene of the alleged trespass power to direct the person or persons whom he or she reasonably believes to have committed the offence to leave the land. A failure to comply with such a direction is an offence, punishable by a prison sentence not exceeding three months and/or a fine.

Although this offence is primarily directed against groups such as hunt saboteurs and other trespassing protesters, it could be used against pickets who trespass on their employer's (or former employer's) land and commit acts intended to intimidate other employees from exercising their lawful right to enter the employer's premises for the purposes of their work.

6.34 Public order offences

The Public Order Act 1986 is relevant to the law of picketing for two reasons. First, it gives the police the power to regulate assemblies and processions with a view to preventing disorder or intimidating conduct. Secondly, the Act abolished the common law offences of riot, rout, unlawful assembly and affray, and replaced them with six equivalent statutory public order offences. While a peaceful picket will commit none of these offences, picketing which becomes aggressive or violent may well incur liability under the Act.

Powers of police to maintain public order. The 1986 Act gives the police wide 6.35 powers to maintain public order by regulating large gatherings in public, such as assemblies or processions. The powers that may be relevant in a picketing context are discussed in outline below.

Public assemblies. The police have the power to regulate a public assembly if they believe that:

- the assembly may result in serious public disorder, serious damage to property or serious disruption to the life of the community, *or*

- the purpose of the organisers is to intimidate others with a view to compelling them to refrain from doing an act they have a right to do, or to do an act they have a right to refrain from doing – S.14(1).

If either of the above applies, the police may, either before the assembly takes 6.36 place or once it is under way, limit the location, duration and numbers involved in the assembly. However, the police have no power to impose conditions that will effectively ban the assembly – Austin v Commissioner of Police of the Metropolis 2005 EWHC 480 (QB), QBD. In England and Wales, a public assembly is defined as any assembly of two or more persons in a public place which is wholly or partly open to the air, including the highway – S.16. A picket of two or more is therefore a public assembly. In Scotland, 20 or more persons are needed to constitute a public assembly – S.16.

Public processions. The police have similar regulatory powers in respect of public processions. While a picket is not a procession, these powers will be relevant whenever unions organise marches or demonstrations in support of a trade dispute. A public procession is defined as a procession in a public place and no minimum number of people is specified – S.16.

Section 11 makes it a requirement that anyone organising a public procession to demonstrate support for or opposition to someone's views or actions, to publicise a cause or campaign, or to commemorate an event, must give *advance written notice* to the police, unless it is not reasonably practicable to do so. It is an offence for organisers to hold the procession if the notice requirements have not been met, or if the actual details of the procession differ from those notified.

The police can impose the same types of conditions upon a procession as they 6.37 can upon assemblies, and for the same reasons – S.12(1). Unlike assemblies, however, the police have the power to seek a ban on all public processions (or any class of public processions) for a period of up to three months if they think it impossible to prevent serious public disorder any other way – S.13.

143

Trespassory assemblies. Finally, S.14B creates an offence of organising or participating in a trespassory assembly, which the accused knows is prohibited by a district council's order. Those found guilty of this offence are liable to a prison sentence of three months and/or a fine.

An assembly is a 'trespassory assembly' if:

- it is intended to be held on land to which the public have no or only a limited right of access

- it is likely to be held without the permission of the occupier of the land or to conduct itself in such a way as to exceed the limits of any permission or the limits of the public's right of access, *and*

- it may result in serious disruption to the life of the community, or, where the land, or a building or monument on it is of historical, architectural, archaeological or scientific importance, in significant damage to the land, building or monument – S.14A(1).

6.38 An 'assembly' for these purposes is an assembly of 20 or more persons – S.14A(9).

If the chief officer of police reasonably believes that a trespassory assembly is intended to be held, he or she may apply to the district council for an order prohibiting for a specified period the holding of the assembly – S.14A(1). Similarly, if a constable in uniform reasonably believes that a person is proceeding to an assembly which has been prohibited by a district council's order, he or she may stop that person and tell him or her not to proceed to the assembly – S.14C. Failure to comply with such an order is an offence.

These provisions are directed primarily at persons organising 'raves' and other similar activities. However, the scope is there for them to be used against the organisers of marches and demonstrations held in support of picketers. It is unclear what sort of activities may amount to a 'serious disruption to the life of the community', but a large-scale demonstration which prevents the public from going about their day-to-day business might arguably fall within this phrase.

6.39 In Director of Public Prosecutions v Jones and anor 1999 2 AC 240, HL, environmental protesters were prosecuted for gathering on a grass verge on the roadside near Stonehenge in defiance of a S.14A order. They denied the charge, arguing that no trespassory assembly had occurred because a peaceful, non-obstructive assembly did not exceed the limits of the public's right of access to the highway. This argument ultimately found favour with a majority of the House of Lords. In the words of Lord Irvine, 'the public highway is a public place which the public may enjoy for any reasonable purpose, provided the activity in question does not amount to a public or private nuisance and does not obstruct the highway by unreasonably impeding the primary right of the public to pass and repass: within these qualifications there is a public right of peaceful assembly on the highway'.

Statutory public order offences. The six public order offences are: riot; violent **6.40** disorder; affray; violent behaviour; intentional harassment, alarm or distress; and disorderly behaviour. These are dealt with in turn below.

Riot. Where 12 or more people use or threaten violence for a common purpose which would cause a 'person of reasonable firmness' to fear for his or her personal safety, then each person *using* violence will be guilty of riot – S.1. The person of reasonable firmness does not actually have to be, or be likely to be, present at the scene, and the offence can be committed in private as well as public places. This is the most serious offence contained in the Act, carrying a maximum penalty of ten years' imprisonment and/or a fine. Charges of riot must have the consent of the Director of Public Prosecutions and the section is therefore used only in the most serious of cases.

Violent disorder. This offence has the same elements as riot, except that it **6.41** applies where only three or more persons are involved, and each person need only be *threatening* violence to be guilty – S.2.

Affray. This follows the same formula as riot and violent disorder, except that here only one person need threaten or use violence for the offence to be committed – S.3. If two or more people commit such acts, it is their conduct taken together that must be considered. For the purposes of this offence only, a threat cannot be made by the use of words *alone*.

Violent behaviour. It is an offence to use threatening, abusive or insulting words or behaviour, or distribute or display any writing, sign, or other visible representation which is threatening, abusive or insulting, to another person, where that act is intended or likely to make that person fear immediate violence against him or herself or someone else, or to provoke immediate violence by that person or another – S.4. An offence under this section can be committed in a public or private place (with the exception of a private dwelling) but another person must in fact be present for the offence to be made out.

Intentional harassment, alarm or distress. Under S.4A(1) a person is guilty of **6.42** an offence if, with intent to cause a person harassment, alarm or distress, he or she:

- uses threatening, abusive or insulting words or behaviour, or disorderly behaviour, or

- displays any writing, sign or other visible representation which is threatening, abusive or insulting,

thereby causing that or another person harassment, alarm or distress.

145

Like S.4, an offence under this section can be committed in a public or a private place (with the exception of a private dwelling) but another person must in fact be present for the offence to be made out. It is a defence for the accused to prove that his or her conduct was reasonable – S.4A(3).

6.43 This offence is very similar to the offence of disorderly behaviour in S.5 (see below). It involves a substantial element of subjectivity in that although the pickets' conduct might not cause distress or alarm to most of the people at whom it is directed, there may be one particularly sensitive individual who suffers distress, and this would be enough to constitute the offence. The scope of the 'reasonable conduct' defence is very uncertain, and it remains to be seen what approach the courts will adopt in respect of it. Presumably issues such as whether the picketing fell outside S.220 TULR(C)A, whether any tort was committed during the picketing, and whether the Code of Practice was breached may be relevant factors in determining whether a picket's conduct was 'reasonable'.

(Note that a person who may not have intended to harass another but who *ought to have known* that his or her actions amounted to harassment may be guilty of an offence under the Protection from Harassment Act 1997 – see under 'Protection from Harassment Act 1997' below.)

Disorderly behaviour. It is an offence to use threatening, abusive or insulting words or behaviour, or disorderly behaviour, or to display any writing, etc (as in S.4 above), within the hearing or sight of a person *likely* to be caused harassment, alarm or distress thereby – S.5 (our stress). It will be a defence if the accused can prove that he or she had no reason to believe there was such a person within hearing or sight or that his or her conduct was reasonable. This offence can be committed if the only person likely to be suffering harassment, alarm or distress is the arresting police officer – Director of Public Prosecutions v Orum 1989 1 WLR 88, Div Ct.

6.44 'Violence' in all these offences means *any* violent conduct, including violence towards property as well as people (except in the case of affray, which applies to violence against people only) – S.8. Conduct which *might well have caused injury* can amount to violence even if it was neither intended to, nor did in fact, cause violence. Thus an action such as throwing a missile towards someone which falls short will amount to violent conduct. On the other hand, violent gestures where there is no possibility of any harm being caused – as where someone shakes a fist at another who is out of reach – would probably not constitute violence, but only a threat of violence.

It is clear that picketing is capable of giving rise to some of the above offences, especially where emotions are running high in the dispute, such as in the 1986 Wapping dispute or during the miners' strike of 1984. Moreover, as is discussed below, a police officer on the scene is entitled, under his or her overriding duty to prevent a breach of the peace, to disperse a picket if he or she suspects on reasonable grounds that one of these offences may be committed.

Dispersal orders
6.45

For the sake of completeness it should be mentioned here that S.30 of the Anti-Social Behaviour Act 2003 gives the police the power, where certain conditions are met, to disperse groups in public places. However, by virtue of S.30(5), this power may not be used to disperse anyone who is lawfully picketing under S.220 TULR(C)A or taking part in a public procession where proper notice under S.11 of the Public Order Act 1986 has been given. Nevertheless, there may be circumstances where an order could be made against pickets who fall outside the protection of S.220; for example, where a constable has reasonable grounds for believing that the presence or behaviour of the pickets has resulted, or is likely to result, in any members of the public being intimidated or harassed in an area where anti-social behaviour is a significant and persistent problem.

Breach of the peace
6.46

The police have a duty to take reasonable steps to preserve the peace. In fulfilling this duty, they are entitled to order a person to stop doing an act which is in itself perfectly lawful if they believe that such an act is likely to lead to a breach of the peace. In relation to picketing, *this duty overrides any right to picket*. Thus the statement in S.220 TULR(C)A to the effect that peaceful picketing is lawful must be read as subject to the police's right to take whatever steps are necessary in carrying out their duty to prevent a breach of the peace. Anyone who refuses to obey an order from the police can be arrested under S.89 of the Police Act 1996 for obstructing a police officer in the execution of his or her duty.

Note that it is not necessary that the breach of the peace is likely to be caused by the pickets themselves. The police may still move the pickets on even if it is the people they picket or other demonstrators or bystanders who are likely to cause the breach of the peace – Kavanagh v Hiscock and anor 1974 ICR 282, Div Ct.

Threatened or actual violence. The power to prevent a breach of the peace 6.47 gives the police considerable discretion and represents probably the greatest limitation on the so-called 'right to picket'. But before the police can act there must be actual violence, or at least a threat of violence, so not every public disturbance will amount to a breach of the peace. As Lord Justice Watkins put it in R v Howell (Errol) 1982 QB 416, CA, 'there is a breach of the peace whenever harm is actually done or is likely to be done to a person or in his presence to his property or a person is in fear of being so harmed'.

The Code of Practice, which deals with the role of the police in the context of picketing in paras 45–47, states that the police have considerable discretionary

147

powers to limit the number of pickets where 'they have reasonable cause to fear disorder'. To support this proposition, it refers to the case of Piddington v Bates 1960 3 All ER 660, Div Ct, which involved a strike at a printing works where eight of a staff of 24 were working. Soon after the arrival of the police, two vehicles arrived with 18 men wearing picket badges. There were two pickets at the front entrance and four at the back. B, a chief inspector of police, told the pickets that two were sufficient at the back and two moved away. Then the defendant, P, said he was going to the back entrance. He was told by B that two pickets were enough but insisted on going and gently pushed past B. He was then arrested for obstructing a police officer in the execution of his duties. The defendant relied on S.220 but was convicted. On appeal, the High Court held that the police officer was entitled to take such steps as he thought proper to preserve the peace. However, it is not enough for the police officer merely to state that he or she believed a breach of the peace was likely: there must be reasonable grounds for that belief. Moreover, there must be a real, as opposed to a remote, possibility of a breach of the peace. On the facts of the case, the police officer did have reasonable grounds for anticipating that a breach of the peace was a real possibility and P's conviction was therefore upheld.

6.48 It is doubtful, however, that this case would be decided the same way today. In R (on the application of Laporte) v Chief Constable of Gloucestershire 2007 2 AC 105, HL, where the House of Lords conducted an in-depth investigation of the common law concept of breach of the peace, the decision was strongly criticised. Lord Bingham remarked that there was no disorder in this case, nor was any violence threatened or offered by any of the pickets or other persons present. (The case was also criticised for finding that a breach of the peace was a 'real possibility', as opposed to being imminent. 'Imminence' is an essential ingredient of the concept of a breach of the peace – see below.) As a result, this part of the Code should be treated with caution.

6.49 **Imminent breach.** The police's duty to take whatever steps are reasonably necessary to prevent a breach of the peace only arises when the police consider that the breach of the peace is *imminent*. In R (on the application of Laporte) v Chief Constable of Gloucestershire (see above), their Lordships stressed that this is an important threshold requirement that must be satisfied before *any* form of preventive action – such as arrest, detention or warning – can be taken. In the words of Lord Rodger, this requirement ensures that the duty to prevent a breach of the peace is not used as 'a recipe for officious and unjustified intervention in other people's affairs'.

Whether a breach of the peace is 'imminent' – i.e. it is reasonably apparent that it is 'about to take place' or 'about to be committed' in the immediate future – has to be judged in the particular circumstances under consideration. The case often cited in this context is Moss and ors v McLachlan 1985 IRLR 76, Div Ct, which concerned the miners' strike of 1984, when miners from other parts of the country travelled to Nottinghamshire with the intention of picketing the pits there. The police set up a cordon at the motorway junction between one to five miles away from the relevant pits, thereby preventing the miners from reaching their destination. The miners were arrested when they tried to force their way through the blockade. The action of the police was held to be a lawful exercise of their right to take necessary steps to prevent an anticipated breach of the peace. The Divisional Court said that for the police to be entitled to stop the miners, it did not have to be clear from the miners' words and deeds that a breach was intended. The police could rely on the experience of others or on what they had read in the papers or seen on television in order to decide whether a breach of the peace was likely. Further, the Court held that the breach of the peace did not have to be imminent, although the immediacy of the threat will be relevant to the reasonableness of the officer's belief. In this case, considering the relative proximity of the pits, the possibility of a breach of the peace was by no means remote.

This case was criticised by the House of Lords in R (on the application of **6.50** Laporte) v Chief Constable of Gloucestershire (see above) in that, according to Lord Brown, it carried 'the notion of imminence to extreme limits'. Nevertheless, their Lordships thought that the decision could still stand on the basis that one belligerent faction of striking miners was less than five minutes (by car) away from another belligerent faction of non-striking miners and, without the police blocking the strikers' onward process, a breach of the peace was about to be committed.

A picket who disobeys a police officer's order where there is no real danger of an imminent breach of the peace occurring will not be guilty of obstructing the officer in the execution of his or her duty. In reality, however, the question of whether or not a breach of the peace is imminent is for the police officer to decide, and the courts are generally reluctant to disagree with the officer's judgement in this matter. The courts will also make allowance for the fact that the officer had to make a spur of the moment decision in an emergency – G v Chief Superintendent of Police, Stroud 1986 86 Cr App Rep 92, Div Ct.

Code of Practice. The Code of Practice emphasises the police's considerable **6.51** discretionary powers, but points out that they have no duty to enforce the civil law. An employer should not require the help of the police in identifying ringleaders against whom the employer wishes to seek an injunction. Nor is it the police's job to enforce the terms of an injunction, although they may decide to assist the officers of the court in this task where they fear a breach of the peace.

Conspiracy 6.52

If a person agrees with another person or persons that a course of conduct shall be pursued which, if the agreement is carried out in accordance with their intentions, either

149

- will necessarily amount to or involve the commission of any offence by one or more of the parties to the agreement, or

- would do so but for the existence of facts which render the commission of the offence impossible,

that person is guilty of conspiracy to commit the offence in question – S.1(1) Criminal Law Act 1977. However, if the offence in question is a summary offence not punishable with imprisonment and is done in contemplation or furtherance of a trade dispute, then S.1(1) of the Criminal Law Act 1977 will not apply (in England and Wales) – S.242 TULR(C)A.

6.53 Protection from Harassment Act 1997

The Protection from Harassment Act 1997 (PHA) was introduced in 1997 to deal primarily with the problem of stalkers. The Act is, however, drafted in very broad terms and potentially covers at least some of the activities associated with picketing.

The PHA introduced three main categories of unlawful act:

- the offence of harassment – Ss.1 and 2

- the tort of harassment – Ss.1 and 3

- the offence of putting a person in fear of violence – S.4.

6.54 Offence of harassment

It is an offence for someone to pursue a course of conduct which amounts to harassment of another and which he or she knows or ought to know amounts to harassment of the other – Ss.1(1) and 2. It is also an offence for someone to pursue a course of conduct which involves harassment of two or more persons, which he or she knows or ought to know involves harassment of those persons, and the purpose of which is to persuade any person (not necessarily one of the persons being harassed) not to do something that that person is entitled or required to do, or to do something that that person is not under any obligation to do – Ss.1(1A) and 2. This provision, which was inserted by the Serious Organised Crime and Police Act 2005, was designed specifically to protect people employed in the biomedical research sector from the activities of animal rights extremists. According to the Explanatory Notes to the 2005 Act, 'the sort of behaviour which will engage the [S.1(1A)] offence is activity involving threats and intimidation which forces an individual or individuals to stop doing lawful business with another company or with another individual'.

'Harassment' is not defined in the Act, although S.7(2) and (4) makes it clear that harassing someone can include 'alarming the person or causing the person distress' and includes speech. According to the Court of Appeal in Veakins v

150

Kier Islington Ltd 2010 IRLR 132, CA, the primary focus is on whether the conduct is '"oppressive and unacceptable" as opposed to merely unattractive, unreasonable or regrettable'. Furthermore, to cross the boundary from the regrettable to the unacceptable, the gravity of the misconduct must be of an order that would sustain criminal liability – Majrowski v Guy's and St Thomas's NHS Trust 2006 ICR 1199, HL.

A 'course of conduct' must involve, in relation to a single person, conduct on **6.55** at least two occasions in relation to that person or, in relation to two or more persons, conduct on at least one occasion in relation to each of those persons – S.7(3). Thus, a picket commits an offence if he or she repeatedly (i.e. at least twice) harasses the *same* person or harasses two or more people on the same occasion.

The test of whether a person *ought to have known* that his or her actions amounted to or involved harassment is whether 'a reasonable person in possession of the same information would think the course of conduct amounted to or involved harassment' – S.1(2).

There are three defences to the offence of harassment. These are:

• that the course of conduct was pursued for the purpose of preventing or detecting crime

• that the course of conduct was pursued under any enactment or rule of law, or

• that in the particular circumstances the pursuit of the course of conduct was reasonable – S.1(3).

The burden of proof is on the person who took the course of action in question **6.56** to show that one of the defences applies.

A person guilty of an offence under Ss.1 and 2 is liable to imprisonment and/or a fine – S.2(2). He or she may also be made subject to a restraining order under S.5. A restraining order may even be made where the person is found not guilty of this offence – S.5A.

As stated above, these provisions are very wide and potentially cover much of what happens on a picket line. However, provided the picketing falls within the scope of S.220 TULR(C)A, it may be possible to argue that the conduct of the pickets was reasonable under S.1(3) PHA.

Tort of harassment **6.57**
Under S.3 PHA, a victim of harassment under S.1(1) may bring a civil claim against the alleged harasser. Someone who is threatened with harassment under S.1(1) may also bring a claim under S.3. The same three defences apply to the

151

tort of harassment under S.3 as apply to the offence of harassment under S.2 – see above.

The remedies available under S.3 are damages and/or an injunction. Damages may include damages for any anxiety caused by the harassment and any financial loss resulting from the harassment – S.3(2). Where, without reasonable excuse, the harasser breaches the terms of an injunction, he or she will be guilty of an offence, punishable by imprisonment and/or a fine – S.3(6) and (9).

6.58 Section 3A provides that a claim in tort may also be brought where an offence under S.1(1A) is threatened or committed (subject to the three S.1(3) defences). However, in these circumstances the only remedy is injunctive relief (and not damages). An application to the High Court or county court can be made either by the person who is or may be the victim of any harassment or any person who is or may be persuaded not to do something that he or she is entitled or required to do or to do something that he or she is not under any obligation to do – S.3A(2). The High Court confirmed in Smithkline Beecham plc v Avery 2009 EWHC 1488, QBD, that this provision is wide enough to allow corporate claimants to apply for injunctive relief to protect employees as well as others. The Explanatory Notes to the Serious Organised Crime and Public Disorder Act 2005, which inserted the section, gives the following practical example: 'where people who work for a particular company are being harassed in order to persuade the company not to supply another company, either the employees themselves or the company in question could apply for an injunction'. Breach of the terms of an injunction, without reasonable excuse, will amount to an offence, punishable by imprisonment and/or a fine – S.3A(3).

6.59 ## Putting a person in fear of violence
Section 4(1) PHA provides that a person whose course of conduct causes another to fear, on at least two occasions, that violence will be used against him or her is guilty of an offence. For this provision to apply, the person must either know, or ought to know, that his or her course of conduct will cause the other person to fear violence. The test of whether a person *ought to have known* that his or her conduct would cause another to fear violence is whether 'a reasonable person in possession of the same information would think the course of conduct would cause the other so to fear on that occasion' – S.4(2).

It is a defence for a person charged under S.4 to show that:

- the course of conduct was pursued for the purpose of preventing or detecting crime

- the course of conduct was pursued under any enactment or rule of law, or

- the pursuit of the course of conduct was reasonable for the protection of him or herself or another or for the protection of his or her property or the property of another – S.4(3).

A person guilty of an offence under this section is liable to imprisonment and/ **6.60** or a fine – S.4(4). He or she may also be made subject to a restraining order under S.5. A restraining order may even be made where the person is found not guilty of this offence – S.5A.

Harassing a person at home
6.61
It is worth noting that S.42A of the Criminal Justice and Police Act 2001 protects people from suffering harassment at home. Arguably, this offence may be of relevance in a picketing context where the employer lives 'above the shop' or a caretaker lives in work premises. A person commits the offence if:

- he or she is present outside or in the vicinity of any premises that are used by any individual as their dwelling ('the resident')

- for the purpose of representing to or persuading the resident or another individual (whether or not using the premises as their dwelling) not to do something that he or she is entitled or required to do or to do something that he or she is not under any obligation to do, and

- he or she intends his or her presence to amount to the harassment of, or to cause alarm or distress to, the resident, or knows or ought to know that his or her presence is likely to have that effect, and

- his or her presence amounts to the harassment of, or causes alarm or distress to, any person in the resident's dwelling or a person in a nearby dwelling, or is likely to have that effect – S.42A(1).

A person ought to know that his presence is likely to result in the harassment **6.62** of, or to cause alarm or distress to, a resident if a reasonable person in the possession of the same information would think that his presence was likely to have that effect – S.42A(4). A person guilty of an offence under S.42A is liable on summary conviction to imprisonment for a term not exceeding six months and/or a fine – S.42A(5).

Section 42 confers powers on the police to issue directions for the purpose of stopping harassment of a person in his or her home. For example, a direction may be given to the harasser to leave the vicinity of the premises and not to return to it for a period of up to three months. However, no directions can be given to any person who is lawfully picketing under S.220 TULR(C)A – S.42(6)(b).

Secondary picketing
6.63

The requirement in S.220 TULR(C)A that pickets attend *at or near their place of work* prohibits secondary picketing in its broadest sense, i.e. picketing somewhere other than the pickets' own place of work. There is one respect, however, in which primary pickets – i.e. those attending at their own place of work – may nonetheless be involved in secondary picketing. This happens

153

where pickets induce breaches of the employment contracts of employees employed by other employers, thereby causing breaches of commercial contracts. Such tortious acts will almost invariably be committed during the course of successful picketing – for example, where pickets persuade drivers of delivery lorries to turn back without delivering their loads. The pickets will retain their immunity in these circumstances provided that:

- the picketing is lawful under S.220, and

- their employer is a party to the dispute – S.224(3).

It should be noted that, following the enactment of the Employment Act 1990, this is the only form of secondary picketing that remains lawful. The trend now is towards the use of consumer boycotts and leafleting campaigns, and as the case of Middlebrook Mushrooms Ltd v Transport and General Workers' Union and ors 1993 ICR 612, CA, shows, such actions are unlikely to give rise to a remedy in tort for the employer affected. In that case, union members picketed a supermarket that stocked mushrooms supplied by the company with whom the union was in dispute, and handed out leaflets to customers asking them not to buy the company's mushrooms. The company sought an injunction on the basis that this action amounted to an inducement to the supermarket to breach its supply contract with the company but this was refused by the Court of Appeal. In the Court's view, the company was not entitled to an injunction because the union had not used any unlawful means – members were free to persuade shoppers to boycott a product in support of their cause. (This case is also discussed in Chapter 2 under 'The industrial torts – causing loss by unlawful means'.)

7 Remedies for unlawful action

Injunctions

Damages

Action by union members

Action by individuals

Employers have few remedies when it comes to dealing with individual **7.1** employees who participate in industrial action and thereby breach their contracts of employment. Short of dismissing them, an employer's only real remedy lies in suing for damages. However, few employers like taking this course, given its detrimental effect on industrial relations and the difficulties of pinning specific loss on individual employees, not to mention the problems of enforcing awards against individuals who are unlikely to have large sums of money available. (Another option might be to permanently withdraw benefits from striking employees. However, this course of action is fraught with legal difficulty and is likely to have a significant negative impact on industrial relations – see further Chapter 9 under 'Detriment short of dismissal'.)

The courts have no power to compel an employee to work by making an order for specific performance of a contract of employment, or by granting an injunction restraining any continued or threatened breach of contract – S.236 Trade Union and Labour Relations (Consolidation) Act 1992 (TULR(C)A). This was highlighted in Barretts and Baird (Wholesale) Ltd and ors v Institution of Professional Civil Servants and ors 1987 IRLR 3, QBD, where it was held that there was an arguable case that a striker's breach of his or her employment contract could constitute 'unlawful means' for the purpose of establishing liability for the tort of interference with the plaintiff's business (now treated as part of the wider tort of causing loss by unlawful means). However, Mr Justice Henry made it clear that even if this were the case, S.236 prevented him from granting an injunction to restrain the breach of contract, which was an essential feature of the tort, and thereby force the employees back to work.

As a rule, much more effective remedies are available for the tortious acts **7.2** committed by the *organisers* of unlawful industrial action. In most cases, liability for such acts rests vicariously at the door of the trade union to which the organisers belong, which can far more easily meet any claim for large-scale damages. Often, though, damages will not really be at issue. In many cases the employer is much more concerned to prevent the unlawful action from starting in the first place, or, if it has already started, from continuing. To achieve this, the employer must obtain an interim injunction from the High Court restraining

155

the union from starting or continuing the action, ostensibly until the question of liability can be decided at full trial – which may not be for quite some time. In practice, though, employers' claims for damages rarely go to full trial as their principal objective is usually realised once an interim injunction has been granted (although, as the House of Lords observed in Dimbleby and Sons Ltd v National Union of Journalists 1984 IRLR 161, HL, since the Employment Act 1982 exposed union funds to actions in tort, there can be no presumption that employers will not press their claims for damages all the way).

In this chapter we discuss first the principles that govern the granting of interim injunctions in trade dispute cases. We then consider the heads of damage under which an award of damages can be made and the rules which apply to such awards in trade dispute cases. Finally, we look at the circumstances in which union members and individuals can bring court actions to restrain unlawful industrial action. It should be noted that some of the terminology differs between the different jurisdictions within the United Kingdom. Where this occurs we generally use that which pertains in England and Wales.

7.3 Injunctions

The most important remedy in the context of industrial action is an injunction. An injunction (or interdict in Scotland) is a court order requiring a party to the proceedings to do or not to do something (apart from paying money). It may be temporary or permanent. An interim injunction will restrain a union from taking, or continuing, industrial action pending full trial which will determine the lawfulness or otherwise of the action). A permanent injunction is a final remedy granted at the full trial itself. In practice, interim injunctions are by far the more effective in trade dispute cases; they will often determine the outcome of the case, which will rarely proceed to a full trial.

Before considering the principles that govern the availability of an injunction, it is important to understand that an interim or permanent injunction granted against a trade union will not prevent the union from taking *any* industrial action against the employer. Rather, the injunction will be limited to the *specific* instance or instances of industrial action in respect of which it was sought. There is nothing in an injunction that prevents a trade union from initiating new action by balloting, or reballoting, members. Thus, an injunction is best viewed as a delaying tactic – it will do nothing to resolve the underlying industrial dispute but it will gain the employer more time, enabling him to better prepare for the disruption or even achieve a resolution.

7.4 Basis on which interim injunctions are granted

The general test governing the granting of interim injunctions – whether in the context of industrial action or otherwise – was established by the House of Lords in American Cyanamid Co v Ethicon Ltd 1975 AC 396, HL. This test

156

requires the court to consider first whether there is a *serious issue to be tried* – i.e. a good arguable claim to the relief sought. Provided the case is neither frivolous nor vexatious, the court must then consider where the *balance of convenience* lies. This requires the court to ask itself whether damages would provide an adequate remedy for the wronged party if its decision whether or not to grant an injunction later proves to be incorrect. In other words, would the party against whom an interim injunction is granted be adequately compensated by an award of damages if it is later proved at trial that the injunction should never have been granted in the first place? Alternatively, if no injunction is granted, would the party who had applied for it be adequately remedied by an award of damages if it later transpires that that party was in the right and that an injunction should have been granted? Finally, if damages would provide an adequate remedy for neither party, then the courts should lean towards maintenance of the status quo. If action has not yet commenced, this will normally mean that an injunction will be granted.

Trade disputes exception. Under the American Cyanamid principles, a court **7.5** should not normally consider the relative strengths of the parties' cases, other than in answering the preliminary question of whether there is a serious issue to be tried. The court's role at the preliminary hearing is simply to decide whether certain action should be restrained until the matter comes to trial, not to prejudge the substantive issues (which will be determined at the trial). There are, however, exceptions to this general rule; one important exception being where the interim proceedings would effectively decide the case. Labour injunctions usually fall into this category. As a result, before deciding whether to grant an interim injunction in a trade dispute case the court must at least consider the question of whether the industrial action is lawful or not. This position is given statutory authority by S.221(2) TULR(C)A, which states that in interim proceedings where the defendant (i.e. the union) claims that he acted in contemplation or furtherance of a trade dispute, the court must 'have regard' to the likelihood of the defendant succeeding at trial with a defence under S.219 (protection from certain tort liabilities) or S.220 (peaceful picketing) – see further 'Grounds on which injunctions normally sought' below.

In NWL Ltd v Woods 1979 ICR 867, HL, the House of Lords considered the relationship between the American Cyanamid test and S.221(2). It concluded that the section does not mean that if a trade dispute defence is more likely than not to be established at trial, then that is an overriding reason for the injunction to be refused. Rather, the likelihood, and the degree of that likelihood, that the trade dispute defence will be established are factors which a court should consider in deciding the balance of convenience in a particular case. However, their Lordships concluded that a judge should normally refuse an injunction where the defendant had shown that it was 'more likely than not' that he or she would succeed with his or her defence of statutory immunity unless the

157

consequences for the employer, third party or public were so serious that a higher degree of probability was needed.

7.6 **Picketing exception.** Where an employer seeks an injunction to restrain unlawful picketing, the court should have regard to the right to freedom of expression and the right to freedom of assembly guaranteed by Articles 10 and 11 of the European Convention on Human Rights. In particular, consideration should be given to S.12 of the Human Rights Act 1998 (a provision aimed primarily at securing freedom of the press), which requires courts to have 'particular regard' to the importance of the Article 10 right to freedom of expression when deciding whether to grant an injunction that may affect the defendant's exercise of that right.

In Cream Holdings Ltd v Banerjee 2005 1 AC 253, HL, the House of Lords explained that the effect of S.12 is that a court should not grant an injunction restraining freedom of expression unless it is probable that the claimant will succeed at trial. But since S.221(2) already requires an employer involved in a trade dispute to show that he is more likely than not to succeed at trial, this is unlikely to add very much in a picketing context.

7.7 **Damages an 'adequate remedy'.** In determining whether damages would be an adequate remedy, the court may have to consider the financial means of the parties: damages will not be an adequate remedy if the unsuccessful party is unable to pay them. Nor will they be an adequate remedy for the employer in trade dispute cases where the maximum limit on a union's liability imposed by S.22 TULR(C)A (see below under 'Damages') is considerably less than the amount of the employer's loss – Mercury Communications Ltd v Scott-Garner and anor 1984 ICR 74, CA. It is interesting to note that unions often find it difficult to argue that they would suffer irrecoverable losses if an injunction were to be granted. This is because it is difficult to quantify the loss that might be suffered by a union if industrial action is restrained. It is arguable, however, that when exercising their discretion to grant an injunction courts should take account of certain costs unions incur when organising industrial action – namely, the expense of holding fully postal ballots and the costs involved in appointing an independent scrutineer.

7.8 **Effect on public.** One factor that may be taken into account in weighing up the balance of convenience is the effect the industrial action may have on the public. For example, in London Underground Ltd v National Union of Rail, Maritime and Transport Workers, unreported 22.12.98, QBD, the High Court, having held that the union was unlikely at trial to establish the lawfulness of planned industrial action, went on to add that the balance of convenience also favoured the granting of an injunction on account of the serious consequences for public safety and convenience of a strike that was due to commence around the New Year period.

Conduct of parties. As an equitable remedy, injunctions are subject to the 7.9 maxim: 'He who comes to Equity must come with clean hands.' What this means is that an injunction is generally not available to a claimant who has acted, or is acting, unconscionably in seeking it. That said, it is clear that the conduct of the parties in the lead-up to industrial action is not a relevant factor for a court to consider when weighing up the balance of convenience. In British Railways Board v National Union of Rail, Maritime and Transport Workers, unreported 17.9.92, QBD, for example, Mr Justice Laws rejected an argument by the union that BRB should be denied an interim injunction because it had acted in a confrontational manner which was not designed to assist good industrial relations. He took the view that this argument confused the balancing of interests as a judicial exercise when interim relief is sought with the formation of views on what good industrial relations require. He stated that the first is the function of the judge. As regards the second, a judge has no more expertise on this issue than anyone else.

A similar line was taken in Ministry of Justice v POA (formerly Prison Officers Association) 2008 ICR 702, QBD. In that case the POA and the Government had entered into a procedural agreement under which the Government undertook, barring exceptional circumstances which included the question of affordability, to implement the non-binding recommendations of a pay review body. In return, the POA undertook not to authorise industrial action in relation to any dispute. In 2007 the review body recommended a 2.5 per cent increase but the Government, citing reasons including affordability, opted to stagger the pay rise, which meant an overall rise of 1.9 per cent. When the POA balloted its membership and took industrial action, the Government sought and obtained an interim injunction restraining the POA from breaking the no-strike agreement.

When an application was made to extend the injunction, the POA argued that 7.10 the Government should not be entitled to equitable relief because of the unconscionable way in which it had overruled the pay review body's recommendation. However, Mr Justice Wyn Williams opted to grant the injunction, holding that when the Government declined to accept the recommendation of the pay review body, it was not acting unlawfully; on the contrary, by opting for a staggered increase on the ground of affordability, the Government was doing what it had undertaken to do in the agreement. Accordingly, it was very difficult to see how the claimant had acted in such a way that it should be deprived of an equitable remedy.

Grounds on which injunctions normally sought 7.11

Given the admonishment in S.221(2) TULR(C)A that, in deciding whether to grant an injunction in trade dispute cases, the court must have regard to the likelihood of the defendant succeeding at trial with a defence under S.219 (protection from certain tort liabilities) or S.220 (peaceful picketing), the pivotal factor in many cases will be the likelihood of the trade union establishing such a defence. It thus falls to those seeking an injunction on behalf of an employer to scrutinise the actions and correspondence of the union and assess whether immunity from liability for the industrial torts is likely to be established at trial. The principles that govern statutory immunity, and the circumstances in which it can be lost, are considered in detail in Chapters 3–6, and do not require substantial restating here. However, it is worth noting that the insertion of S.232B into the TULR(C)A by the Employment Relations Act 1999 has made it more difficult for employers to gain injunctions, since failures in the balloting process that are 'accidental and on a scale which is unlikely to affect the result' can be disregarded. Previously, minor errors in the selection of members to be balloted amounted to a breach of the requirements and were often sufficient to ground an injunction. Now, however, an employer seeking an injunction will realistically have to show some evidence of one of the following:

- a breach of the balloting requirements which is not accidental

- an error in the selection of members to ballot or in the balloting process which is on a scale that may affect the result

- a breach of a contractual agreement with the employer not to engage in strike action

- a failure to include the correct information in a notice to the employer

- strike action being taken for the purpose of enforcing union membership, supporting employees dismissed for taking part in unofficial action, or enforcing union recognition

- commission of a tort or torts that fall outside the scope of the statutory immunity

- secondary action

- unlawful picketing.

7.12 Generally speaking, trade unions are well aware of the legal restrictions on industrial action taken for a prohibited purpose and of the ban on secondary action, so it will only be in exceptional circumstances that an alleged breach of these provisions will be the subject of an application for injunctive relief. The stringent ballot and notice requirements, however, have continued to flummox unions and most applications in a trade dispute context will allege one or more failure(s) to comply with these requirements. Two recent cases:

- **British Airways plc v Unite the Union** 2009 EWHC 3541, QBD: Mrs Justice Cox granted BA an injunction restraining a 12-day strike by cabin crew. Having examined correspondence between Unite and its members and between Unite and BA, she considered that BA was likely to establish at trial that, in balloting approximately 900 cabin crew who had accepted voluntary redundancy and would have left BA before industrial action took place, Unite had not done all that was reasonably practicable to ballot only the relevant members of the union and to provide accurate lists of the categories and number of those engaging in industrial action

- **Metrobus Ltd v Unite the Union** 2010 ICR 173, CA: the Court of Appeal upheld the decision to grant an injunction restraining a strike by bus drivers. Unite had not supplied M Ltd with the correct information in the notice of ballot and notice of industrial action, having conflated the information that should be provided in respect of those union members who paid union dues via payroll deductions with the obligation in respect of members who paid union dues by other means.

The law governing industrial action ballots is discussed in detail in Chapter 5.

Picketing is another activity in respect of which injunctive relief is often sought – see for example, Gate Gourmet London Ltd v Transport and General Workers' Union and ors 2005 IRLR 881, QBD. Picketing will be lawful provided it falls within the narrow confines of S.220 TULR(C)A, which permits peaceful picketing in contemplation or furtherance of a trade dispute at or near the pickets' place of work. If pickets lose this limited statutory protection, they expose themselves and potentially their trade union to liability for a number of industrial and other torts. Picketing is dealt with in Chapter 6.

Breach of contract. Although the provisions of collective agreements are often **7.13** incorporated into individual employees' contracts of employment, it is rare for such agreements to have contractual force in their own right – unions and employers are generally wary of entering into a contractually enforceable bargain with one another. However, in circumstances where a collective agreement *has* attained contractual status, a party to the agreement can seek an injunction restraining the other party from breaching its terms. This was demonstrated in Ministry of Justice v POA (formerly Prison Officers Association) 2008 ICR 702, QBD, where the MoJ applied successfully for an injunction preventing the POA from breaching the terms of a 'no-strike agreement'.

Judicial discretion   7.14

The granting of an injunction is discretionary. Thus, even where the trade dispute defence is almost certain to succeed, the court still retains a residual discretion to grant an interim injunction in the exceptional cases of immediate and serious threat to public safety or health or to a fundamental public right – Duport Steels Ltd and ors v Sirs and ors 1980 ICR 161, HL. In that case, however, a threatened steelworkers' strike that was likely to have a very serious effect on the national economy was not so immediate as to justify the granting of an injunction to prevent the strike where the trade dispute defence was highly likely to succeed.

Conversely, even where it is more likely than not that the union's trade dispute defence will fail, the judge is still entitled to exercise his or her discretion and refuse to grant an injunction against the union. In Hadmor Productions Ltd and ors v Hamilton and anor 1982 ICR 114, HL, the House of Lords held that even where the union's defence is unlikely to succeed the judge should still consider whether an injunction would do the claimant any good. Injunctions are an equitable remedy, and it is said that 'Equity does nothing in vain'. This principle will influence how a judge chooses to exercise his or her discretion. In Marfax Ltd v Amalgamated Union of Enigineering Workers, unreported 16.7.86, QBD, for instance, the High Court judge refused to grant an injunction despite the union's refusal to hold a ballot because, in his view, it was inconceivable that members would vote so differently from the 62–2 vote in favour of action already registered by a show of hands.

The judge's discretion belongs to the judge at first instance. Appellate courts are entitled to interfere only where the judge's view was based on a misunderstanding of the law or the evidence before him or her, or upon facts that have materially changed by the time of the appeal; or where his or her decision was such that no reasonable judge, acting judicially, could have reached it – Hadmor Productions Ltd v Hamilton (above).

7.15 Scope of injunction

Apart from its general powers to order a party to refrain from taking certain action, a court hearing injunction proceedings against a union has the power under S.20(6) TULR(C)A to require the union to take such steps as the court considers appropriate in order to ensure:

- that there is no, or no further, inducement of persons to take part or to continue to take part in industrial action, and

- that no person engages in any conduct after the granting of the injunction because he or she was induced to take part or continue to take part in industrial action before the injunction was granted.

It is not entirely clear what these provisions add to the existing powers of the High Court and Court of Session. They appear to mean that the court will have the power to direct a union to take disciplinary action against those who continue to induce or participate in industrial action after it has been repudiated by the union.

7.16 Procedure

A full explanation of the detailed procedural rules governing the granting of interim injunctions by the courts is beyond the scope of this Handbook. (See the Civil Procedure Rules 1998 SI 1998/3132, Parts 23 and 25, and Practice Directions 23 and 25A.) Briefly, the normal procedure for obtaining an interim injunction (interdict in Scotland) is by motion in the Chancery Division of the

High Court (or Court of Session in Scotland). It is considered good practice to first seek an undertaking from the union not to engage in industrial action pending a full trial. If no such undertaking is forthcoming, the claimant (i.e. the employer) must normally give the defendant (i.e. the union) two working days' clear notice of his or her intent and the hearing should be inter partes (i.e. the parties to the proceedings should be present before the court).

In urgent cases the claimant may apply to either the Chancery Division or the Queen's Bench Division for an injunction without notice to the other side and therefore without giving the other side the opportunity to put forward any arguments for refusing the injunction. In such cases the injunction will only be granted until such time as the claimant can give the defendant proper notice of his or her application. Because of the potentially very serious effect the granting of an injunction without notice can have on the outcome of a trade dispute – a union can lose the impetus for industrial action without ever having had the chance to argue that the dispute was lawful – the power to grant such injunctions in labour law cases is severely limited by S.221(1). That section states that where the defendant claims (or the court thinks the defendant is likely to claim) a trade dispute defence to an application for an injunction (or interdict), the court must not grant it without notice unless it is satisfied that all reasonable steps have been taken to notify the union and give it a chance to state its case. It does not matter whether there is in fact a trade dispute; what does matter is whether it is likely that the union will claim that it proposed to act in contemplation or furtherance of such a dispute – Gouriet v Union of Post Office Workers and ors 1977 3 All ER 70, HL.

Timing. It is a general principle of equity that a claimant should not delay **7.17** unnecessarily in seeking an injunction, and that such a delay may give a court grounds to refuse to grant the injunction. Generally speaking, however, delay is unlikely to occur in trade dispute cases where employers will normally seek injunctions at an early stage in order to limit the damage. An injunction can be sought as soon as a breach of notice or ballot requirements is suspected, as there is no requirement to wait until either the results of the ballot or notice of the strike has been given to the employer:

- **EDF Energy Powerlink Ltd v National Union of Rail, Maritime and Transport Workers** 2010 IRLR 114, QBD: the RMT wrote to EDF Ltd – the company that manages London Underground's power network – giving notice of its intention to ballot all members who fell into the category of 'engineer/technician'. EDF Ltd considered this category to be too broad to comply with the notice requirements in S.226A, and sought an injunction before the ballot had been completed. Among the grounds on which the RMT opposed the injunction was that EDF Ltd had acted prematurely in seeking injunctive relief before the results of the ballot were known, and therefore before any decision to take industrial action was reached.

However, in granting the injunction, Mr Justice Blake held that the rapid pace at which the industrial dispute had moved to a strike ballot meant the prospect of industrial action was 'sufficiently imminent' to warrant the granting of an injunction at an early stage.

7.18 **Target of injunction.** Typically, an employer will seek an injunction against a trade union and rely on the coercive effect of S.20(6) (see 'Scope of injunction' above) to force the union to prevent members engaging in industrial action. There may, however, be situations where an injunction against the union will not suffice – for example, a union cannot physically remove members who are engaged in unlawful picketing or unofficial action. In such circumstances, the employer has effectively two options: he can either seek an injunction against 'representatives' or apply for an injunction against 'persons unknown'.

Rule 19.6 of the Civil Procedure Rules 1998 allows for claims to be brought against one or more persons as representatives of a group where all members of that group share the 'same interest'. The problem that can arise for an employer, however, is establishing that all of the individuals involved in the unlawful action or unlawful picketing share the same interest. In News Group Newspapers Ltd and ors v Society of Graphical and Allied Trades '82 and ors (No.2) 1987 ICR 181, QBD, the employer sought, among other things, an injunction against three members of SOGAT branches as representatives of those branches, restraining them from engaging in unlawful picketing. The application was refused because the different members of the branches would have different defences to the application, and so did not share the same interest.

7.19 Where a court is willing to grant an injunction against a representative party, that order will bind all the members of the represented group – Rule 19.6(4)(a). However, a claimant must seek the court's permission to enforce the injunction against a person who was not originally a party to the proceedings – Rule 19.6(4)(b).

The alternative to a representative action is to seek an injunction against 'persons unknown'. Such actions are a fairly new legal development, having only been possible since the introduction of the Civil Procedure Rules in 1998, and we know of only one case to date where a court has granted such an injunction in the context of industrial action:

● **Gate Gourmet London Ltd v Transport and General Workers' Union and ors** 2005 IRLR 881, QBD: a large number of GGL Ltd's employees were dismissed after taking part in unofficial industrial action. This led to wide-scale picketing of GGL Ltd's premises, some of which was aggressive and intimidating in nature. In addition to seeking an injunction restricting the defendant union to lawful and peaceful picketing, GGL Ltd sought an injunction restraining unidentified individuals – persons unknown – from engaging in unlawful picketing. In granting the injunction, Mr

Justice Fulford was satisfied that the group of persons unknown which the claimants sought to restrain – those engaging in unlawful picketing and/ or otherwise assaulting, threatening, intimidating, harassing, molesting or otherwise abusing the employees of GGL Ltd or its associated companies – was sufficiently clear that those who were included and those who were not could be readily identified.

Contempt of court   7.20

The deliberate failure by a union to obey the terms of an injunction is a contempt of court and is punishable by an unlimited fine and/or imprisonment (for individuals) or a fine and/or sequestration of assets (for corporate bodies or associations like trade unions). The defendant must be shown beyond reasonable doubt to have known of the court order. However, a telephone call giving details of the injunction will be enough. In Kent Free Press v National Graphical Association and ors 1987 IRLR 267, QBD, a union official was made aware of the terms of an injunction when its details were dictated over the telephone to his secretary on the day it was granted. Actual copies of the order were received the next morning. The High Court held that the obligation to comply with an injunction takes effect when the defendant knows with sufficient certainty of the details and that this does not require actual service of the order.

In Richard Read (Transport) Ltd v National Union of Mineworkers (South Wales Area) 1985 IRLR 67, QBD, the High Court made it clear that it is no defence to an alleged breach of an injunction for the union to claim that the breach was unknowingly committed. Nor can a union merely allege that it did its best to comply if its best falls short of what the court orders to be done – Howitt Transport Ltd and anor v Transport and General Workers' Union 1973 ICR 1, NIRC. Reasonable belief that the order was made by mistake does not excuse contempt either – Austin Rover Group Ltd v Amalgamated Union of Engineering Workers (Technical, Administrative and Supervisory Section) 1985 IRLR 162, QBD.

Fines for contempt in civil proceedings are usually made to coerce or encourage **7.21** the party in contempt to comply with the court's order. But where there is 'wilful disobedience' of the order and 'a measure of contumacy on the part of the contemnor', then the fine can take on a penal dimension – Phonographic Performance Ltd v Amusement Caterers (Peckham) Ltd 1963 3 WLR 898, ChD. As for liability, the only relevant question is: has the alleged contemnor breached the terms of the court order after having received notice of it? – Express and Star Ltd and ors v National Graphical Association (1982) and anor 1986 IRLR 222, CA.

Unions liable in contempt. Injunctions tend to cover the union, its officers, **7.22** servants and agents. So if a union falls short of publicly distancing itself from any acts done by its officers or members in breach of the injunction, then it may

165

itself be liable in contempt. Threats of disciplinary action against members or withdrawal of a steward's credentials might be sufficient evidence that the union has refused to countenance contempt – Heatons Transport (St Helens) Ltd v Transport and General Workers' Union 1972 ICR 308, NIRC and HL. A union that appears to reject contemptuous acts but which, in reality, sanctions those acts with 'clandestine nods and winks' will not escape liability, however – see Express and Star Ltd v National Graphical Association (1982) and anor (above).

7.23 **Sequestration for contempt.** There are no limits to the amount a union can be fined for contempt. Any of its property is liable to be seized in satisfaction of unpaid fines. In practice, refusal to pay fines has frequently led to orders for sequestration of the union's assets, out of which the amounts due are taken – see Con-Mech (Engineers) Ltd v Amalgamated Union of Engineering Workers (Engineering Section) (No.3) 1974 ICR 464, NIRC. The writ of sequestration must name at least four commissioners who are charged to take possession of all or such amounts of the contemnor's property as the court directs.

An order for sequestration is not normally discharged until the union has 'purged its contempt' by apology to the court. However, judges generally take a pragmatic approach, recognising that a genuine undertaking to comply in the future with the court's order matters more than a public apology.

7.24 ## Damages

We noted above that interim injunctions are the most commonly sought remedy in the context of industrial action. However, actions for damages in tort are also an attractive remedy where a person has suffered loss as a result of unlawful industrial action. Claims can be brought against both trade unions, which can be sued in their own right just like ordinary persons, and individual participants. However, in reality it is highly unlikely that an individual participant would be sued since he or she is unlikely to have the resources to meet a large bill for damages. Accordingly, an action for damages will normally be brought against a union. However, such an action will only succeed if the union is legally responsible for the action under either the common law or the statutory principles of vicarious liability described in Chapter 2.

Section 22 TULR(C)A puts limits on the level of damages a court may award in any one tort action against a union arising out of unlawful industrial action. These limits vary with the union's size:

- £10,000 if the union has less than 5,000 members

- £50,000 for 5,000 or more but less than 25,000 members

- £125,000 for 25,000 or more but less than 100,000 members

- £250,000 for 100,000 or more members – S.22(2).

These figures may be varied from time to time by statutory instrument issued **7.25**
by the Secretary of State for Employment, but have remained at their existing
level since the TULR(C)A came into force in October 1992.

It should be noted that the S.22(2) figures only apply to damages. They do not
apply to legal costs and expenses or to fines imposed for contempt of court.
Nor do they apply to any additional award of interest made on top of the
damages – Boxfoldia Ltd v National Graphical Association (1982) 1988
ICR 752, QBD.

Moreover, where more than one claimant sues it is not clear whether damages up
to the maximum can be recovered by each successful claimant. S.22(1) merely
states: 'This section applies to *any proceedings in tort* brought against a trade
union' (our stress). Is a consolidated action, in which several employers' separate
actions are joined against the one defendant union, one set of proceedings or
several? And if one claimant issues different writs in respect of several torts,
would a court award damages up to the maximum in respect of each tort if the
torts arose in respect of the same industrial action? In regard to the latter problem,
a union could ask the court to consolidate the proceedings into one action so as
to avoid multiple awards of damages. To date there appear to have been no cases
addressing these particular problems and judicial guidance is awaited.

There are three exceptions to the limitation on damages. These are where the **7.26**
action is:

- for personal injury arising out of negligence, nuisance or breach of duty

- for breach of duty in connection with the ownership, occupation, possession,
  control or use of property, or

- for breach of duty in connection with product liability – S.22(1).

The first exception clearly covers a union's vicarious liability for its officials'
acts committed during the course of union business. The second covers such
matters as trespass, nuisance or occupiers' liability. The third covers proceedings
brought under Part I of the Consumer Protection Act 1987.

Protected property. Where damages, costs or expenses are awarded against (i) **7.27**
the union, (ii) trustees in whom property is vested in trust for a union (except
in actions for breach of trust against such persons), or (iii) members or officials
of a trade union on behalf of themselves and of all the union's members, then
recovery of damages cannot be enforced against certain property of the union
– S.23(1). This so-called 'protected property' comprises:

- the personal property of the trustees otherwise than in their capacity as
  trustees; the personal property of members other than that held jointly or
  in common with other members; and the personal property of officials who
  are neither members nor trustees

167

- the political fund – so long as, under the rules of the union, the fund's property cannot be used for financing industrial action

- any provident benefits fund – so long as it is a separate fund which can only be used for the purpose of providing provident benefits such as sick pay or superannuation or payments made to dependants of deceased members – S.23(2) and (3).

In addition, property held by union branch or district trustees may be protected if it is in fact the separate property of the branch or district and not held on trust for the union as a whole – News Group Newspapers Ltd and ors v Society of Graphical and Allied Trades '82 1986 ICR 716, CA. The protection provided by S.23 is not restricted to proceedings in tort, although fines for contempt of court are not covered.

7.28 Heads of damage

Damages are limited to losses attributable to torts that do not attract statutory immunity under S.219 or which have lost that immunity – Norbrook Laboratories Ltd v King 1984 IRLR 200, NICA. In that case the Northern Ireland Court of Appeal held that the trial judge had erred in assessing damages by failing to distinguish between damage caused by the inducement to breach contracts of employment – a tort which was protected by statutory immunity – and damage caused by other torts such as trespass and nuisance.

The general purpose of damages – in both actions for breach of contract and tort – is essentially the same. In contract, it is not to punish the guilty party but to place the innocent one in the same position that he or she would have been in if the contract had been performed, so far as monetary compensation can do this – Robinson v Harman 1848 1 Exch 850, Court of Exchequer. In tort, the equivalent purpose is to award 'that sum of money which will put the [injured] party... in the same position as he would have been in if he had not sustained the wrong for which he is now getting compensation or reparation' – Livingstone v Raywards Coal Co 1880 5 App Cas 25, HL. In both types of claim, the loss compensable by way of damages must be caused by, and not be too remote a consequence of, the guilty party's breach of contract or tortious act. In other words, a claimant employer will be entitled to recover the losses that can be shown to be the reasonably foreseeable consequence of unlawful industrial action – subject, of course, to the claimant's duty to mitigate (i.e. lessen) the loss and to the maximum limits set out in S.22 where applicable.

7.29 The scope of 'foreseeable harm' caused by unlawful industrial action appears to be fairly wide. In Falconer v Associated Society of Locomotive Engineers and Firemen and National Union of Railwaymen 1986 IRLR 331, Sheffield County Court, for instance, a commuter, though only an incidental victim of the union's tortious and unballoted action, was nevertheless entitled to damages on the basis that the loss he sustained through being unable to travel was a reasonably foreseeable consequence of the unlawful action.

Aggravated damages may be awarded over and above the amount strictly necessary to compensate a claimant for proven loss. These damages may be obtained by a person whose 'proper feelings of dignity and pride' are injured. Here the object of the award remains compensatory. But punitive or exemplary damages are penal and can be imposed to teach a defendant that tort does not pay. Awards are only made where 'oppressive, arbitrary or unconstitutional' action by Government servants is shown; where a defendant 'with a cynical disregard for a claimant's rights has calculated that the money to be made out of his wrongdoing will probably exceed the damages at risk'; or where such damages are provided for by statute – Rookes v Barnard 1964 AC 1129, HL. Moreover, following the Court of Appeal's decision in AB and ors v South West Water Services Ltd 1993 1 All ER 609, CA, it is clear that, in respect of the first two categories above, exemplary damages will only be awarded in respect of torts for which exemplary damages had been awarded prior to 1964. Torts such as trespass and private nuisance can therefore ground an award of exemplary damages as, it seems, can the tort of intimidation.

In Messenger Newspapers Group Ltd v National Graphical Association (1982) 1984 IRLR 397, QBD, a newspaper publisher was faced with industrial action and picketing undertaken to coerce it into accepting a closed shop. The Court found that the union had unlawfully interfered with the claimant's business and held that the union was a deliberate tortfeasor whose pursuit of its own objective was reckless and in 'jubilant' defiance of a previous court injunction. The judge, in awarding exemplary damages of £25,000 for the defendant's tortious conduct involving intimidation and aggravated damages of £10,000, saw no reason why a limited company should not be awarded these just like an ordinary person. The aggravated damages were not to compensate for injury to feelings (how can a company suffer this?), but rather for the 'insolence or arrogance' that accompanied the union's manner in injuring the claimant company. However, this decision seems to be inconsistent with the general approach to aggravated damages and should therefore be treated with some caution. In AB and ors v South West Water Services Ltd (above), for example, the Court of Appeal refused to award the claimant aggravated damages because it had not suffered pain and suffering – the accepted ground on which awards of such damages are usually made.

Action by union members   7.30

Union members have a right at common law to take action against their union if it acts in contravention of the union rule book when calling industrial action. During the miners' strike there was a spate of cases in which members successfully enforced their common law rights. For example, in Taylor and ors

169

v National Union of Mineworkers (Derbyshire Area) and ors 1984 IRLR 440, ChD, T and two other union members obtained an injunction and declaration against the NUM because the union had called a strike in disregard of a ballot majority against such action, and in contravention of the union rule book.

Section 62 TULR(C)A gives union members a separate statutory right to take court action against their union in respect of industrial action where it has failed to obtain approval in a proper ballot. For the purposes of bringing a claim under S.62, industrial action will be regarded as having the support of a ballot only if:

- the union has held a ballot in respect of the action in relation to which the requirements of S.226B (appointment of scrutineer) and Ss.227–231 (entitlement to vote; separate workplace ballots; voting papers; conduct of ballot; information as to result of ballot) were satisfied

- the union has held a ballot in respect of the action in which the majority voting in the ballot answered 'Yes' to the question specified in S.229(2), which relates to the kind of industrial action the applicant has been, or is likely to be, induced to take part in

- the requirements contained in S.226B (appointment of scrutineer) and S.231B (scrutineer's report) that should have been complied with when the application under S.62 was made, have been complied with; and

- the requirements of S.233 (calling of industrial action with support of ballot) are satisfied – S.62(2).

(For detailed consideration of the above balloting provisions, see Chapter 5.)

7.31 The right under S.62 is to apply for a court order requiring the union to take certain steps. It is available to any union member who has been or is likely to be induced by the union to take part in any industrial action which is unsupported by a ballot – S.62(1). It is not restricted to action which is in breach of contract, so an inducement not to work voluntary overtime, for example, would be caught. 'Inducement' also has a wide meaning and includes an inducement that is, or would be, ineffective, such as where the union member simply ignores it or is unwilling to be influenced by it – S.62(6). Furthermore, a member can bring a claim before his or her union has made any effort to induce him or her to participate. All the member need show is that it is 'likely' that he or she will be induced to join the action. 'Industrial action' means a strike or other industrial action by persons employed under a contract of employment, which includes any contract under which one person personally does work or performs services for another – S.62(6) and (8).

Where the court is satisfied that the claim is well founded, it must make an order requiring the union to take steps to ensure:

- that there is no, or no further, inducement of members of the union to take part or to continue to take part in the industrial action to which the application relates, and

- that no member engages in conduct after the making of the order by virtue of having been induced before the making of the order to take part or to continue to take part in the action – S.62(3).

The court has no specific power to order a union to hold a ballot, but only to order it to refrain from instigating or continuing action which is unsupported by a proper ballot. The court can also grant injunctive relief if it upholds a member's complaint – S.62(4). The usual principles applying to the granting of interim injunctions will apply (see 'Injunctions' above), although it will not be open to a defendant opposing an application for an injunction to argue that damages would be an adequate remedy for the complainant because damages are not available as a remedy in this type of action.

For the purposes of proceedings under S.62, an act shall be taken to have been **7.32** done by a trade union if it is authorised or endorsed by the union. The provisions of S.20(2)–(4) – discussed in Chapter 2 under 'Union liability in tort' – apply for the purposes of determining whether an act was so authorised or endorsed.

The statutory right to apply for a court order under S.62 is additional to any right a member may have at common law when a union's action is in breach of its rule book. It is only available to union members when the union has induced (or is likely to induce) them to take part in industrial action without holding a ballot at all or after holding a ballot that does not comply with the statutory requirements. Provided that the formalities are complied with, there is no statutory right for a union member to challenge industrial action on the ground that it is unlawful for some other reason – e.g. as being unlawful secondary action.

Action by individuals 7.33

Section 235A(1) TULR(C)A provides that an individual may apply to the High Court or the Court of Session for an order to restrain industrial action if:

- a trade union or any other person has done, or is likely to do, an unlawful act to induce any person to take part, or continue to take part, in industrial action, and

- an effect, or a likely effect, of the action is or will be (i) to prevent or delay the supply of goods or services, or (ii) to reduce the quality of goods or services supplied, to the individual making the claim.

It is immaterial whether or not the individual is entitled to be supplied with the goods or services in question – S.235A(3). Furthermore, there is no requirement

171

that the individual demonstrate that he or she (or anyone else for that matter) has incurred any material loss or suffered any damage as such. The individual only has to show that an effect, or a likely effect, of the industrial action is, or will be, to interfere with the supply of goods or services to the individual or reduce the quality of those goods or services.

7.34 The right is restricted to individuals and does not apply to a company or corporation. However, an individual employee of a company has the right to bring a claim, provided all the other relevant statutory requirements are satisfied.

An individual may only apply for a court order restraining industrial action if the action is 'unlawful'. S.235A(2) states that industrial action is unlawful if it is actionable in tort by one or more persons – i.e. the action is outside the scheme of the statutory immunities or the union has lost protection because it has failed to comply with all the statutory requirements – or if a member of the union taking the industrial action would be entitled to apply for a court order under S.62 on the grounds that he or she has been, or is likely to be, induced by the union to take part in industrial action that does not have the support of a valid ballot. (S.62 claims are discussed in the preceding section.)

Where a court is satisfied that a claim is well founded it must make an order against the person who has induced or is likely to induce the action to take steps to ensure:

- that no, or no further, act is done by him or her to induce any persons to take part or to continue to take part in the industrial action, and

- that no person engages in conduct after the making of the order by virtue of having been induced by him or her before the making of the order to take part or continue to take part in the industrial action – S.235A(4).

7.35 The court does not have the power to award damages under S.235A but can grant such interlocutory relief as it considers appropriate – S.235A(5). The usual principles applying to the granting of interim injunctions will apply here (see above), although it will not be open to a defendant opposing an application for an injunction to argue that damages would be an adequate remedy for the complainant because, as already noted, damages are not available as a remedy in this type of action. Orders may be made against individuals or trade unions responsible for inducing unlawful industrial action. In this regard, S.235A(6) provides that an act of inducement shall be taken to be done by a trade union if it is authorised or endorsed by the union and that S.20(2)–(4) applies for the purpose of determining whether such an act is to be taken to be so authorised or endorsed. S.20(2)–(4) are described in Chapter 2 under 'Union liability in tort'.

Section 235A is very unusual in that it allows an individual against whom *no civil wrong*, whether in tort or contract, has been committed to step into a dispute where one of the parties has been the victim of a tortious act and effectively use that party's remedy of obtaining an injunction to stop the union from continuing the action. However, despite the provision having been in force since 1993, it is rarely used. Indeed, as far as we know, there has been only one reported case brought under the section:

- **P (A Minor) v National Association of Schoolmasters/Union of Women Teachers** 2003 ICR 386, HL: following persistent disruptive behaviour by P, a pupil, NASUWT balloted its members at a London school, with the result that they refused to teach him. P sought an injunction under S.235A, arguing that the industrial action was unlawful because (a) a dispute about whether the teachers should have to teach P was not a 'trade dispute' within the meaning of S.244 and (b) the union had failed to send ballot papers to two members at the school who were entitled to vote. The High Court rejected the application for an injunction, finding that the dispute was about 'terms and conditions' of employment and therefore within the ambit of S.244, and that the failure to send ballot papers was accidental and could be overlooked in line with S.232B. On appeal, both the Court of Appeal and House of Lords upheld the decision.

In P's case, the potential availability of an injunction under S.235A made a lot of sense – if a pupil's access to education is going to be limited by industrial action, natural justice requires that the pupil should be able to test the legality of that action. However, S.235A has far more wide-ranging and damaging implications. Where industrial action is not lawful, the person best placed to take legal action is the employer directly affected by the dispute. An employer who chooses not to exercise this option may have very good industrial relations reasons for letting the dispute run its course. An injunction obtained by an individual who has no connection whatsoever with the dispute other than the fact that, for example, his or her garbage has not been collected by refuse workers taking industrial action may well serve to inflame the dispute and prolong it rather than hasten its resolution.

8 Industrial action dismissals

Dismissal during unofficial action

Dismissal during 'protected' official action

Dismissal during 'non-protected' official action

The law does not give employees a positive right to take part in industrial **8.1** action. On the contrary, any participation in industrial action seriously affects both their contractual and their statutory employment rights. So far as the contractual position is concerned, going on strike almost invariably constitutes a repudiatory breach of the contract of employment which entitles the employer to dismiss the striking employee without notice. Other forms of action falling short of a complete withdrawal of labour usually constitute a breach of contract too, but whether they are serious enough to be repudiatory will depend on the nature and terms of the contract involved.

Even if the breach is not serious enough to warrant summary dismissal, the employer may still terminate the contract with notice in the usual way. What is important is that in none of these situations will the employee concerned have any remedy against dismissal in *contract law*. The employee will also find that the industrial action has serious implications for his or her statutory employment rights, such as the right not to be unfairly dismissed and the right to a redundancy payment. In this chapter we look in detail at the effect of industrial action on employees' rights to claim unfair dismissal where they have been expressly dismissed while, or as a result of, taking action. The question of whether an employee can claim constructive dismissal where the employer has retaliated by subjecting him or her to some other detriment short of dismissal is dealt with in the following chapter under 'Detriment short of dismissal'. Chapter 9 also focuses on the effect of industrial action on other statutory employment rights, including redundancy pay, and on an employee's right to be paid under the contract. For further discussion on the effect of industrial action on the contract of employment see Chapter 2 under 'Breach of contract'.

The right of employees dismissed during or as a result of industrial action to claim unfair dismissal are contained in the Trade Union and Labour Relations (Consolidation) Act 1992 (TULR(C)A). The relevant provisions, which have been significantly amended over the years since that Act came into force, provide that:

- an employee has no right to complain of unfair dismissal if at the time of dismissal he or she was taking part in *unofficial industrial action* unless the

175

reason for the dismissal was one of certain protected reasons such as health and safety – S.237 TULR(C)A

- an employee who is dismissed for taking part in *protected industrial action* (i.e. lawfully organised official action) will be treated as having been automatically unfairly dismissed if the dismissal took place during the protected period, or after the end of that period where certain specified conditions are met – S.238A

- an employee who is *selectively dismissed* when taking part in official industrial action or locked out by his or her employer, in circumstances where S.238A does not apply, is entitled to claim unfair dismissal – S.238.

8.2 The term 'official' is used here to denote industrial action that is not rendered unofficial by virtue of S.237.

We examine these three scenarios in turn below.

8.3 Dismissal during unofficial action

As mentioned above, an employee who is dismissed while taking part in unofficial industrial action has no protection against dismissal, even where other employees who are also taking part are not dismissed, or are re-engaged at a later date. This is because S.237 TULR(C)A states that: 'An employee has no right to complain of unfair dismissal if at the time of dismissal he was taking part in an unofficial strike or other unofficial industrial action.' An employer can thus 'pick and choose' with apparent impunity. He can select those employees he considers to be organisers of the strike or general troublemakers in order to be rid of them. Furthermore, there is nothing in the Act to prevent the employer from deliberately provoking unofficial action in order to bring these dismissals about: the crucial question is whether the employee was 'taking part' in unofficial industrial action, not why. (On the question of whether an employee is 'taking part' in industrial action, see below under 'Dismissal during "non-protected" official action – relevant employees'. 'Industrial action' is defined below under 'Dismissal during "non-protected" official action – strikes, lock-outs and other industrial action'.)

8.4 **Exceptions.** Section 237(1A) sets out a number of exceptions to the rule that an employee cannot complain of unfair dismissal if at the time of dismissal he or she was taking part in unofficial industrial action. These exceptions are where the employee can show that the reason for dismissal, or the reason why he or she was selected for redundancy, was a reason falling within one of the following provisions of the Employment Rights Act 1996 (ERA):

- S.98B (jury service)

- S.99 (maternity and family leave)

- S.100 (health and safety) (see further 'Health and safety issues' below)

- S.101A(d) (employee representatives for purposes of working time provisions)

- S.103 (employee representatives for purposes of redundancies and transfers of undertakings)

- S.103A (protected disclosures ('whistleblowing'))

- S.104 (assertion of a statutory right), in so far as it applies to time off work to take care of dependants under S.57A.

The reasons for dismissal in this context will include the circumstances of dismissal – S.237(1A).

A redundancy case for these purposes has the same meaning as that contained **8.5** in S.105(9) ERA, namely that:

- the reason, or principal reason, for the dismissal is that the employee was redundant, and

- the circumstances constituting the redundancy applied equally to one or more other employees employed in the same undertaking in similar positions who have not been dismissed – S.237(1A).

If one of the above exceptions applies, the employee may claim automatically unfair dismissal, even though he or she was taking part in unofficial industrial action at the time of the dismissal. Note that in all other circumstances the *reason* for the dismissal is irrelevant. The crucial question is whether the employee was 'taking part' in the action. (For further information on S.99 ERA, see IDS Employment Law Handbook, 'Maternity and Parental Rights' (2009); on Ss.98B, 100, 103 and 104, see IDS Employment Law Handbook, 'Unfair Dismissal' (2005), Chapters 9, 10 and 11; on S.101A(d), see IDS Employment Law Supplement, 'Working Time' (2009), Chapter 7; and on S.103A, see IDS Employment Law Supplement, 'Whistleblowing at Work' (2004)).

Unofficial action   8.6
Section 237(2) states that a strike or other industrial action will be unofficial in relation to an employee *unless*:

- he or she is a member of a trade union and the action is authorised or endorsed by that union, or

- he or she is not a member of a trade union but there are among those taking part in the industrial action members of a trade union by which the action has been authorised or endorsed.

Therefore, any action that is authorised or endorsed by a union will not be unofficial in relation to the members of that union or to individuals who are

177

not members of any union. However, members of a union that has not authorised or endorsed industrial action will be caught.

These definitions are subject to the proviso that a strike or other industrial action is *not* to be regarded as unofficial if *none* of the participants is a union member. It will only be unofficial if at least one of the participants is a union member (and the action has not been authorised or endorsed by that union).

8.7 Employees who were trade union members when the action began will continue to be treated as union members for the purpose of determining whether the action is unofficial even if they have since ceased to be union members – S.237(6). This prevents union members suddenly resigning their membership in an attempt to turn unofficial action into official action. However, membership of a trade union for purposes unconnected with the employment in question will be disregarded – S.237(6). This presumably means, to take a hypothetical example, that an out-of-work actor who is working on a building site, but who happens to be a member of Equity, would not be considered a union member for the purposes of S.237 were he or she to take part in industrial action at the building site.

The effect of S.237 is that if at least one of the participants in the industrial action is a member of a union (for purposes connected with the employment in question) and the action has not been authorised or endorsed by the union, the action will be unofficial.

8.8 **'In relation to an employee'.** Section 237 states that action will be unofficial 'in relation to an employee' unless one of the two exceptions listed above is made out. It is therefore possible for the same action to be official in relation to one employee but unofficial in respect of another. This situation is likely to arise where there is more than one union involved but not all have endorsed or authorised the action. In Balfour Kilpatrick Ltd v Acheson and ors 2003 IRLR 683, EAT, for example, a group of workers walked off site because of health and safety concerns arising from excessive water on site, insufficient facilities for drying themselves and their clothes, and the risk of Weil's disease. They continued to refuse to work for the remainder of the week and were all dismissed as a result. The shop steward of the engineering union AEEU, which was the recognised union for the site, authorised the action and the action was not repudiated. Many of the workers, however, were members of the TGWU, and because their spokesperson was not a union official his involvement did not amount to authorisation of the industrial action. The result was that members of the AEEU, and any non-union members involved, were entitled to pursue claims of unfair dismissal but the TGWU members were not. The EAT, Mr Justice Elias presiding, expressed considerable sympathy for the workers, who it found were justified in seeking an improvement in unsatisfactory health and welfare conditions. It was prompted to comment that the operation of the legal rules, by leaving a significant majority of the workforce without redress, had 'not met the justice of the case'.

Authorisation and endorsement

The question of whether an act has been authorised or endorsed by a trade union is determined in accordance with the rules set out in S.20(2) by reference to the facts as at the time of dismissal – S.237(3) and (4). These rules are discussed at length in Chapter 2 under 'Union liability in tort' but it is important to appreciate that they cover acts authorised by lay officials. This means that the kind of industrial action that most employers and unions tend to regard as 'unofficial' is in fact official for these purposes. For example, action called by a shop steward, without a ballot and even in breach of the union rules, is deemed official industrial action for the purposes of the Act. The action will only become unofficial after the union has *repudiated* it (which it must do if it is to avoid liability for the torts committed by union members organising or taking part in the action).

Repudiation. Section 21(1) provides that an act will *not* be taken to have been 8.10 authorised or endorsed if it has been repudiated by the union. To repudiate action a union must do three things:

- it must send a written notice of repudiation to the committee or official in question without delay

- it must 'do its best' to give individual written notice of the fact and the date of the repudiation – again 'without delay' – to every union member who it has reason to believe is, or might be, taking part in the industrial action, and

- it must give similar written notice to the employer of every such union member – S.21(2).

The notice given to union members must contain a statutory written statement, the wording of which must be as set out in S.21(3), constituting a warning that employees dismissed while taking unofficial action will have no right to claim unfair dismissal – S.21(3).

A failure to comply with these requirements means that the repudiation will be 8.11 ineffective – S.21(4). In Balfour Kilpatrick Ltd v Acheson and ors (above) the union sent written notice of repudiation to the employer and the shop steward which was then read out to the employees in the canteen and posted by the clocking station. The EAT upheld the tribunal's finding that the union had not 'done its best' to give written notice to each individual and that the industrial action had therefore not been repudiated. The official could have attended the site and given out individual notices; alternatively, the shop steward could have been instructed to photocopy the letter and hand it out to individual employees.

179

Timing of repudiation. Even when industrial action is repudiated by a union, it does not become unofficial immediately. Where an act has been repudiated in accordance with S.21, for the purposes of unfair dismissal the action is not taken as being unofficial action before the end of the next working day after the day on which the repudiation takes place – S.237(4). In this context, a working day is strictly defined as any day not a public holiday or Saturday or Sunday – S.237(5). This applies even if these excepted days are, in practice, normal working days for the employees concerned. Thus, action that is repudiated on a Monday will not become unofficial until the Wednesday morning, while action repudiated on a Friday will not become unofficial until the Tuesday morning. Equally, the end of the working day means midnight and not the end of the shift – Balfour Kilpatrick Ltd v Acheson and ors (above).

The exact purpose of this 'day of grace' is not entirely clear. However, one effect is that it gives employees the chance to reconsider their position before the action becomes unofficial and their jobs are put at risk. Whatever the purpose, it is still possible for employees to be dismissed under S.237 before they have in fact received the union's notice of repudiation since, under S.21(2), the union is merely required to 'do its best' to give written notice to every union member.

8.12 **Ineffective repudiation.** If the repudiation is ineffective, any employees dismissed for taking part in the industrial action will have dismissed while participating in official industrial action and the dismissal may be unfair under S.238 (see 'Dismissal during "non-protected" official action' below).

A union's repudiation of industrial action may be ineffective for one of three reasons. First, it will be ineffective if it does not comply exactly with the conditions laid down in S.21 as set out above. Secondly, a repudiation which satisfies all the formal conditions may still be ineffective, or subsequently rendered so, under S.21(5). This states that industrial action will not be treated as repudiated if, at any time after the purported repudiation by the union, the principal executive committee, president or general secretary behaves in a manner which is inconsistent with that repudiation. This provision is aimed at stopping unions going through the formalities of repudiating industrial action while still giving it full support behind the scenes. Thirdly, S.21(6) provides that industrial action will not be considered repudiated if the union does not immediately confirm the repudiation in writing after a request made within three months by anyone party to a commercial contract that may be interfered with as a result of the action.

8.13 Clearly, then, an effective repudiation – making the action unofficial – may be rendered ineffective by the subsequent behaviour of the union, so that the action becomes official again. The Act does not specify at what point industrial action becomes official again following an act by the union that is considered inconsistent with the repudiation. Yet it is crucial for S.237 purposes to know whether the action was unofficial at the time the employee was dismissed. Moreover, what is the position of an employee who is dismissed once the action has become unofficial following union repudiation, but subsequent to the dismissal the union does something inconsistent with the repudiation? It is arguable that the inconsistent act renders the repudiation ineffective from the start, so that in reality there never was any repudiation. If that is the case, then the employee would have been participating in official industrial action all along. Presumably the statement in S.237(4) to the effect that whether or not action is to be regarded as unofficial is to be determined 'by reference to the facts as at the time of dismissal' could be used to refute such an argument, but the matter is not entirely clear.

Timing of dismissal   8.14

There are two issues involved here. First, as with official action dismissals, the employee must be taking part in the action at the time of his or her dismissal. In deciding this question, the same considerations will no doubt apply as with dismissals during official action – see below under 'Dismissal during "non-protected" official action – timing of complainant's dismissal'. Secondly, the action must be unofficial at the time of the dismissal, since S.237(4) states that whether or not industrial action is to be regarded as unofficial is to be determined by reference to the facts as at the time of dismissal. Thus, it is likely that the question of whether or not the action was unofficial at the relevant time will be treated as one of fact for the tribunal to decide.

The 'time of dismissal' is defined as:

• when dismissal is with notice, when the notice is given

• when dismissal is without notice, when the dismissal takes effect

• when the employee is employed under a fixed-term contract which expires without being renewed, the date of expiry of the contract – S.237(5).

As with official action, a dismissal cannot take effect until it is communicated to the employee (or he or she has a reasonable opportunity to learn of it).

Whether the action was unofficial at the time of dismissal may not always be   8.15
clear-cut. Action which involves union members but was not called by a union official or committee will be unofficial from the outset – S.237(2). But in the vast majority of cases, the action will start off as official, only becoming unofficial one working day after the union has repudiated it. In these cases the real problems arise where the purported repudiation by the union is in fact ineffective.

No action in support of employees dismissed under S.237   8.16

Finally, S.223 states that a union will have no immunity from proceedings in tort in respect of industrial action if the reason – or one of the reasons – for calling the action was the fact or belief that the employer had dismissed one or

181

more employees in circumstances in which they have no right to complain of unfair dismissal because they were taking part in unofficial action at the time of dismissal. Thus, even if there is a ballot in favour of the second action, a union will not be able to enter into a lawful dispute in support of members who were dismissed while taking part in unofficial action. The purpose of this provision is to bolster the S.237 provisions. The employer's sanction of dismissal might lose its bite if unions could threaten to take lawful industrial action in retaliation. The provision may also have the effect of further alienating unions from their members: not only will unions have been forced to repudiate the action and thereby expose their members to dismissal without remedy, they will also be prevented from taking supportive action on behalf of the dismissed employees.

8.17 Effect of S.237 on unofficial action

Much industrial action is by its very nature of short duration and so the provision in S.237(4) for a 'day of grace' before the action becomes unofficial following repudiation may result in much unofficial action slipping through the net. This is particularly true for industries for which Saturdays and Sundays are regular working days, since any action called on a Friday and repudiated the same day would still not become unofficial until Tuesday. The 'day of grace' also means that the union remains at risk of damages in respect of action that it has already disowned. Union liability for industrial action is discussed in Chapter 2.

One clear intention of the Act is to allow employers to dismiss those employees they consider to be the regular organisers of unofficial action. It is not certain, however, that the Act is wholly effective in this respect. As explained in relation to dismissals under S.238 (see 'Dismissal during "non-protected" official action – timing of complainant's dismissal'), the complexities involved in ensuring that employees' dismissals are communicated to them while they are still taking part in industrial action are many. The problem is even more acute where the action in which the employees are taking part must also be unofficial at the relevant time. Since employees are likely to know if they are near the top of the employer's hit list for selective dismissals, it may be that those employees will be able to make themselves scarce – for instance, by going on a brief holiday – so that the employer is not capable of communicating the dismissal to them while the unofficial action is still taking place.

8.18 Employer-provoked strikes

Section 237 permits no examination by the tribunal into the merits of the industrial action that is taken. Therefore an employer can deliberately provoke industrial action in order to gain immunity from unfair dismissal claims. The section seems to provide more scope for the unscrupulous employer than was probably intended. It appears to allow an employer to manufacture a situation in order to provoke unofficial action so that he can dismiss undesirable members of the workforce. In particular, he can dismiss trade union activists with impunity, which makes something of a mockery of the S.152 provisions which provide that dismissal for a trade union reason is automatically unfair.

Note, however, that Ss.237, 238 and 238A only bar unfair dismissal claims. If an employer selects employees for dismissal on the grounds of sex, race, disability, religion or belief, sexual orientation or age during industrial action, he will still be liable under the discrimination laws. Similarly, there is nothing to stop claimants from claiming redundancy payments should an employer decide to implement redundancies during industrial action, as long as redundancy is the true reason for dismissal and not the industrial action – this is explained further in Chapter 9.

Health and safety issues   8.19
As explained above, there are a number of exceptions to the bar on unfair dismissal claims if the employee was taking part in unofficial industrial action. These include where the reason for the dismissal or selection for redundancy falls within the health and safety provisions of S.100 ERA. However, the circumstances covered by S.100 are limited to the activities of certain safety representatives (or, where there is no such representative or safety committee, those who brought concerns to their employer so long as they did so 'by reasonable means') or to where there is a 'serious and imminent' danger. This means that there will be situations in which employees refuse to work because of immediate health and safety concerns that are not protected.

The problem arises where employees refuse to work in order to exert pressure on the employer to improve safety standards but the safety hazard or health risk does not pose a threat of 'imminent and serious danger' at that time. Since the question of what amounts to industrial action is purely one of fact for the tribunal, it is possible that a tribunal would consider such conduct to be unofficial industrial action, and thereby deprive the dismissed employees of the right to claim unfair dismissal. It can only be hoped that tribunals will adopt a commonsense approach and find that this kind of protest is not industrial action. However, it should be noted that in Wilkins and ors v Cantrell and Cochrane (GB) Ltd 1978 IRLR 483, EAT, the EAT upheld a tribunal's decision that the refusal of lorry drivers to drive lorries that were overloaded under the Road Traffic Act 1930 amounted to industrial action. And in Balfour Kilpatrick Ltd v Acheson and ors 2003 IRLR 683, EAT, a group of workers who refused to work in circumstances that could amount to a serious and imminent danger were not able to pursue claims of unfair dismissal because by the time of their dismissals, although working conditions remained far from satisfactory, the imminent danger had passed.

183

8.20 Dismissal during 'protected' official action

As outlined above, unless one of the limited exceptions applies, an employee has no right to complain of unfair dismissal if he or she is dismissed while taking part in unofficial industrial action – S.237. Where, however, the action is official (in the sense that it is not unofficial by virtue of S.237), he or she retains the right to complain of unfair dismissal in the two circumstances set out in Ss.238 and 238A.

The first is where he or she is *selectively dismissed* while taking part in official action – S.238. However, the right to claim unfair dismissal under this provision does not apply if the employer dismisses *all* employees taking part in the action. As with S.237, the *reason* for the dismissal under S.238 is irrelevant – what matters is whether the employee was taking part in the industrial action at the time of his or her dismissal. Dismissals under S.238 are dealt with under 'Dismissal during "non-protected" official action' below.

8.21 The second situation is where the employee is taking or has taken 'protected' official industrial action that is 'not actionable in tort' by virtue of S.219 and the reason for the dismissal is that the employee has taken part in such action – S.238A. (Action that is 'not actionable in tort' is explained fully in Chapters 3 and 4 but, briefly, it means that the union has complied with all the procedural requirements set out in the Act, including the complicated balloting and notice provisions, and immunity has not been lost for any reason.) However, the right to claim unfair dismissal under this section exists only if the dismissal occurs within a 'protected period' of 12 weeks (although dismissal after the end of that period remains protected in certain specified circumstances). After this, the employer can dismiss all employees involved with impunity.

It is worth emphasising here that S.238A is concerned with dismissal *for* taking part in industrial action, whereas Ss.237 and 238 are concerned simply with dismissal *while* taking part in industrial action. In other words, Ss.237 and 238 apply whenever an employee is dismissed during industrial action, but S.238A only applies if the participation in the action was the reason for the dismissal. S.238A differs from S.238 in that the reason for the dismissal *is* relevant and it does not preclude employers from dismissing employees for an unrelated reason during a period of industrial action. Nevertheless, many of the cases decided under S.238 – for example, on the definition of industrial action and on what constitutes participation in industrial action – are also of relevance to cases decided under S.238A.

8.22 Automatically unfair dismissal

Section 238A provides that a dismissal will be *automatically* unfair if the reason (or, if more than one, the principal reason) for the dismissal is that the employee took 'protected industrial action' (see below), provided the dismissal occurred:

- within the 'protected period' – S.238A(3) (see below)

- after the end of the protected period, but the employee had ceased to take part in the industrial action before the end of that period – S.238A(4) , or

- after the end of the protected period, but the employer had not taken such procedural steps as would have been reasonable for the purposes of resolving the dispute – S.238A(5) (see below).

Furthermore, a redundancy dismissal will be unfair if the reason (or principal reason) the employee was selected for redundancy was that he or she took protected industrial action and one of the above provisions applied – S.105(7C) ERA.

Thus, there are no circumstances in which an employer may fairly dismiss an employee for taking protected industrial action unless the action has lasted more than 12 weeks and the employer has tried to resolve the dispute. **8.23**

As with the majority of other types of automatically unfair dismissal, there is no qualifying period of employment or upper age limit applicable to claims brought under S.238A – S.239(1).

'Protected' industrial action **8.24**

Section 238A applies only to lawfully organised industrial action. S.238A(1) attempts to make this clear by stating that an employee takes protected industrial action 'if he commits an act which, or a series of acts each of which, he is induced to commit by an act which by virtue of S.219 is not actionable in tort'. This means action which the employee is induced to commit by his or her union, provided the union's action in doing so is protected under S.219 from liability in proceedings in tort for inducement to break, or interfere with, contracts (see further Chapters 3 and 4).

If a union repudiates the protected industrial action, the status of the action will change from official to unofficial in the same way as it does under S.237 (see the discussion on repudiation under 'Dismissal during unofficial action', above). To prevent employees losing the protection of S.238A in such circumstances, S.238A(8) gives them a day's grace in which to cease their action. That is, they will only lose the protection of S.238A if they continue the action beyond the end of the next working day after the day on which the repudiation took place. ('Working day' for these purposes is defined in S.237(5) as any day not a public holiday or Saturday and Sunday.) So if, for example, the union repudiates the action on a Monday, the entitlement to claim unfair dismissal under S.238A would be lost if the employees take action on or after the following Wednesday.

The S.238A(1) definition of protected industrial action envisages that industrial action will only be taken by a trade union. Yet S.237(2) makes it clear that **8.25** industrial action that involves no union members is to be regarded as official action. Thus industrial action that is taken, for example, by just a few workers in a non-unionised workforce would be official industrial action for the purpose of the 'picking and choosing' provisions in S.238 (discussed in the next section), but would not be protected official action within the meaning of S.238A. Although industrial action that involves no union members may be comparatively rare, this does seem to create something of an anomaly.

8.26 The protected period

The protected period was originally introduced by the ERelA 1999 and was initially eight weeks in total. However, it was later extended to 12 weeks by the ERelA 2004, which also introduced an extension period where striking workers are locked out by their employer. The protected period is now a basic period of 12 weeks beginning with the first day of protected industrial action, plus any extension period in relation to that employee – S.238A(7A–B). An extension period is a period equal to the number of days during the basic protected period on which the employee was subjected to a lock-out by his or her employer – S.238A(7C).

The 'first day of protected industrial action' for these purposes means the day on which the employee starts to take protected industrial action (even if on that day he or she is locked out by the employer) – S.238A(7D).

8.27 Reasonable steps for resolution of dispute

Even if the industrial action dismissal takes place outside the protected period, S.238A will still apply if the employer has not taken such procedural steps as would have been reasonable for the purposes of resolving the dispute – S.238A(5). S.238A(6) sets out a number of factors to be taken into account in determining whether an employer has taken appropriate steps, and it is clear that the behaviour of the union will be just as relevant as the employer's behaviour for these purposes. The factors are:

- whether the employer or union had complied with procedures established by any applicable collective or other agreement – S.238A(6)(a)

- whether the employer or union offered or agreed to commence or resume negotiations after the start of the protected industrial action – S.238A(6)(b)

- whether the employer or union unreasonably refused, after the start of the protected industrial action, a request that conciliation services be used – S.238A(6)(c)

- whether the employer or union unreasonably refused, after the start of the protected industrial action, a request that mediation services be used in relation to procedures to be adopted for the purposes of resolving the dispute – S.238A(6)(d).

Where there was agreement to use conciliation or mediation services (see subsection (c) and (d)), regard should also be had to:

- whether the employer or union was represented by an appropriate person at meetings arranged by the conciliation or mediation service provider. An 'appropriate person' for these purposes is:
  - for the employer, a person with authority to settle the matter on the employer's behalf, or a person authorised by such a person to make recommendations to him or her regarding settlement
  - for the union, a person responsible for handling the matter subject on the union's behalf

- whether the employer or union cooperated, as far as requested to do so, in making arrangements for meetings to be held with the conciliation or mediation service provider

- whether the employer or union fulfilled any commitment given during conciliation or mediation process to take particular action. Consideration may be had to any agreed timetable or, if no timetable was agreed, to how long it was before action was taken

- whether the representatives of the employer or union answered any reasonable question put to them at conciliation or mediation meetings concerning the matter subject to conciliation or mediation – Ss.238A(6)(e) and 238B.

8.28 Section 238B(8) protects the position of the conciliation or mediation service provider in the following terms:

- notes taken by or on behalf of the service provider are not admissible in evidence

- the service provider must refuse to give evidence as to anything communicated to him or her in connection with the performance of his or her functions if, in his or her opinion, it would involve making a damaging disclosure. A 'damaging disclosure' is a disclosure of commercially sensitive information or information that relates to a position taken by one of the parties on the settlement that has not previously been disclosed, where the disclosure has not been consented to by the person who communicated it – S.238B(9)

- he or she may refuse to give evidence as to whether a particular question was a reasonable one for the purpose of deciding whether a representative has answered it.

In determining whether the employer has taken the appropriate steps, a tribunal should not become involved in judging the merits of the dispute – S.238(7).

8.29 Reinstatement

A successful unfair dismissal claimant may apply to an employment tribunal for an order of reinstatement to his or her old job or, failing that, re-engagement in a comparable job (S.113 ERA). In the case of an unfair dismissal for participation in protected industrial action, a tribunal cannot make an order for reinstatement or re-engagement until after the conclusion of the protected industrial action by any employee in relation to the relevant dispute – S.239(4)(a).

8.30 Tribunal procedure

Section 239(4) also contains a couple of provisions dealing with tribunal practice and procedure in relation to the hearing of claims under S.238A. It allows provisions to be made under Ss.7 and 9 of the Employment Tribunals Act 1996 requiring tribunals to carry out pre-hearing reviews in specified circumstances, and enabling or requiring tribunals to adjourn cases in specified circumstances. The DTI (Department of Trade and Industry – now the Department for Business, Innovation and Skills) Explanatory Notes on the Employment Relations Bill 1999 stated that it was envisaged that this power would be used to require pre-hearing reviews in all cases where the grounds for the claim fall under S.238A, and to require tribunals to adjourn such proceedings where they become aware that the courts are considering actions brought by the employer or others challenging the legitimacy of the union's organisation of the industrial action in question. No such provisions have been made to date.

8.31 Qualifying period

The period of one year's continuous service normally required to pursue a claim for unfair dismissal under the ERA does not apply to claims brought under S.238A for dismissal for taking part in protected industrial action – S.239(1).

8.32 Time limits

The time limit for bringing a claim under S.238A is the same as that for S.238. The usual three-month time limit is disapplied and instead the claim must be presented before the end of six months beginning with the complainant's date of dismissal – S.239(2)(a). The date of dismissal is the date when notice is given, if dismissal is with notice. In other cases, it is the effective date of termination – S.238(5). A tribunal may hear a complaint presented outside the relevant time limit if it considers that it was not reasonably practicable to present it within the time limit and it was presented within a reasonable period after that – S.239(2)(b).

188

Dismissal during 'non–protected' official action 8.33

Where industrial action is official but the dismissal provisions of S.238A (see 'Dismissal during "protected" official action' above) do not apply (because, for example, the dismissal has occurred outside the protected period or the action is not 'protected'), then the rights of an employee dismissed during the action will be governed by S.238. 'Official' in this context means not 'unofficial' by virtue of S.237 (see 'Dismissal during unofficial action' above), so would include, for example, action where no trade union members are involved as well as spontaneous action by union members that has been endorsed by a workplace shop steward and not repudiated by the union.

Briefly, S.238 provides the employer with immunity from unfair dismissal claims so long as he dismisses *all* those taking part in the action and does not selectively re-engage any of them within a three-month period. S.238 includes dismissals by reason of redundancy. S.238 also applies where the employee was dismissed while the employer was conducting or instituting a lock-out – see below.

If the employer is selective, the S.238 immunity will be lost and an employment 8.34 tribunal will then be able to hear unfair dismissal complaints brought by those who have been dismissed, or not re-engaged, in the normal way. (Note that, unlike dismissals under S.238A, a dismissal that falls foul of the S.238 'picking and choosing' provisions is not automatically unfair and the normal test of reasonableness contained in S.98 ERA will apply – see below under 'Reasonableness of dismissal'.)

The *reason* for the employee's dismissal is generally irrelevant for the purposes of unfair dismissal law in this context. The simple fact that an employee is *taking part* in industrial action (or the employer is conducting a lock-out at the time of dismissal) is enough to warrant dismissal (provided all those taking part are dismissed and none are re-engaged within three months). However, this rule is subject to virtually the same exceptions that apply to dismissals during unofficial action under S.237. These exceptions are where the principal reason for the dismissal, or the reason why the employee was selected for redundancy, was a reason falling within S.98B, 99, 100, 101A(d), 103, 104C or 104 (in so far as it relates to time off to take care of dependants) ERA – S.238(2A) (see under 'Dismissal during unofficial action' above). However, unlike S.237, there is no exception in respect of the right not to be dismissed for 'whistleblowing' under S.103A ERA.

Where one of these exceptions applies, the employee can claim automatically unfair dismissal, even though he or she was taking part in industrial action at the time of the dismissal.

8.35 Note that the limits imposed by S.238 apply only to unfair dismissal law. An employee who can show that the reason for dismissal was related to his or her sex, race, disability, religion or belief, sexual orientation or age will still have a claim under discrimination law.

The rules governing official industrial action contained in S.238 provide that, where at the date of dismissal:

- the employer was conducting or instituting a lock-out, or

- the complainant was taking part in a strike or other industrial action

a tribunal shall not determine whether the dismissal was fair or unfair unless it is shown that:

- one or more relevant employees have not been dismissed, or

- any such employee has, before the expiry of three months beginning with that employee's date of dismissal, been offered re-engagement and that the complainant has not been offered re-engagement.

8.36 These provisions are fairly complex and the definitions of several of the crucial terms have caused some difficulty. Matters have not always been helped by the courts' frequent insistence that the issues involved are solely ones of fact (and not law) for the tribunal to decide. This means that it is difficult to challenge a tribunal's decision as it will only be overturned by the EAT or a higher appellate court if the decision is perverse – that is, one that no reasonable tribunal could have come to on the facts. This has led, as we shall see, to a good deal of uncertainty in this area of the law.

This section is laid out as follows. First we consider the meaning of the terms 'strikes', 'lock-outs' and 'other industrial action'. We then turn to the definition of 'relevant employees'. The question of whether an employee is 'taking part' in industrial action is considered under this head. Next we consider the timing of the relevant dismissals before finally turning to the question of selective re-engagement.

8.37 Strikes, lock-outs and other industrial action

In order for Ss.237 and 238 to operate to give employers immunity from unfair dismissal claims, it must be shown that, at the time of dismissal, the complainant was taking part in a strike or other industrial action, or, in the case of S.238, that the employer was conducting a lock-out. The Act only defines the term 'strike', which is unfortunate because the distinction between the three different forms of action can be decisive in determining the parties' rights. For example, it is essential to know whether employees are taking some form of industrial action or the employer has instituted a lock-out because the definition of 'relevant employees' differs in each case – see below. The only guidance as to which form of action is being taken (if any) is provided by judgments of the EAT and the Court of Appeal, which we discuss below. (Note that the terms 'strike' and 'industrial action' are also considered in Chapter 1 in a more general context.)

Lock-outs. The question of what constitutes a lock-out was specifically **8.38** addressed by the Court of Appeal in Express and Star Ltd v Bunday and ors 1988 ICR 379, CA. In that case, employees had been instructed by their union not to handle material produced by a new process, the introduction of which had been the subject of a dispute between the employer and the relevant trade union. The company closed the premises the next day and informed the employees that, unless they agreed to handle the material, they would be dismissed. They refused and were suspended, and later some of them were dismissed. The tribunal decided that the employer's conduct was designed merely to put pressure on the workforce to encourage them to perform their duties and in these circumstances there was industrial action rather than a lock-out. In so deciding, they took into account the fact that the employer, by seeking to introduce the new process, had not been in breach of the contracts of employment.

On appeal, however, the EAT held that a breach of contract was not a prerequisite for either a strike or a lock-out and that the tribunal had erred in focusing on that issue. It held that, although there was no definition of 'lock-out' as the phrase is used in S.238, the relevant definition could be extracted from that given in S.235(4) ERA. This defines a lock-out for continuity of employment purposes as '(a) the closing of a place of employment, (b) the suspension of work, or (c) the refusal by an employer to continue to employ any number of persons employed by him in consequence of a dispute, done with a view to compelling persons employed by the employer, or to aid another employer in compelling persons employed by him, to accept terms or conditions of or affecting employment'. On this basis, the EAT reasoned that the question of whether there was a lock-out resolved itself into the simple issue of 'Who stopped work continuing?' In the instant case, the EAT took the view that the employer had taken the initiative by suspending the workforce and so, contrary to the tribunal's finding, there had been a lock-out.

The Court of Appeal overturned the EAT's ruling and restored the tribunal's decision. In the Court's view, it is a matter of fact (not law) for the tribunal to decide in each case whether, on the ordinary meaning of the term, a lock-out has in fact taken place, and in deciding this issue they are not to be fettered by any one rigid definition. The definition of 'lock-out' contained in S.235(4) ERA should be used as a guide only. Similarly, the fact that an employer may have been in breach of contractual obligations to employees is not conclusive proof that there has been a lock-out, although it is a material consideration.

Tribunals therefore have a wide discretion in deciding whether, in any particular **8.39** case, a lock-out has occurred. In so deciding, they will look at a number of

191

factors, including the S.235(4) ERA definition, the contractual position and the employer's intentions. If the evidence shows that the employer's intention is to keep the business and the jobs open, and the close-down is to force changes on the workforce, then it is likely that the situation will be characterised as a lock-out – Webb and ors v Sundaw Products Ltd and anor EAT 477/79.

In another case, while accepting that whether there was a lock-out is a question of fact for the tribunal the EAT nevertheless decided that a situation where the employer was simply refusing to allow employees to work otherwise than in full compliance with their contracts of employment was not capable of constituting a lock-out. In Manifold Industries Ltd v Sims and ors 1991 ICR 504, EAT, the employer tried to interview all staff to ask them whether they intended to cooperate over new terms and conditions which were to be imposed as a result of a work study that the company had carried out. Those who did not agree were dismissed. This led to a complete stoppage of work. The tribunal found that the employer had conducted a lock-out but, on appeal, the EAT upheld the employer's argument that the cooperation sought by the company was a legitimate requirement of the employees' contracts and could not therefore amount to a lock-out.

However, this did not settle the matter. The employees argued that in reality the employer had refused to allow them to work unless they submitted to an interview and agreed to cooperate. The interviews were carried out in breach of the employees' contracts, which, among other things, gave them rights of representation. In the employees' view, therefore, the tribunal had been entitled to hold that there was indeed a lock-out. The EAT was not prepared to say that this argument stood no chance of success, but the tribunal had not made sufficient findings of fact for it to decide whether or not it should succeed. The case was therefore remitted to a different tribunal for it to reconsider whether the employer's actions could properly be regarded as a lock-out.

8.40 In Barrett and ors v M Bolas Ltd and anor ET Case Nos.2103645–7/97 the tribunal was called upon to decide whether employees asked to leave the premises after refusing to work in protest at a change from weekly to monthly pay, and dismissed with immediate effect, were involved in a strike or a lock-out at the date of dismissal. The tribunal held that, since the employees were engaged in a 'concerted stoppage of work', they were taking part in industrial action at the relevant time.

8.41 **Strike.** The Court of Appeal's decision in Express and Star Ltd v Bunday (above) essentially redefined the way in which tribunals should approach the question of whether a strike was taking place at the time of dismissal. Prior to this decision, tribunals had relied on the definition of 'strike' contained in what is now S.235(5) ERA, which, like the definition of 'lock-out', is concerned with continuity of employment. This defines a strike as: '(a) the cessation of work by a body of employed persons acting in combination, or (b) a concerted refusal, or a refusal under a common understanding, of any number of employed persons to continue to work for an employer in consequence of a dispute, done as a means of compelling their employer... to accept or not to accept terms or conditions of or affecting employment'. The Court of Appeal stated that this definition should be confined to its context – continuity of employment – and that the question of whether a strike is taking place for the purposes of S.238 TULR(C)A – and presumably S.237 – is one of fact, not law, for the tribunal to decide.

Accordingly, it is for the tribunal to use its industrial experience and to look to **8.42** all the circumstances of the action and the surrounding events when deciding whether a strike was actually under way when the dismissal took place. Guidance can be found in S.246 TULR(C)A, which defines the word 'strike' as 'any concerted stoppage of work'. This echoes the definition of a strike provided by Lord Denning MR in Tramp Shipping Corp v Greenwich Marine Inc 1975 ICR 261, CA. In that case a strike was defined as 'a concerted stoppage of work by men done with a view to improving their wages or conditions, or giving vent to a grievance or making a protest about something or other, or supporting or sympathising with other workmen in such endeavour'. Lord Justice Stephenson noted that a strike could also be over a political issue and this definition seems to have met with Parliamentary approval since S.246 applies to *any* concerted stoppage of work. (Note that, for the purpose of S.238A, action over a political issue will not amount to protected industrial action since it is not 'in contemplation or furtherance of a trade dispute' and does not therefore attract the immunities under S.219.)

'Other industrial action'. Action short of a strike will also activate the special **8.43** dismissal rules contained in Ss.237 and 238 if it amounts to 'other industrial action'. There is no definition of the term and, as with strikes and lock-outs, whether action constitutes 'other industrial action' is a question of fact, not law, for the tribunal to decide according to the circumstances – Coates and anor v Modern Methods and Materials Ltd 1982 ICR 763, CA.

However, two important factors to be taken into account in determining the issue are the nature and effect of the acts and the intention behind them. The EAT in Rasool and ors v Hepworth Pipe Co Ltd 1980 ICR 494, EAT, put more emphasis on the nature and effect of the concerted action than on the employees' intentions. It went on to decide that holding a meeting to discuss pay in defiance of the management's instructions was not industrial action. However, the Court of Appeal in Power Packing Casemakers Ltd v Faust and ors 1983 ICR 292, CA, attached greater importance to the purpose of the action. If the intention is to put concerted pressure on the employer in relation to some dispute or grievance, then it is likely to be characterised as industrial action.

Thus, although tribunals will take into account the nature and effect of the **8.44** action, the key issue is whether the facts support a finding that the actions of

193

the employees constituted a concerted effort to put pressure on the employer. Determining this issue can be a difficult task. Some examples:

- **Butterworth and anor v FA Gill Ltd** COET 1854/141: two pork cutters refused to do non-contractual overtime and they were dismissed. A factor which led the tribunal to hold that the employees were not engaged in industrial action was that the employees were not intent on putting pressure on the employer or disrupting his business in support of an ongoing dispute

- **Singh and ors v Pennine Fur Fabrics Ltd** ET Case No.15418/85: some employees organised a deputation to discuss grievances with management. The tribunal held that this was not industrial action because it was merely a deputation seeking information; they had not threatened to refuse to work or pressured the company in any way

- **Glenrose (Fish Merchants) Ltd v Chapman and ors** EAT 245/89: the employees decided to refuse to work voluntary overtime in protest at various acts of the company. The EAT, by a majority, overruled a tribunal's finding that a refusal to work non-compulsory overtime was not 'other industrial action'. The fact that the action was premeditated and was in effect an overtime ban meant that it fell on the side of the line constituting 'other industrial action' rather than being a mere protest by individuals

- **Holt and ors v First Peterloo Housing Association Ltd and anor** ET Case Nos.65860/94 and others: the employees were employed at a residential unit that their employer planned to close, with a consequent loss of jobs. The employees continued to book in new residents in direct contravention of a management instruction not to do so, changed the locks of the building and barred management from free access to it, and continued to work at the premises without management's authority. The tribunal found that the purpose of this action was to put pressure on the employer not to close the building; it was concerted action and consequently amounted to industrial action.

In Midland Plastics v Till and ors 1983 ICR 118, EAT, the Appeal Tribunal provided a list (which it stressed was not exhaustive) of the kinds of activity short of a strike which may constitute 'other industrial action'. This included go-slows, working to rule, overtime bans and picketing. Concerted disruptive acts on the shop-floor can also amount to industrial action: for example, in Thompson and ors v Eaton Ltd 1976 IRLR 308, EAT, the EAT decided that surrounding new machinery to prevent management testing it could fall within the statutory term.

It must therefore always be borne in mind that what constitutes 'other industrial action' will vary according to the particular situation and the tribunal's judgment. As the Court of Appeal recognised in the Coates case (above), it is quite possible for two different tribunals to come to two different conclusions on the same set of facts. Both would be upheld on appeal provided the decisions were not perverse. The EAT in Naylor and ors v Orton and Smith Ltd and anor 1983 ICR 665, EAT, accepted that this was the approach which should be adopted following the Court of Appeal's ruling, but found it unsatisfactory because it meant that employers and their advisers cannot predict in advance which way a tribunal is likely to exercise its discretion. In the EAT's view, the question of what amounts to industrial action is essentially one of principle and it is absurd to treat it as one of fact.

Must employees be acting in breach of contract? It is not an essential **8.45** requirement of industrial action that the employees are acting in breach of contract. However, as most forms of industrial action will involve a breach of contract, the question of whether a breach is a necessary ingredient does not normally arise. For example, a ban on overtime will clearly constitute a breach where overtime is required by the contract. But the question that faced the Court of Appeal in Power Packing Casemakers Ltd v Faust and ors (above) was whether a collective withdrawal of voluntary overtime as a result of a dispute over wages, which was not in breach of contract, could amount to industrial action under S.238.

The Court decided that it was not necessary for the employees' actions to be in breach of contract for the action to fall within the meaning of 'other industrial action'. In the words of Lord Justice Stephenson: 'If [the employee] merely refuses to do something which he is not contractually bound to do, he cannot be taking part in industrial action… if he refuses because he has a private commitment to visit a sick friend, or a personal preference for a football match, he is not taking industrial action. But that is not this case. If he refuses because he and others who refuse with him hope to extract an increase of wages out of his employers because their business will be disrupted if they do not grant it, that continued application of pressure is industrial action in the common sense of the words.'

Contrast that case with Knowles and anor v Fire Brigades Union 1996 IRLR **8.46** 617, CA, in which the Court of Appeal held that a union's ban on full-time fire-fighters taking on additional fire-fighting duties in their spare time because the extra work might affect their ability to do their full-time work satisfactorily did not amount to industrial action. The ban did not involve employees departing from the terms of their existing contracts, but merely prevented them from undertaking work under additional contracts. In the Court's view, the fact that a union's policy applies pressure on an employer and inhibits his freedom of action is not a sufficient test of industrial action. Moreover, in this case negotiations were continuing and there had not occurred that breakdown in negotiations which, said the Court, is almost implicit in the taking of industrial action. (Note, however, that this case was concerned with the definition of industrial action for the purposes of the provisions on unjustifiable discipline by a union of its members under S.65 TULR(C)A.)

Similarly, in Burgess and ors v Stevedoring Services Ltd 2002 IRLR 810, PC, a case heard by the Privy Council under Bermudan law and therefore persuasive but not binding on UK courts, the Privy Council held that an overtime ban that was not in breach of contract did not amount to industrial action, even though it arose over an industrial dispute. However, peculiar to this case was that the union was responsible for assigning workers to overtime gangs and had refused to do so; consequently workers had not actually refused to perform any work.

8.47 **Does a threat to take action amount to industrial action?** Since the decision of the EAT in Lewis and Britton v E Mason and Sons 1994 IRLR 4, EAT, it is no longer clear whether a threat to take industrial action at some point in the future amounts to taking part in action for the purposes of the TULR(C)A. In Midland Plastics v Till and ors (above) the EAT was clear that it did not. It was generally assumed, therefore, that industrial action did not take place until the participants were actually due to carry out their contractual obligations. This principle was slightly modified by the EAT in Winnett v Seamarks Brothers Ltd 1978 ICR 1240, EAT, but in circumstances where collective action had already begun at the time of the dismissals and had, therefore, gone beyond a mere threat. In that case, all the employees involved in the action were held to have been participating, even though, for some, the time for performing their contractual duties was not yet due as their shift had not started.

Uncertainty in this area of the law crept in when the EAT in the Lewis case (above) upheld a tribunal's decision that a group of drivers who were dismissed when they told their employer that they would not work the following day unless two previously dismissed employees were reinstated were taking part in industrial action. At the time of the dismissal the drivers were off duty and were not due to work until the following morning. The tribunal relied on the Winnett case as authority for the proposition that employees were on strike from the moment they expressed their intention not to carry on working.

8.48 On appeal to the EAT, the employees argued that the tribunal had misdirected itself in law. In particular, the tribunal had not considered the Midland Plastics case. The EAT began by emphasising that, even though the decision of the Court of Appeal in Coates had been subject to some criticism, the question of whether there had been industrial action was a question of fact, not law, for the tribunal to decide. The EAT then went on to note that the tribunal had considered two particular facts to be relevant to its conclusion. The employer had already allocated work for the following day and believed that there was no realistic prospect of further negotiation between the time the threat was made and the time when work was due to commence. The employer did not, therefore, expect the drivers to turn up. On the facts, the EAT was unable to find the tribunal's decision perverse.

However, despite the EAT's finding, it is arguable that the principle established in Winnett should not have been applied to this case because, unlike here, in Winnett no action was actually under way at the time of dismissal.

Can an individual employee take industrial action alone? In Bowater **8.49** Containers Ltd v Blake EAT 552/81 the EAT stated that the 'relevant employee' definition in S.238 (see below) assumes that at least one other employee is involved in concerted action. Thus a solitary employee taking action alone will not come within the definition. However, in Lewis and Britton v E Mason and Sons (above), the EAT upheld a tribunal's conclusion that one person was participating in industrial action on his own. The facts were that B, a driver, was dismissed when he refused to take a lorry without an overnight heater from Wales to Edinburgh unless the employer paid him an extra £5 to enable him to take bed and breakfast accommodation. Another driver also refused to make the trip and when he was dismissed L and other drivers threatened not to work the following day unless their colleagues were reinstated. The tribunal pointed out that the words of S.238 were not limited to the definition in S.235 ERA. All that was required was conduct designed to coerce the employer to improve existing terms and conditions. As B had refused to carry out the work allocated to him unless he was paid more money, he was involved in industrial action. The EAT took the view that one person may be involved in industrial action on his own and that the tribunal was entitled to reach the conclusion it did on the facts.

If this is right, it means that any refusal by an employee to carry out an employer's lawful instructions unless certain terms are agreed could be categorised as industrial action. In Pigott v Yonex UK Ltd ET Case No.56223/94, for example, P was dismissed following his refusal to do what he considered to be extra work unless he was paid for it. The tribunal found that the work in question in fact constituted part of P's contractual duties and that his refusal to do it constituted industrial action, with the result that he was barred by S.238 from claiming unfair dismissal.

End of industrial action. In some cases it may be difficult to pinpoint when **8.50** industrial action has ended. This can cause problems for employers, as the following cases demonstrate:

- **South East Kent Health Authority v Gillis and ors** EAT 927/83: a health authority issued an ultimatum to striking porters that they would be dismissed if they did not sign an undertaking formally accepting new working arrangements and return to work. They returned to work but refused to attend a meeting because they objected to its being held outside the porters' lodge. The EAT held that the industrial action actually ended when the employees clocked in for work and their refusal to attend the meeting was merely an expression of resentment at the employer's 'officious

197

and unnecessary' requirement. The dismissals did not occur during industrial action and so the employer lost immunity from unfair dismissal claims

- **Glenrose (Fish Merchants) Ltd v Chapman and ors** EAT 245/89: C and 17 other employees worked from 7 am to 4 pm, with a voluntary overtime scheme in the evenings as and when required. They came into dispute with management over a proposed change in working hours and decided to refuse the next request to do overtime. Despite the employer's warning that such a refusal could lead to dismissal, the overtime ban took place one evening. However, the employees told management that they would return to work as normal the next day. When they turned up the following morning, they were dismissed. The EAT upheld the tribunal ruling that the employees were not taking part in industrial action at the time of their dismissal. Because the employees had made clear their intention to work as normal in the morning, the employer could not satisfy the tribunal that the action was still continuing at that time

- **Mainland Car Deliveries Ltd v Cooper and ors** EAT 492/96: the employees decided to take industrial action in relation to a pay claim. Their union informed the employer that the action would consist of a one-day strike on 1 May and, from 2 May, a restriction on overtime work until the dispute was resolved. In response the employer threatened to dismiss any employee who refused to sign a letter dissociating him or herself from 'all industrial action'. None of the employees signed that letter and the strike on 1 May went ahead. On 2 May the employees reported for work but were locked out and given letters of dismissal. The EAT, by a majority, upheld a tribunal's decision that the employees were not taking industrial action at the time of their dismissal. The one-day strike and the overtime restriction constituted two separate stages of action. At the time of the dismissals on 2 May the strike was over but the union had yet to decide how the overtime restriction was to be implemented. Moreover, the employees' refusal to sign the letter dissociating themselves from the action was understandable given that it was drafted in such wide terms.

8.51 Industrial action and trade union activities

It may sometimes be difficult to draw the line between industrial action and participation in trade union activities. In Drew v St Edmundsbury Borough Council 1980 ICR 513, EAT, the Appeal Tribunal held that a dismissal cannot be for both reasons but must fall within one or other of the categories. The distinction is a vital one since a dismissal for trade union activities is automatically unfair – S.152(1)(b), whereas a dismissal for taking part in industrial action may mean that the tribunal cannot hear the case at all. Once again, it will be a question of fact for the tribunal to decide. In a borderline case, two different tribunals may reach opposite conclusions as to the reason for the dismissal. Yet both will be correct in that the EAT will not intervene. An example of a borderline case is Naylor and ors v Orton and Smith Ltd and anor 1983 ICR 665, EAT, in which the EAT found that a tribunal could reasonably decide that attendance at a meeting that voted for an immediate overtime ban did not amount to industrial action. It went on to note that the contrary view was equally reasonable and a tribunal could not be faulted at law whichever way it decided this issue of fact. Two further cases:

- **Crowther v British Railways Board** EAT 762 and 1118/95: four employees who were organising industrial action were dismissed. The action was taken without any regard to the recognised procedures for negotiation. A tribunal rejected the employees' claim that they had been dismissed for trade union activities. The reason for the dismissals was the employer's belief that the employees, in organising the industrial action, were guilty of gross misconduct. The EAT upheld the decision, noting that the employees' authorised duties as union representatives did not include the incitement or organisation of industrial action without reference to accepted negotiating procedures. The fact that at the time of the dismissals the action was official in that it had not yet been repudiated by the union did not necessarily mean that the dismissals had been for trade union activities

- **Vascroft Contractors Ltd v Falvey and Clarke** EAT 176/94: the employer recognised three trade unions: UCATT, the EETPU and the TGWU. C and F, who were members of UCATT and the TGWU respectively, were among a number of employees who took industrial action after the employer had withdrawn permission for a union meeting at the last minute. The employer then announced that a single union agreement had been reached with the EETPU and warned that those taking part in the industrial action would be dismissed if they did not return to work within two hours. C and F turned up before the deadline but were dismissed anyway. The EAT upheld a tribunal's decision that the employees had been dismissed for trade union activities. The single union agreement was a sham and the employer's strategy was to secure the workforce's return to work on the condition that those employees who were UCATT or TGWU members forswore their union. The reason for the dismissals was 'to deter and discourage membership of the two active unions'.

Relevant employees   8.52

Once a tribunal has decided that there was an official strike, other industrial action or a lock-out, it must then go on to determine whether all the 'relevant employees' have been dismissed, or whether any have been selectively re-engaged within three months. S.238 defines 'relevant employees' differently according to the type of action taking place:

- in relation to a lock-out, the 'relevant employees' are those employees with a *direct interest* in the dispute which led to the lock-out – S.238(3)(a)

199

- in relation to a strike or other industrial action, the 'relevant employees' are those employees at the same establishment as the complainant who are *taking part* in the industrial action at the time the complainant was dismissed – S.238(3)(b).

The definition of 'relevant employees' for the purposes of a lock-out is, therefore, much wider than that for a strike or other industrial action. Consequently, it is to the employee's advantage to show that a lock-out was under way at the time of dismissal and to the employer's advantage to show that there was a strike taking place.

8.53 Below, we take a more detailed look at the meaning of the key phrases used in the above definitions and at other relevant points that have emerged from the case law in determining who is a relevant employee.

8.54 **Direct interest.** It is clear that there may be more employees who are directly interested in the outcome of a dispute than are in fact locked out by the employer. In Fisher and ors v York Trailer Co Ltd 1979 ICR 834, EAT, the Appeal Tribunal decided that 'directly interested' meant those employees who had at some time been involved in the dispute which led to the lock-out. Similarly, in H Campey and Sons Ltd v Bellwood and ors 1987 ICR 311, EAT, employees were given an ultimatum to return to work or be dismissed after being locked out by their employer. The EAT decided that the relevant employees included the employees who had returned to work before dismissal, as these employees were directly interested at the commencement of the lock-out.

Whether or not an employee has a direct interest will depend on the facts of each case. One case in which the employees were found to have only an indirect interest is Saunders and ors v Commercial Dry Dock Enterprises ET Case No.6708/80. Here, existing riggers were locked out and subsequently dismissed when they refused to work alongside 'helpers'. When none of the helpers were dismissed, the riggers argued that there had been discrimination in respect of the lock-out because the helpers had a direct interest in the dispute. The tribunal held that although the helpers had an interest – they had the prospect of better-paid work if the employer won the dispute – this interest was only indirect.

8.55 The concept of direct interest in a trade dispute has received its most comprehensive analysis in the context of social security law, where employees can avoid the 'trade dispute disqualification' from unemployment benefit if they can show that they are not directly interested in the trade dispute causing the stoppage of work. In Presho v DHSS 1984 IRLR 74, HL, the House of Lords held that where a dispute is between an employer and one group of workers, an employee belonging to another group of workers would be directly interested in the dispute where two conditions were satisfied:

- the outcome of the dispute would be applied to all employees whether or not they belonged to the union involved in the dispute

- this would come about as a result of a collective agreement or an established custom or practice.

Consequently, it is probably right to say that if an employer wishes to dismiss workers whom he has locked out and still retain S.238 immunity from unfair dismissal claims, he must look wider and dismiss all those employees who will be directly affected by the outcome of the dispute which has led to the lock-out.

Taking part in industrial action. For the special dismissal rules in Ss.237, 238 and 238A to come into play, the complainant and, in relation to S.238, other 'relevant employees' must have been 'taking part' in a strike or other industrial action. The Court of Appeal established in Coates and anor v Modern Methods and Materials Ltd 1982 ICR 763, CA, that the issue of whether an employee is taking part in industrial action is a matter of fact for the tribunal to decide and that it is quite possible for two tribunals, dealing with identical facts, to reach different conclusions without either of them being wrong in law. **8.56**

Unlike the question of whether an act amounts to industrial action (where the purpose of the act will be relevant), the employee's motives are irrelevant to the question of whether or not he or she was taking part in the action. What is needed is an objective evaluation of the circumstances. In the Coates case (above) an employee stayed away from work because she was afraid to cross a picket-line, although she had gone to the factory intending to work. The Court of Appeal ruled that she was participating in the action. The Court said that 'participation in a strike must be judged by what the employee does and not by what he thinks or why he does it. If he stops work when his workmates come out on strike and does not say or do anything to make plain his disagreement, or which could amount to a refusal to join them, he takes part in their strike... In the field of industrial action those who are not openly against it are presumably for it.' The EAT has subsequently emphasised, however, that those remarks of the Court of Appeal were concerned with the facts of that case. They were not intended to be a sweeping statement of principle that anyone who is not present at work during industrial action and has not declared him or herself openly against the action is necessarily taking part – Hulse and anor v E Hillier and Son (Engineering) Ltd and ors EAT 273/94.

In one unusual case, which clearly demonstrates the irrelevance of an employee's motive, the EAT upheld a tribunal's decision that an employee who was taking part in strike action at his employer's request as an informant was taking part in the action at the time of the others' dismissals. The employee had all the appearances of taking part in the action: his motives were irrelevant – Wood Group Engineering Contractors Ltd v Byrne EAT 447/92. **8.57**

Similarly, an employer's knowledge is irrelevant for the purposes of Ss.237 and 238. In Manifold Industries Ltd v Sims and ors 1991 ICR 504, EAT, the Appeal Tribunal stressed that it was irrelevant whether an employer thought that an

201

employee was participating in industrial action. The question that had to be decided was whether, on the facts, the employee was actually taking part and this must be decided solely on an objective view of the employee's acts or omission and not by reference to what the employer knew. This view was accepted by the EAT in Jenkins v P and O European Ferries (Dover) Ltd 1991 ICR 652, EAT, where Mr Justice Wood resiled from his earlier decision in McKenzie v Crosville Motor Services Ltd 1990 ICR 172, EAT, in so far as he had held in that case that the knowledge of the employer is important in answering the question posed by S.238.

It is important to note that whether an employee is taking part in industrial action is a matter of fact for the tribunal to decide. Some examples:

- **New Venture Carpets Ltd v Vincent and ors** EAT 733/83: the day and night shifts met and decided that they would not work if the temperature dropped below 60°F. The night shift went home when the temperature did drop below this level, but the day shift later worked as the temperature had risen above 60°F. The EAT upheld a tribunal's decision that, by dismissing only the night shift, the employer had not dismissed all the relevant employees. Since the day shift would have gone home if the temperature had fallen below 60°F, they were held to be taking part in the action

- **Glenrose (Fish Merchants) Ltd v Chapman and ors** EAT 245/89: the EAT upheld a tribunal's decision that employees who refused to work overtime one evening but made it clear that they would be working normally the next day were not taking part in industrial action when they were dismissed the next day

- **Vascroft Contractors Ltd v Falvey and Clarke** EAT 176/94: the employer informed employees participating in industrial action that they would be dismissed if they did not return to work within two hours. C and F turned up before the deadline but were dismissed anyway. The EAT held that, although the employees had not in so many words told their employer that they were intending to resume their duties immediately, the tribunal had been entitled to find that before their dismissal the employees had by their actions adequately conveyed to the employer that they had stopped taking part in the action.

8.58 Employees who are off duty but who inform the employer that when they are next due to work they will join existing industrial action will be treated as taking part from the time the statement of future intention is made – Winnett v Seamarks Brothers Ltd 1978 ICR 1240, EAT. This was taken one step further in Lewis and Britton v E Mason and Sons 1994 IRLR 4, EAT, where the EAT upheld a tribunal's decision that off-duty employees were taking part in industrial action when they threatened not to work the following day. No action had commenced, but the tribunal took into consideration the employer's belief that, since there was no prospect of further negotiation, the employees would not have turned up for work when they were due.

Taking part when legitimately absent from work. Employees need not be acting in breach of their contracts of employment to be taking part in industrial action. Some of the most complex cases on participation have concerned situations where the employee was lawfully absent from work at the time that he or she was dismissed for taking part in industrial action. The key issue here is whether or not the employee is regarded as being associated with the action. Some examples of cases where employees were found to have been associated with the action:

- **Bolton Roadways Ltd v Edwards and ors** 1987 IRLR 392, EAT: the employer dismissed 13 striking employees but offered re-engagement to one who was sick at the time of dismissal. It sought to preserve its S.238 protection by claiming that the re-engaged employee was not taking part when the others were dismissed because he was absent due to illness. Technically he was not in breach of his employment contract. The EAT said that the fact that an employee is in breach of his or her obligation to attend work may be relevant to whether he or she was taking part in industrial action but it is not an essential ingredient. An employee who is not contractually required to work because of sickness (or holidays) can still be viewed as taking part in a strike if he or she associates him or herself with the strike

- **Cowan v T Bailey Forman Ltd** ET Case No.7066/79: a journalist who helped organise and took part in picketing was held to be participating even though he was on holiday at the relevant time and not acting contrary to his contract of employment

- **Williams v Western Mail and Echo Ltd** 1980 IRLR 222, EAT: the EAT rejected the employee's contention that because he was ill during a strike he could not be regarded as having taken part in it. Once he had become associated with the action, he would be regarded as continuing to participate in it until he 'indicated to the contrary'

- **Doctor and ors v Labour Pump Co Ltd** EAT 38/85: a sick shop steward went into work because of his position as a union official when a strike broke out. The tribunal found that he was participating even though he was sick. The evidence showed that he had asked not to be paid and used the term 'We' when referring to the strikers.

Some examples of cases where employees were found *not* to have been associated with the action:

- **Hindle Gears Ltd v McGinty and ors** 1985 ICR 111, EAT: an employee who had been sick from the start of the strike merely chatted to striking pickets while going to and from work to deliver a sickness certificate. The

EAT held that he was not participating in the action. It also held that in such a situation – where an employee has been off sick since before the strike began – the burden is on the employer to show that the employee was in fact participating. It should be noted, however, that this emphasis on the employer's knowledge of the employee's actions was disapproved by a differently constituted EAT in Bolton Roadways Ltd v Edwards and ors (above). In that case, the EAT held that the issue of whether an employee was taking part in the action is to be determined by the evidence of what the employee was or was not doing; this could not be invalidated according to the employer's knowledge of what he or she was doing

- **Jenkins and ors v Phillips Rubber Ltd** COET 1646/142: an employee was off sick during a strike and his employer claimed he was participating because he had received and cashed union strike pay. The tribunal nonetheless held that he was not participating because he had not applied for strike benefit and only received it because an unidentified person applied on his behalf without his approval

- **Atkins and ors v Abram Alloys Ltd** EAT 370/89: an employee voted for industrial action but left on Territorial Army leave before the strike started and remained on leave for the duration of the strike. At one point he had been seen on the picket line backing the other employees but this was after the complainants had been dismissed. The EAT held that he was not a relevant employee because he was on leave from the outset and had only started taking part after the complainants had been dismissed

- **Hulse and anor v E Hillier and Son (Engineering) Ltd and ors** EAT 273/94: an employee had a day's holiday booked for the day subsequently selected by the union for strike action. On that day he contacted management to check that the holiday was still available to him, then popped into the workplace to collect some tools. On leaving he chatted to the strikers at the factory gates for about half an hour and indicated his general support for them. A tribunal found that the employee had not by these actions associated himself with the strikers in any way. He had made a positive decision to take a holiday and not join the strike. The EAT held that there was sufficient evidence to justify the tribunal's conclusion

- **Pointon and ors v BBA Friction Ltd** EAT 1380/00: the claimants argued that a colleague, W, who was on long-term sick leave at the time of the industrial action, was a 'relevant employee'. W had been balloted while he was on sick leave and had not returned by the time the action commenced; in fact, he had been told that his post had been filled by someone else and he was in 'suspense' pending redeployment. The EAT rejected the idea that W could be taking part in the action, since he had no obligation to attend work while he was on sick leave. It described the logic of the claimants' case, which was that the employee on sick leave should have been dismissed, as 'astonishing'.

Because of the uncertainty surrounding employees who are ill or on holiday, it **8.59** will often be difficult for an employer to decide who is taking part in industrial action. The employer need only omit to dismiss one participant for the S.238 protection to be lost. To minimise the risk of this occurring, many employers are inclined to send all employees who might conceivably be involved a letter giving them the opportunity to 'dissociate' themselves from the action. But employers need to make sure they send such a notice to all the potential participants. In New Venture Carpets v Vincent (above) the employer sent letters to the night shift workers but not to all those on the day shift. Since the latter were also held to be taking part, the letters were of no help to the employer.

Where there is wide-scale industrial action an employer may resort to blanket dismissals. This approach was endorsed by the EAT in Sehmi v Gate Gourmet London Ltd; Sandhu and ors v Gate Gourmet London Ltd 2009 IRLR 807, EAT, where it was held that in circumstances of mass industrial action which is causing enormous disruption to an employer's business and which requires an immediate and firm response, a policy of summarily dismissing any employee who is absent without leave or explanation and trying to sort out the exceptional cases of genuine non-participation by way of an appeal process can constitute a reasonable response.

Taking part at the date of complainant's dismissal. An employer will only lose the protection of S.238 in industrial action situations if he fails to dismiss, or re-engages, employees who were participating in the action *at the date of the complainant's dismissal* – S.238(3)(b). Employees who originally participated in the action, but returned to work before the complainant was dismissed, are not 'relevant employees' and so an employer will not lose S.238 protection by not dismissing them. In Hindle Gears Ltd v McGinty and ors 1985 ICR 111, EAT, two striking employees returned to work while letters of dismissal to all strikers were in the post. Because the two employees returned to work before the other strikers received their dismissal letters they were held not to be participating on the complainants' date of dismissal. In the case of a lock-out, however, 'relevant employees' are those who have participated *at any time* when the lock-out is in progress – a much wider definition.

At the same establishment. The 'relevant employees' for industrial action **8.60** dismissals are those taking part in the action at the same establishment as the complainant when the complainant was dismissed. S.238 does not define 'establishment' except to give it the meaning of 'the establishment of the employer at or from which the complainant works'. Cases on failure to consult unions on impending redundancies under S.188 TULR(C)A may be relevant when considering the meaning of 'establishment', particularly in multi-site operations – see IDS Employment Law Handbook, 'Redundancy' (2008),

205

Chapter 11. For example, in Athinaiki Chartopoiia AE v Panagiotidis and ors 2007 IRLR 284, ECJ, it was held that an establishment may consist of a distinct entity, having a certain degree of permanence and stability, which is assigned to perform one or more given tasks, and which has a workforce, technical means and a certain organisational structure allowing for the accomplishment of those tasks. That entity does not need to have any legal, economic, financial, administrative or technological autonomy, however. (It should be borne in mind, though, that the ECJ emphasised in that case that the definition was necessarily broad in order to limit the instances in which the EU Collective Redundancies Directive (No.98/59) does not apply.)

'Relevant employees' must take part in the same action as the complainant. Even if striking employees are at the same establishment as the complainant they will not be 'relevant employees' unless they are taking part in the same industrial action as the complainant. In McCormick v Horsepower Ltd 1981 ICR 535, CA, an engineer went on strike in sympathy with the striking boilermakers at his company. The engineers were not in dispute with the employer and the Court of Appeal held that he was not a relevant employee because he did not act in concert with the boilermakers and had no obligation to stay out on strike with them. His union had not organised sympathetic action and the Court of Appeal concluded that the engineer had not in effect taken part in the same strike.

8.61 Timing of complainant's dismissal

Employers will only lose their S.238 protection if they have selectively dismissed (or re-engaged) relevant employees who were participating in the strike or industrial action at the complainant's date of dismissal. Further, the dismissal of the complainant must have taken place during the industrial action (or lock-out). Thus, the timing of the complainant's dismissal is crucial.

Section 238(5) specifically provides that in the context of industrial action dismissals 'date of dismissal' means:

- where an employee's contract of employment was terminated by notice, the date on which the employer's notice was given, and

- in any other case, the effective date of termination.

8.62 This effectively means that employees will usually be taken to have been dismissed on the date they were informed of the dismissal. In Bolton Roadways Ltd v Edwards and ors 1987 IRLR 392, EAT, the employer gave striking employees an ultimatum that they would be considered dismissed if they did not turn up to work on the following day's shift. Before the EAT, the employer tried to argue that the ultimatum constituted a notice and so the date of dismissal was when the employees received it. The EAT rejected the argument and held that 'notice' meant notice of some period. The employer's ultimatum was a warning that the employees would be dismissed without notice if they failed to comply, rather than a notice of dismissal. Therefore the date of dismissal was not when the ultimatum was given but the effective date of termination, which occurred when the employees did not turn up to work.

Unlike other areas of employment law, it may be relevant to look not only at the day of dismissal but also at the specific time of dismissal. This was made clear by the National Industrial Relations Court in Heath and anor v JF Longman (Meat Salesmen) Ltd 1973 ICR 407, NIRC. In that case H and two others walked out on strike and received an ultimatum that, unless they returned to work, they would be dismissed. They decided that they would return to work and sent one of their number to inform the employer that the strike was over. On receiving this information, the employer told them that they were dismissed. The tribunal hearing their claim decided that the employees were taking part in industrial action on the date of dismissal. The NIRC decided that in this context there were special reasons for taking account of fractions of a day, as opposed to taking the day as a whole. In the NIRC's view, it is the time of dismissal which is relevant for S.238 purposes. Therefore, the employees were not taking part in the strike at the time of their dismissal.

Communicating the dismissal. A dismissal will not take effect until it is **8.63** actually communicated to the employee or he or she has had reasonable opportunity to learn of it. Thus, where dismissal letters reach employees *after* they have returned to work, they will not have been taking part in the action at the time of their dismissal and the tribunal will have jurisdiction to hear the claim. In Hindle Gears Ltd v McGinty and ors 1985 ICR 111, EAT, two employees returned to work while their dismissal letters were in the post. The EAT held that the employees had to receive the letters or at least have had an opportunity to learn of their dismissal before they could be said to be dismissed.

The potential complexity of determining the date of dismissal and all the relevant employees at that date is illustrated by Ramalheira and ors v Bloomsbury Health Authority EAT 698/87. In that case eight domestic assistants refused to work as a result of a dispute with their employer. They congregated outside a disciplinary hearing on Friday 9 August, at which it was decided that they should be dismissed. M, one of the eight, along with a union official, went to see the committee and was told of the decision to dismiss, which he then communicated to the other seven outside. Letters of dismissal, dated Monday 12 August, were written and received. During the intervening weekend, P, one of the eight, returned to work.

It was crucial, on the above facts, to determine when the date of dismissal of **8.64** the six employees, excluding M and P, occurred. If it fell on the Friday, the tribunal would have jurisdiction to hear the claims of the six since a relevant employee – namely P – would not have been dismissed. However, if they were dismissed on the Monday, the tribunal would only have jurisdiction to hear the

207

claim of M, who had been specifically and personally told of the dismissals. The tribunal, upheld by the EAT, decided that it could not be said that M was acting as an agent of the health authority in communicating the decision to dismiss to those assembled outside the disciplinary hearing. Consequently, M was dismissed on the Friday and the rest when they received their dismissal letters on the Monday and the tribunal only had jurisdiction to hear the claim relating to M's dismissal, as P was still taking part in the industrial action when M was dismissed but not when the others were dismissed.

The dismissal of individuals who have indicated that they will be taking industrial action, but have not yet commenced any collective action at the time of the dismissals, will not usually fall within S.238. The threat to take action does not usually constitute action, although it was held to do so in Lewis and Britton v E Mason and Sons 1994 IRLR 4, EAT (see further 'Does a threat to take action amount to industrial action?' above). However, once the action has commenced, then employees may be assumed to be taking part in it unless they have made their non-participation clear, even if they have not actually been due at work because, for example, they were on a different shift – Winnett v Seamarks Brothers Ltd 1978 ICR 1240, EAT.

8.65 Successive industrial action. It may be more difficult to determine whether an individual is taking part in industrial action at the date of dismissal where there is a series of, for example, one-day strikes or one-day works-to-rule. In Sams and ors v Chamberlain Phipps Coatings Ltd ET Case No.39351/81 the tribunal held that in a programme of such action an employee can be dismissed even when, on the day of dismissal, he or she is prepared to work normally, unless the employer has been told that his or her participation is at an end. But if the employer knows that one-off action will last only for a short while (for example, a protest walk-out for the remainder of the working day), the EAT has held that the employer will only be able to rely on S.238 where the employees are effectively dismissed during that action – Lookers of Bradford Ltd v Mavin and ors EAT 332/80.

In the case of a threat by a union to hold a one-day strike every week until a better pay offer is received, it is arguable that the reasoning in the Lookers of Bradford case should apply – i.e. the individuals must actually be on strike so that the employer can rely on S.238. This is because on the days between the strikes the employees are prepared to work normally and the next strike will only take place if a better offer is not forthcoming.

8.66 Dismissal of relevant employees

Under S.238 a tribunal will not have jurisdiction to hear a complainant's unfair dismissal claim unless the employer has selectively dismissed (or re-engaged) some of the relevant employees involved in the industrial action, but not all. The time for deciding whether the employer has been 'picking and choosing' is at the conclusion of the tribunal hearing to determine jurisdiction. This was established by the Court of Appeal in P and O European Ferries (Dover) Ltd v Byrne 1989 ICR 779, CA. In that case 1,025 employees (including B) were dismissed while on strike. B claimed that one relevant employee – referred to as 'Mr X' – had not been dismissed and that therefore S.238 did not apply. The company requested details of the identity of Mr X so that it could know the case it had to meet. The Court of Appeal granted the order for particulars of Mr X's identity, and the employer swiftly dismissed him, thereby frustrating all 1,025 claims. The Court ruled that the time for deciding whether all relevant employees had been dismissed was the end of the substantive hearing, which involves determining the jurisdiction point as well or, where appropriate, the end of the preliminary jurisdictional hearing prior to going on, or not going on, as the case may be, with the substantive hearing. Accordingly, the employees would have had to disclose Mr X's identity at some point during the hearing anyway.

The Court added that it was necessary and proper that the particulars should be given, even though they might also have the effect of enabling the employer to take action to frustrate the employees' claims. That was the inevitable result of the legislation. The effect of this decision is essentially to provide employers with the necessary time and relevant information to dismiss any employees whom they had not already dismissed and thus preserve their immunity from unfair dismissal claims. Note, however, that where an employer dismisses an employee after the strike or other action is over in order to maintain his immunity, the real reason for dismissal may in fact not be connected with the dispute at all. Accordingly, employees so dismissed may claim unfair dismissal in the normal way.

8.67 Another problem arises where a relevant employee has stopped working for the employer before the employer has had a chance to dismiss him or her. This situation arose in Manifold Industries Ltd v Sims and ors 1991 ICR 504, EAT, where two employees, W and T, had been participating in the industrial action at the time of the claimants' dismissals and were therefore relevant employees for the purposes of S.238. However, they had not been dismissed but had voluntarily resigned at some point after the dismissals. The claimants argued that the tribunal therefore had jurisdiction to hear their claims because W and T were two relevant employees who had not been dismissed. The EAT rejected this argument. It stated that when, at the hearing to determine jurisdiction, the tribunal looked to see whether any relevant employees had not been dismissed, only those still in the employ of the employer should be considered. It should disregard any employees who had voluntarily resigned since the complainant's dismissal. The EAT accepted that S.230(1) ERA specifically defined 'employee' to include ex-employee (the same definition of employee is also contained in S.295(1) TULR(C)A), but stated that for the present purposes 'employee' should have 'its normal meaning of an individual who is engaged under a

209

contract of employment and thus those who are dead, have retired or have voluntarily resigned all fall to be disregarded'. To rule otherwise, claimed the EAT, would be to frustrate the whole purpose of the section's provisions, which is to expose employers who selectively dismiss employees during industrial action, while protecting those who have not so discriminated.

The burden of proving that all relevant employees were dismissed is neutral. In Smith v Lex Wilkinson Ltd EAT 661/84 an employee argued that a tribunal had erred in law because it appeared to hold that the employee had the burden of proving that all relevant employees had been dismissed. The employee argued to the contrary that the burden should be placed on the employer. The EAT held that the language of S.238 denoted a neutral burden and so it lay on neither employer not employee. Accordingly, it was for the tribunal to decide on the evidence whether all relevant employees had been dismissed.

8.68 Selective re-engagement

Under S.238(2)(b), tribunals will acquire the jurisdiction otherwise lost when an employer dismisses all the 'relevant employees' but then offers some, but not all, of them re-engagement within three months of their dismissal. (Note that it is the date of dismissal of the re-engaged employee(s), not of the complainant, that is important here.) After the three months have elapsed, the employer can pick and choose by offering re-engagement to only some of the employees whom he dismissed for taking part in the industrial action and S.238 will defeat any unfair dismissal claims from those dismissed employees not re-engaged.

In order for there to be a re-engagement of a dismissed person who has participated in industrial action (i.e. a relevant employee), it is necessary for the employer either to have actual knowledge of the circumstances of the dismissal or constructive knowledge of those circumstances – Bigham and anor v GKN Kwikform Ltd 1992 ICR 113, EAT. In that case B was re-engaged two months after being dismissed while taking part in industrial action. While accepting that the manager who re-engaged B did not know he had been dismissed previously, the EAT found that, as all that had been necessary was a telephone call to another depot, the manager ought to have known that there had been a dismissal. Consequently, an employee who had not been re-engaged and who had been dismissed with B could claim unfair dismissal.

8.69 **Offers of re-engagement.** The first point to note is that the employer only has to *offer* re-engagement – it does not matter if the offer is refused. Nevertheless, the offer must satisfy the statutory requirements of S.238(4), which defines an offer of re-engagement as 'an offer (made either by the original employer or by a successor of that employer or an associated employer) to re-engage an employee, either in the job which he held immediately before the date of dismissal or in a different job which would be reasonably suitable in his case'.

210

Section 235(1) ERA defines 'job' as 'the nature of the work which [the employee] is employed to do in accordance with his contract and the capacity and place in which he is so employed'. The job does not have to be offered on exactly the same terms and conditions as before since 'capacity' covers the kind of task required to be done rather than the relationship with the employer or the terms of the contract itself.

In Williams and ors v National Theatre Board Ltd 1982 ICR 715, CA, a re-engagement offer was made on the basis that the strikers would return to work but would be treated as being on the final warning stage of the disciplinary procedure. W and others argued that this offer did not count as a proper offer of re-engagement and that since another striker had been re-engaged without any alteration in her disciplinary status, the employer had selectively re-engaged, so that the tribunal had jurisdiction to hear their unfair dismissal complaints. The Court of Appeal held that the definition of 'job' did not include the employee's disciplinary status or employment terms which did not relate to the nature of the work, capacity or workplace. It was irrelevant that another employee had been offered re-engagement on different terms. **8.70**

Where the terms and conditions offered do amount to a change in the job, the second limb of the definition of a re-engagement offer in S.238(4) will apply – i.e. the different job will have to be reasonably suitable for the employee. This will obviously be a question of fact in each case but very few instances have come before the tribunals. However, it is clear that changes in the form rather than the substance of the contract will not make the job unsuitable, nor will changes in conditions necessarily do so. In one case a changed job title (which reflected the kind of work actually done before dismissal) and the additional conditions that unfair dismissal complaints would be withdrawn and that employees would not be paid for the period between dismissal and re-engagement were held not to affect the suitability of the job – Vine and ors v Harris (Ipswich) Ltd COET 906/188. However, in another case an offer that did not take into account health problems which had been accommodated before dismissal was held not to be 'reasonably suitable' for the employee – Wadkin v George Armitage and Sons plc ET Case No.18104/82.

What amounts to an offer of re-engagement? While it is clear that an offer must have been made by the employer, tribunals have sometimes taken a liberal approach as to what amounts to an offer. For example, it does not necessarily have to be in writing. In Marsden and ors v Fairey Stainless Ltd 1979 IRLR 103, EAT, as a result of an oversight an employee did not receive a letter offering re-engagement that had been sent to all other strikers. He did, however, know of the terms of the offer and believed that it applied to him. The EAT decided that he had sufficient time to respond to the offer and that there had been no selectivity in the offers of re-engagement. By contrast, in Tomczynski v JK Millar Ltd 1976 ITR 127, EAT, the employee was unable to understand the **8.71**

211

nature of an oral offer on account of his deafness. The EAT held that no effective offer had been made in his case.

Furthermore, an offer of re-engagement does not have to be a positive offer but may be tacit or implied. In Bolton Roadways Ltd v Edwards and ors 1987 IRLR 392, EAT, the employer thought that an employee was on strike when he was dismissed. The employee subsequently informed the employer that he was in fact sick and he was duly reinstated. The employer argued that no offer of re-engagement to the employee had been made but that he had 'slid back into employment' when he informed the company of his excuse, which was accepted as genuine. It claimed that an offer for S.238 purposes had to be couched in genuine terms and was more than a tacit acceptance of continuing employment. The EAT held that an offer of re-engagement meant no more and no less than that the employee's job was being held open for him, which is what happened in this case.

8.72   In some circumstances an employer may be held to have made an offer when acceding to a request by an ex-employee for re-engagement. In Golden Sunrise (Pies) Ltd v W and S Hamill EAT 640/80 a friend of the dismissed employee asked her employer to re-engage her. When she was re-engaged, other dismissed employees claimed that the tribunal had jurisdiction to hear their unfair dismissal complaints because she had been offered re-engagement and they had not. The EAT held that she had in effect been made an offer, notwithstanding the fact that the initiative had come from the employee, because the ultimate decision whether or not to re-employ her lay with the company.

Tribunals will construe whether an offer has been made from the general circumstances and the intent of the employer. In Mills and ors v Lloyds British Testing Co Ltd ET Case No.4478/83 a tribunal held that the employer's attitude merely showed that it wanted to open amicable negotiations with an employee and it made no clear-cut offer of employment. The tribunal further stressed that an offer could not have been made because the person holding the negotiations did not have the authority to make such an offer. An offer from an employer to re-engage must be made by someone with the requisite authority.

A highly publicised recruitment campaign does not constitute an offer to any particular person. In Crosville Wales Ltd v Tracey and ors 1993 IRLR 60, EAT, following the dismissal of 73 employees who refused to call off their strike action, the employer conducted a highly publicised recruitment drive. The ex-employees were well aware that the employer was recruiting from those who applied for the jobs, even if they had just been dismissed for striking, and they knew that if they applied they stood a good chance of being re-engaged. The EAT held that all that the employees had been presented with was the opportunity of having an offer made to them, should they choose to apply, and that this was not the same as an offer of a job. This was to be contrasted with Williams and ors v National Theatre Board Ltd 1982 ICR 715, CA, where each employee received an individual letter inviting him or her to apply for re-engagement. Those letters were considered offers of re-engagement.

Timing of offer of re-engagement. An employer is not obliged to offer re-engagement to all dismissed strikers at the same time. It is simply necessary for all the relevant employees to have been offered re-engagement within three months of their dismissal. In Highland Fabricators Ltd v McLaughlin 1985 ICR 183, EAT, the employer re-engaged the dismissed employees gradually within a three-month period. One employee was not re-engaged in the first batch of employees and by the time he was offered re-engagement he had found another job. He claimed that the tribunal had jurisdiction to hear his unfair dismissal claim because he had not been offered re-engagement at the same time as many of his colleagues. The EAT disagreed and held that it was irrelevant that he had been offered re-engagement later than his workmates. The EAT further noted that the three months were a cooling-off period to enable unions and employers to pick up the pieces after a dispute. This process would be wrecked if employees who are overlooked in the first batch of re-engagements are immediately entitled to enter unfair dismissal claims. **8.73**

Similarly, in Engineering Utilities and Installations Ltd v Rosser EAT 553/84, E Ltd dismissed 12 employees and later offered nine of them re-engagement. A fortnight later, after being told by Acas of the consequences of selective re-engagement, they offered re-engagement to the other three, one of whom, R, declined the offer and claimed unfair dismissal. The EAT, overturning the tribunal's decision, decided that R had clearly been offered re-engagement within three months and so the employer was still afforded the protection of S.238. This reasoning is borne out by the fact that the time limit for bringing a claim under the selective re-engagement provisions is six months from the date of dismissal – as opposed to the usual three months in unfair dismissal claims – as employees will not know whether they effectively have a claim until the lapse of three months from their dismissal – S.239(2).

Reasonableness of dismissal
8.74

If the tribunal's jurisdiction to hear a claim of unfair dismissal is not barred by S.238, then the tribunal must decide whether the dismissal was fair in accordance with the normal rules under S.98 ERA – see generally IDS Employment Law Handbook, 'Unfair Dismissal' (2005). The employer will first have to show a potentially fair reason for dismissal and the tribunal will then have to decide whether dismissal for that reason was a reasonable response in the circumstances. However, going on strike or taking part in industrial action will not usually be capable of amounting to such a reason because if dismissal for one employee was justified, it would have been justified for all those who had participated. The employer must therefore justify dismissal on other grounds such as 'misconduct' during the action or 'some other substantial reason'. Selective dismissals have been held to be fair in cases where the employee has been involved in violence on the picket line – Hameed v Sunblest Bakeries (Stevenage) Ltd ET Case No.3578/79, or has damaged the employer's premises during the strike – Wilson and anor v Acres the Bakers Ltd ET Case No.1336/79. Continuing a strike after a national agreement has settled the dispute can also make selective dismissal fair – Barnes and ors v Metal Box Ltd ET Case No.18221/78.

In Glenrose (Fish Merchants) Ltd v Chapman and ors EAT 467/91 the EAT upheld a tribunal's finding that an employer who did not investigate employees' grievances concerning a change in their employment terms relating to overtime unfairly dismissed them when they carried out an overtime ban. The purpose of the ban was a protest to get the employer to discuss the changing situation with them. The tribunal was satisfied that the employer had shown a potentially fair reason for dismissal, namely the employees' conduct, but found the dismissal unfair because the employer had refused their several attempts to have a meeting and had done nothing to find out why his long-serving and loyal employees had decided to take such a stand.

8.75 **Procedure.** A fair procedure leading to the dismissal is still essential when employers dismiss employees for taking part in a strike or other industrial action. This was emphasised by the Court of Appeal in McLaren v National Coal Board 1988 IRLR 215, CA, where it stated that employers cannot deprive striking employees of their opportunity to answer charges of misconduct merely because they are participating in a heated industrial dispute. The Court of Appeal did concede that 'industrial warfare' might create a situation in which conduct not normally justifying dismissal might become conduct justifying dismissal, but standards of fairness are unchangeable. Employers cannot ignore procedural constraints merely because relations between management and unions are at a particularly low ebb.

8.76 **Fair selective re-engagement.** In the case of selective re-engagement it is specifically provided that the consideration of fairness applies to the reason for not offering re-engagement, rather than to the original reason to dismiss – S.239(3), although the surrounding circumstances of that dismissal may be relevant – Edwards and ors v Cardiff City Council 1979 IRLR 303, EAT. The employer must justify his grounds for not offering the complainant re-engagement and the same sorts of considerations will apply as apply to all unfair dismissal claims. For example, where an employee's work record would not have justified dismissal before the strike it would be unfair not to re-engage him or her on account of that conduct – Laffin and anor v Fashion Industries (Hartlepool) Ltd 1978 IRLR 448, EAT.

It may be possible for employees to invoke procedural factors in relation to their non-selection for re-engagement. In Goundry v Graham Charles Sportswear Ltd ET Case No.25184/30 G was told that she would not be re-engaged on account of her poor attendance and work record. A tribunal decided that refusing re-engagement in these circumstances was equivalent to dismissing her with no previous warning that her job was in danger and so her dismissal was unfair.

Compensation 8.77

In Courtaulds Northern Spinning Ltd v Moosa 1984 IRLR 43, EAT, the Appeal Tribunal held that the fact of an employee's participation in industrial action could not constitute contributory conduct warranting a reduction in the employee's compensation for unfair dismissal. This was because, in the EAT's view, the policy behind the special provisions on industrial action dismissals in S.238 was that an employment tribunal should be prevented from going into the rights or wrongs of an industrial dispute. A similar view was taken by the House of Lords in Tracey and ors v Crosville Wales Ltd 1997 ICR 862, HL, although for slightly different reasons. In their Lordships' view, it was simply impossible to allocate blame between those individuals taking part in industrial action, particularly in view of the fact that the collective blame for the action is shared by those employees who have been selectively re-engaged. This conclusion merely reflected the statutory requirement that the compensatory award must be such as is 'just and equitable'. However, while the mere fact of an individual's participation in industrial action cannot amount to contributory fault, there is an exception where the individual is guilty of blameworthy conduct that is additional to, or separate from, the mere act of participation. Such conduct may be capable of amounting to contributory fault.

An example of the kind of conduct their Lordships appear to have had in mind is provided by Crowther v British Railways Board EAT 762 and 1118/95, in which the EAT decided that the employee's actions in inciting industrial action outside the normal procedures for the industry could amount to conduct justifying a reduction in his compensation. As this decision suggests, it is the person who incites industrial action, as opposed to merely participating in it, who will be the most likely to have his or her compensation reduced. While, from one perspective, this certainly has a degree of logic about it, from another perspective it sets a dangerous precedent. The organisers of industrial action are those who are most likely to be victimised for taking industrial action and, as such, should not be unduly penalised if UK law is to genuinely protect the right to organise lawful industrial action. It is to be hoped, therefore, that so long as an individual is acting within the scope of normal procedures for calling industrial action and is not offending against the criminal law, the exception to the general rule set out by the House of Lords in the Tracey case will not be invoked.

The rules governing the award of compensation for unfair dismissal generally **8.78** are discussed at length in IDS Employment Law Handbook, 'Unfair Dismissal' (2005), Chapters 14–18.

215

8.79 Time limits

The general rule is that claims of unfair dismissal must be presented to the tribunal before the end of three months beginning with the effective date of termination – S.111(2) ERA. However, claims of unfair dismissal where the dismissal is connected with industrial action, or which are based on selective re-engagement after industrial action, are an exception to this rule. Such claims must be presented before the end of *six months* beginning with the complainant's date of dismissal – S.239(2)(a) TULR(C)A. The date of dismissal is the date when notice is given, if dismissal is with notice. In other cases, it is the effective date of termination – S.238(5). This extended time limit recognises the fact that a selective re-engagement may take place at any time up to three months after dismissal.

A tribunal may hear a complaint presented outside the relevant time limit if it considers that it was not reasonably practicable to present it within the time limit and it was presented within a reasonable time after that – S.239(2)(b).

8.80 The rules governing time limits generally are discussed in IDS Employment Law Handbook, 'Employment Tribunal Practice and Procedure' (2006), Chapter 3.

9 Industrial action and employment rights

Detriment short of dismissal

Pay

Redundancy payments

Guarantee payments

Continuity of employment

Notice rights

Time-off rights

9.1 Industrial action can have an effect on a wide range of employment rights other than the right not to be unfairly dismissed. This chapter looks at the effect of industrial action on pay, redundancy payments, guarantee payments, continuity of employment, notice rights and time-off rights. First, however, we consider the position of employees who suffer a detriment short of dismissal as a result of taking part in industrial action.

Detriment short of dismissal 9.2

As explained in the previous chapter, an employee has some protection from dismissal for taking part in industrial action under Ss.237, 238 and 238A of the Trade Union and Labour Relations (Consolidation) Act 1992 (TULR(C)A). However, there is no statutory protection for an employee who is subjected to a detriment short of dismissal by his or her employer because he or she has taken part in industrial action. The TULR(C)A contains specific provisions protecting individuals from both detriment and dismissal on grounds related to union membership or activities – Ss.146 and 152 respectively. But it was established in Drew v St Edmundsbury Borough Council 1980 ICR 513, EAT, that for the purposes of unfair dismissal law, there is a distinction between trade union membership or activities on the one hand and industrial action on the other and that the reason for dismissal must fall within one or the other, but not both. And in London Borough of Islington v Hutchings EAT 34/01, a case concerning suspension without pay, the EAT found that the same distinction applied in respect of detriment falling short of dismissal.

Consequently, an employee who is subjected to a detriment short of dismissal for taking industrial action is left without a remedy in so far as statutory rights

217

are concerned. (The question of whether this complies with Article 11 of the European Convention on Human Rights and Fundamental Freedoms is discussed below.) However, employees may have some comeback – albeit less than satisfactory – where the employer's retaliation amounts to a *breach of contract*. To take a hypothetical example: in retaliation for an employee taking strike action, the employer decides to withhold an annual performance bonus, which forms part of the employee's contractual terms. Since the removal of a contractual benefit amounts to a breach of contract, in the normal course of events (i.e. where no industrial action is taking place), an employee faced with such an action may have a remedy for breach of contract in the civil courts. However, where the employee is taking part in industrial action, the employer is likely to argue that the employee is him or herself in fundamental breach of contract and therefore cannot rely on his or her rights under the contract. In these circumstances a court may well be reluctant to uphold the employee's claim.

9.3 Another avenue open to an employee who suffers a detriment short of dismissal as a result of taking industrial action would be to treat his or her contract as terminated and pursue a claim of unfair constructive dismissal under S.98 of the Employment Rights Act 1996 (ERA). In order for a constructive dismissal claim to succeed, the employer's action would have to amount to a repudiatory breach of contract entitling the employee to resign. Once a constructive dismissal is shown, the issue becomes one of fairness under the ERA.

The timing of the employer's action will make a difference here. In our hypothetical example, if the employer withdraws the employee's contractual benefits *during* protected industrial action, the resulting constructive dismissal will be unfair under S.238A TULR(C)A since the question of reasonableness under S.98(4) ERA does not arise. This is because under S.238A, if the reason for the dismissal is that the employee took protected industrial action, the dismissal is automatically unfair.

If, on the other hand, the employer withdraws the bonus once the industrial action has *finished* and is therefore acting outside the protected period for the purpose of S.238A, the reason for the constructive dismissal will be 'some other substantial reason of a kind such as to justify dismissal of the employee' under S.98(1)(b) ERA. The tribunal would then have to decide whether the employer acted reasonably in dismissing for that reason. This will depend to a large extent on whether the tribunal is of the opinion that the dismissal was justified in light of the fact that the employee had taken industrial action.

9.4 It would seem, therefore, that the success of an action in the civil courts for breach of contract or in the tribunal for unfair constructive dismissal will depend in large measure on whether the court or tribunal takes the view that the removal of the contractual benefit was justified by the fact that the employee was taking industrial action. In domestic law this may well lead to an unfavourable outcome for the employee.

However, Article 11 of the European Convention on Human Rights may be of relevance here. In Enerji Yapi-Yol Sen v Turkey (Application No.68959/01), ECtHR, the European Court of Human Rights held that the right to strike under Article 11 is a fundamental (albeit qualified) human right. Since then there have been several decisions of the Court holding that national law permitting the imposition of a detriment for exercising that right is an impermissible impediment and amounts to an unjustified breach of Article 11(1). (See, for example, Danilenkov v Russia (Application No.67336/01), ECtHR, where the detriment involved the assignment of less work, resulting in reduced income, and discriminatory selection for redundancy; and Kaya and Seyhan v Turkey (Application No.30946/04), EctHR, where the detriment took the form of a written disciplinary warning 'to be more attentive to the accomplishment of his/her functions and in his/her behaviour'.) Article 11 is discussed further in Chapter 1 under 'International obligations'.

It is arguable therefore that the absence of protection from suffering a detriment short of dismissal for taking industrial action is inconsistent with Article 11. There are obvious difficulties in a court or tribunal asserting that an employee's exercise of his or her human rights amounts to a reason justifying a breach of contract by the employer or a constructive dismissal. A similar argument would arise if, rather than bringing a constructive dismissal claim, the employee argues (or the employer alleges) that he or she has been expressly dismissed and immediately re-engaged on different terms.

9.5 An untested question is whether an employee can claim constructive dismissal as a result of the employer's repudiatory breach of contract where he or she is almost certainly already in breach of contract him or herself (since industrial action will almost always amount to a breach of contract). In RDF Media Group plc and anor v Clements 2008 IRLR 207, QBD, the High Court held that an employee could not accept repudiation by an employer where he or she was already in repudiatory breach of a mutual obligation – in this case, the implied obligation not to destroy mutual trust and confidence. However, the Court there was clearly concerned with *mutual* obligations and it is arguable that an employee would not be prevented from pursuing a claim where the employer sought to unilaterally impose a contractual variation – such as, in our hypothetical example, the removal of the contractual bonus.

In any case, there may be an argument that any breach of contract committed by the employee in taking industrial action has been accepted by the employer, thereby affirming the contract, on the basis that the new terms can only apply if it is accepted that the employment relationship continues. Under that analysis, the employee's breach effectively disappears and his or her legal position would be the same as if the industrial action had never occurred.

9.6 Pay

The right to be paid is dependent upon the employee being ready and willing to work. Employees are not, therefore, entitled to be paid for any period during which they are on strike. However, when employees take industrial action short of a strike and perform some, but not all, of their contractual duties, the position is not quite so straightforward. Action falling short of a complete withdrawal of labour usually amounts to a breach of contract and the employer, when faced with such a breach, can choose whether or not to accept the partial performance which is offered, or has been undertaken, by the employee. The question then arises as to the extent to which the employer is entitled to deduct wages from the employee in order to reflect his losses in not having the work performed, or not performed properly.

The right to remuneration during periods of industrial action is determined solely in accordance with the contractual principles set out below. The statutory protection against deductions from wages contained in Part II of the Employment Rights Act 1996 (ERA) does not apply where the reason for the deductions is that the worker has taken part in a strike or other industrial action – S.14(5) ERA (see Sunderland Polytechnic v Evans 1993 ICR 392, EAT, affirmed in Scott v Strathclyde Fire Board EAT 0050/03, in which the EAT confirmed that this is the correct interpretation of the legislation). That said, S.14(5) does not prevent an employment tribunal from hearing a claim in order to establish whether the claimant was in fact taking part in such action for the purposes of determining jurisdiction – Gill and ors v Ford Motor Co Ltd; Wong and ors v BAE Systems Operations Ltd 2004 IRLR 840, EAT.

9.7 Where an employer refuses to accept partial performance, the employee is not entitled to be paid for any services rendered. The contractual right to remuneration depends on the employee being ready and willing to perform *all* of his or her contractual duties. This principle was established by the House of Lords in Miles v Wakefield Metropolitan District Council 1987 ICR 368, HL. In that case M, a registrar of births, deaths and marriages, worked a normal 37-hour week, which included three hours on Saturday mornings – the most popular time for weddings. During a period of industrial action he refused to conduct weddings on Saturdays, although he remained willing to do other work at these times. For the rest of the week he worked normally. The Council made it clear to M from the start that it would not accept partial performance of his duties. So long as he remained unwilling to fulfil all of his duties, he need not work Saturdays at all as he would not be paid for this time. M attended on Saturdays nevertheless but the Council deducted 3/37ths of his salary during the period of the industrial dispute. The issue to be decided was whether the Council was permitted to make this deduction from M's pay.

The House of Lords stated that where an employee, as a form of industrial action, refuses to perform his or her full contractual duties and offers only partial performance, the employer can choose whether or not to accept the partial performance. If he chooses not to accept it, then the employee is not entitled to remuneration even for those services which he or she does perform. To be entitled to remuneration, the employee must be prepared to perform all the work he or she is contractually obliged to do. Accordingly, since M was not prepared to carry out all his duties on Saturdays, he was not entitled to be paid for those days. The Council was therefore entitled to make the deductions that it did.

Where an employer does accept partial performance, he cannot refuse to pay the employee. This principle was established by the Court of Appeal in Wiluszynski v Tower Hamlets London Borough Council 1989 ICR 493, CA. W was a housing officer employed by Tower Hamlets Council. During a pay dispute he took part in limited industrial action in the form of a refusal to answer enquiries from councillors. These enquiries were only a minor part of W's duties (at the end of the month-long strike it took him only three hours to make good the backlog). In all other respects he performed his duties normally. The Council, however, informed W that it was not prepared to accept partial performance and refused to pay him any salary at all for the period of the industrial action. W brought a claim for breach of contract which succeeded in the High Court but was overturned by the Court of Appeal. Lord Justice Fox, giving the leading judgment, held that, in accordance with the Miles decision (above), W was not entitled to any pay because he had not been willing to perform all his contractual obligations. However, the position would have been different had the Council given W directions to work or acted in any other way which would have disentitled it from asserting that W had no right to be paid. In other words, an employer may not accept partial performance offered by an employee and then refuse to pay anything at all.

The vital consideration, then, is whether the employer has made it clear to the employee that he is not accepting partial performance, and does in fact refuse to accept it. However, what amounts to acceptance may not always be clear cut. In the Wiluszynski case the employer wrote to the employee telling him that his partial performance would not be accepted and that any work he did carry out would be considered purely voluntary. It also went through something of a ritual by repeating this warning to W every morning when he turned up for work during the period of industrial action. Nevertheless, W continued to perform all but a tiny part of his contractual obligations and his head of section continued to provide him with work, although this was against the express instructions of the Council. In deciding whether the Council had accepted this partial performance, the Court of Appeal stressed that it is necessary to assess the genuineness of the employer's rejection of the partial performance – employers cannot simply state that they are refusing to accept **9.8**

221

it when their actions tell another story. The Court came to the conclusion that in this case W had been adequately warned that he would receive no pay unless he performed his contract to the full and the Council as a whole did nothing contrary to its avowed intention not to accept partial performance, despite the actions of W's manager.

It is clear from the above cases that an employer who declines to accept partial performance may accept the breach of contract and send the employees home without pay without having to terminate their contracts – Miles v Wakefield Metropolitan District Council (above). If, however, the employees continue to turn up for work, the employer cannot be expected to take action physically to prevent them from doing so, but must make it absolutely clear that partial performance is not accepted and that any work they do do will be treated as having been done on a purely voluntary basis – Wiluszynski (above).

9.9 Withdrawal of goodwill

Industrial action may take many different forms but in most cases it will be possible to determine from the terms of the contract of employment whether the work that the employee carries out amounts to full or partial performance. However, the position is not so clear where employees go on a deliberate 'go-slow' or otherwise work in a manner which is less than satisfactory. Lord Bridge in Miles v Wakefield Metropolitan District Council (above) declined to express any opinion on an employee's entitlement to remuneration in these circumstances, saying that 'there may be no single, simple principle which can be applied in such cases irrespective of differences in circumstances'. However, in British Telecommunications plc v Ticehurst and anor 1992 ICR 383, CA, the Court of Appeal held that the withdrawal of goodwill constituted partial performance.

In that case T, a manager, took part in action which consisted of a period of one-day strikes and a general withdrawal of 'goodwill' in dealing with the employer. The union issued guidelines to its members as to how they could most effectively withdraw goodwill – such as refusing to cooperate with new working practices and adhering strictly to all health and safety procedures – and advised its members that withdrawing goodwill would not constitute a breach of contract. The Court of Appeal did not share the union's view. It noted that, under T's contract, she had a discretion whether or not to carry out certain functions. Her failure to carry out some of those tasks did not, therefore, amount to a breach of an express term of the contract. Nevertheless, her work-to-rule was 'not in honest exercise of choice or discretion for the faithful performance of her work but in order to disrupt the employer's business or to cause the most inconvenience that can be caused'. The Court held, therefore, that her withdrawal of goodwill was a breach of the implied term of faithful service to the employer.

Three further examples (all brought under the unlawful deductions from wages **9.10** provisions in Part II of the ERA):

- **Cambridge and ors v Turners Turkeys Ltd** ET Case Nos.2601360/97 and others: the claimants worked as turkey butchers and were paid piece work. As a result of a dispute about the size of the birds and damage done to them before they arrived, the claimants operated a go-slow whereby they butchered only two birds an hour. They refused to sign an agreement that they would work normally and were barred from the premises for three days, as a consequence of which they were unable to earn wages for that period. The employment tribunal held that the workers were taking part in industrial action and, in any case, were not entitled to be paid as they had failed to comply with a contractual obligation to work to the best of their skill and ability

- **Baker and ors v North-East Derbyshire District Council** ET Case No.2801606/98 and others: the Council introduced a new refuse collection system designed to do away with the 'task and finish' system whereby a crew could go home early on a Friday if all its work was finished but still be paid a full week's pay and receive a bonus. The Council made it clear that workers who disrupted the new system would be sent home without pay. Crews continued to turn up for work to carry out their normal collections but refused to clear the backlog and as a result were sent home without pay. The tribunal held that the workers' refusal to carry out instructions to clear the backlog amounted to 'other industrial action' for the purpose of S.14 ERA, since it was connected with the reluctance to use the new working system, and they were therefore excluded from pursuing their claims for unlawful deduction of wages

- **Bradley and anor v Derbyshire County Council** ET Case Nos.2601039/00 and 2601192/00: a large number of home helps refused to participate in a trial of a new time-recording system. The Council wrote to them warning that they were in breach of contract and that it proposed to reduce their wages by 15 per cent if they continued their refusal. It asked them to complete a certificate stating that they would use the new system and if the certificate was not returned it would assume that the home help had decided not to use it and would receive only 85 per cent of his or her salary. Two home helps who were found to be acting independently of the union – one because she was not a member, the other because she disagreed with the union's stance and had voted against industrial action – pursued claims for unlawful deduction of wages. The tribunal found that the claimants' 'independence' was irrelevant since each had aligned herself with the hundreds of home helps who had acted in the same manner by refusing to participate in the new recording system. Both had refused to sign the certificate. Consequently, they were taking part in industrial action.

223

Since the intention behind all industrial action is to disrupt the employer's business or to inconvenience him in some way, it is difficult to envisage any form of industrial action that would not involve some sort of breach of contract. Where such a situation arises, the employer is entitled to send the employees home without pay – which is tantamount to forcing them to go on strike – and, more importantly as far as their wages are concerned, deprive them of the opportunity to receive any remuneration. The Court of Appeal's ruling in British Telecommunications plc v Ticehurst and anor (above) therefore provides employers with a very strong weapon in their armoury against industrial action.

9.11 Payment for partial performance

One issue that none of the above cases has fully resolved is whether, and on what basis, an employer who does accept partial performance can nevertheless deduct a proportion of the employee's salary. One approach, adopted by Mr Justice Scott in Sim v Rotherham Metropolitan Borough Council 1986 ICR 897, ChD, is to apply the doctrine of equitable set-off, thereby entitling employers to deduct appropriate sums for the losses suffered as a result of the employee's breach of contract. The doctrine of equitable set-off allows a party to withhold the whole or part of a sum he or she has contracted to pay to another party in circumstances where he or she would have a valid defence or counterclaim if that other party were to sue for breach of contract.

The difficulty with such an approach lies in quantifying what loss is actually suffered by an employer as a result of an individual employee's breach. For instance, in Wiluszynski v Tower Hamlets London Borough Council (above) the loss could not be readily apportioned to any part of the working week. And in Miles v Wakefield Metropolitan District Council (above) the employee argued that the employer had suffered no loss at all from his breach because its effect was merely to inconvenience members of the public. The House of Lords thought little of this argument, however, stating that the loss of services of a worker taking industrial action was in itself damage to the employer, and that the value of that loss will always be at least equal to the salary payable for the employee's services. Their Lordships held that since an employee is only entitled to be paid when he or she is ready and willing to work, he or she is not entitled to recover wages for a period during which he or she is not willing to perform his or her contractual obligations. Accordingly, the employer was entitled to deduct 3/37ths of M's salary for each Saturday on which he refused to work normally.

9.12 An alternative approach, favoured by Lords Templeman and Brightman in the Miles case, is that an employee who only partially performs his or her contract is not entitled to be paid anything under the contract as such, but is entitled to be paid for the services he or she has provided on a quantum meruit basis ('as much as he deserves'). However, Lord Bridge was sceptical of this approach since the application of the doctrine of quantum meruit presupposes that the

224

contract of employment has been superseded in some way by a new agreement, which is not the reality of the situation during industrial action. This view was echoed by the county court in Spackman v London Metropolitan University 2007 IRLR 744 where the proposition that quantum meruit applied was rejected on two grounds: first, per Lord Bridge, because the contract of employment subsists during the industrial action; and secondly, because industrial action relies on its collective effect rather than the withdrawal by one individual of his or her labour, and an assessment of the value of work undertaken by an individual fails to address this reality.

In Cooper and ors v Isle of Wight College 2008 IRLR 124, QBD, the High Court held that the amount of the deduction should be limited to the sum that the workers would be able to sue for under their contracts had they not been on strike (but had not been paid), and should not, as the employer had contended, reflect the overall losses to the employer as a result of the strike action. Since the claimants' contracts apportioned salary over the days of the normal working week throughout the year, the College was entitled to deduct a day's pay in the sum equivalent to 1/260 of the claimants' salary to take account of weekends but not in the sum equivalent to 1/228 to take account of holidays as well. The Court also rejected an argument that the additional deduction could be justified by way of equitable set-off, distinguishing this case from Sim v Rotherham Metropolitan Borough Council (above) because there was no counterclaim for damages for breach of contract.

Remedies   9.13

Where an employer has withheld some or all of an employee's pay on account of participation in industrial action, the employee can challenge that deduction in the High Court or county court. An employee will only be able to bring a claim in the employment tribunal for breach of contract if the claim is outstanding on the termination of the employee's employment and does not exceed £25,000 (S.3 of the Employment Tribunals Act 1996 and the Employment Tribunals Extension of Jurisdiction (England and Wales) Order 1994 SI 1994/1623; Employment Tribunals Extension of Jurisdiction (Scotland) Order 1994 SI 1994/162). As mentioned above, no claim can be made under the protection of wages provisions contained in Part II of the ERA.

In exceptional circumstances, employees who believe that their wages have been improperly withheld by their employer may be able to obtain a High Court injunction. Injunctions are occasionally granted as an interim measure to oblige the employer to pay full wages pending the full hearing of a breach of contract claim. There are two types of injunction: mandatory and restraining. A mandatory injunction requires the employer to pay the wages, while a restraining injunction has the effect of preventing it from withholding them. Mandatory injunctions are rarely granted, as was emphasised by Mr Justice Auld in Jakeman and ors v South West Thames Regional Health Authority and

225

London Ambulance Service 1990 IRLR 62, QBD, where ambulance workers involved in a pay dispute refused to comply with the procedure laid down by their employer for making radio contact in emergency situations. The employer subsequently withheld two weeks' wages for the period of this limited industrial action, arguing that the ambulance workers' partial performance had not been accepted and that they were therefore not entitled to be paid. The High Court refused to grant a mandatory interim injunction ordering the employer to pay the wages withheld pending the full trial. Auld J held that a party seeking such an injunction needed, in the absence of special circumstances, to have a clear case in law, i.e. it must be apparent that the defendant has no prospect of making out a defence. The case was far from clear here and temporary hardship did not amount to a special circumstance.

9.14 Auld J went on to state that courts are disinclined to grant mandatory injunctions in cases arising from industrial disputes as to do so is likely to give one side much greater bargaining power than the other. Restraining injunctions are apparently less likely to have this effect. Thus, in situations where an employer proposes to withdraw wages, employees would do best to apply for a restraining interim injunction, the granting of which is governed by the less stringent 'balance of convenience' test. Clearly, though, if the employer has already withheld wages, the only option is to seek a mandatory injunction, and the employee's chances of success would appear to be slim.

When employees refuse to carry out their full contractual duties, the courts are unlikely to grant an injunction unless there is clear evidence that the employer has accepted partial performance. In MacPherson v London Borough of Lambeth 1988 IRLR 470, ChD, the introduction of a new housing benefit scheme led the Council to invest in a new computer system. Negotiations between the employer and the employees' union broke down and the Council issued instructions to all housing officers involved in the new system requiring them to undertake the necessary duties to ensure that the system went online. The Council stated that a failure to do this would result in pay being withheld. The employees applied to the High Court for an interim injunction to compel payment of wages already withheld and to prevent the Council from withholding their pay in the future. Mr Justice Vinelott refused the application. The officers were unable to perform their full contractual duties without using the new computer system and there was no evidence that the Council had accepted partial performance. If the issue remained in dispute, then it could be resolved at the full trial of the action.

Note that courts do not have the power to compel an employee to work. S.236 of the Trade Union and Labour Relations (Consolidation) Act 1992 prohibits a court from ordering specific performance of a contract of employment or from granting an injunction restraining a breach or threatened breach of such a contract.

226

Redundancy payments 9.15

A dismissal by reason of redundancy will normally give rise to entitlement to a redundancy payment, even if it takes place in the context of industrial action. But if the true reason for the dismissal is the employee's participation in industrial action, then there will be no right to a redundancy payment. If, however, the employer dismisses for redundancy but would have been justified in dismissing the employee summarily for gross misconduct – which will normally include participation in industrial action – then a special statutory scheme applies. This is discussed in detail below. First, though, we consider the approach tribunals take when deciding whether the reason for dismissal is redundancy or industrial action.

Reason for dismissal 9.16

Industrial action may force an employer to close the business or cut the workforce, thereby giving rise to a redundancy situation. The question has arisen of whether the employees who took the action and who, in a sense, caused the redundancy situation are still entitled to redundancy payments. The reason for the redundancy situation is irrelevant to the question of whether a redundancy payment is due; it is the reason for the dismissal which counts. Therefore, if the employees were truly dismissed for redundancy they are entitled to redundancy payments. The question of whether an employee was dismissed by reason of redundancy or for taking part in the industrial action is one for the tribunal to decide on the evidence. Two illustrations:

- **Fenn v Mirror Group Newspapers Ltd** EAT 28/81: after a long history of unofficial action the employer decided to dismiss the participants in one particular strike. It also closed down the magazine on which the strikers worked and made the rest of the staff redundant. The EAT held that the reason for dismissing the strikers was that they were a disruptive influence. Although they had caused other people to be made redundant, the reason for dismissal of the strikers was not redundancy

- **Sanders and ors v Ernest A Neale Ltd** 1974 ICR 565, NIRC: some employees took industrial action and the employer threatened to dismiss them unless they undertook to work normally. No such undertaking was given and the threat was carried out. The employer subsequently closed the factory and wound up the business altogether, giving redundancy payments to those employees who had not taken part in the industrial action. The NIRC said that there was clearly a redundancy situation, but it had not caused the dismissals of those taking industrial action.

In Webb and ors v Sundaw Products Ltd and anor EAT 477/79 the EAT had to consider a lock-out by the employer, followed by closure of the business, when the employees refused to accept new terms and conditions of employment. It

227

upheld the tribunal's finding that action meant to compel the acceptance of new terms was inconsistent with an intention to close the business, so that it was the refusal of the new terms that caused both the closure and the accompanying dismissals, and not the closure that caused the dismissals. It followed that the employees had not been dismissed because of redundancy.

9.17 Where an employer may have more than one motive for deciding to dismiss employees involved in industrial action, it is a question of fact which was the dominant or principal reason. An example:

- **Baxter and ors v Limb Group of Companies** 1994 IRLR 572, CA: the employees imposed an overtime ban after a long-running dispute with management over bonus payments. The company warned them that the action might lead to their dismissal and when the employees refused to call it off they were summarily dismissed. Subsequently, the employer decided to dispense with directly employed labour and the work done by the dismissed employees was contracted out. A tribunal held that the employer's decision to contract the work out meant that there was a redundancy situation at the time of the dismissals and awarded the employees a redundancy payment. The EAT overturned the tribunal's decision and a majority of the Court of Appeal also thought that the tribunal had erred. In Lord Justice Dillon's view, the test was quite simple – if the employer dismisses all the employees who refuse to call off industrial action and engages new employees, the reason for the dismissal is industrial action. In his opinion it made no difference to that reason that the employer chose to obtain the replacement workers as contract labour from another company, rather than directly employing new staff.

It is clear in the above case that there was a redundancy situation as soon as the employer made the decision not to replace the workforce with directly employed labour. The difficulty only arises in determining the real or principal reason for the dismissals. If the employer dismissed the employees simply because the company could no longer tolerate industrial action from the employees, that was the real reason and the employees were not redundant. If, on the other hand, the employer simply chose that moment to change the means by which labour was bought, and that was the dominant motive, then a redundancy situation would be the cause of the dismissals. The Court of Appeal concluded, on the facts of the case, that the industrial action was the principal cause of the dismissals.

9.18 Redundancy and misconduct

Section 140(1) ERA provides that an employee loses the right to a redundancy payment if his or her conduct is such that the employer is entitled to dismiss without notice – i.e. if the employee is guilty of gross misconduct – and the employer does dismiss:

228

- without notice, or
- with shorter notice than required by contract or statute, or
- by giving full (or more than full) notice accompanied by a written statement that the employer would, because of the employee's conduct, have been entitled to dismiss without notice.

This is a puzzling provision. As stated above, an employee is only entitled to a redundancy payment if he or she is dismissed because of redundancy. If the employee is dismissed for gross misconduct – and industrial action will usually fall within this category – it stands to reason that he or she will not be in a position to claim a redundancy payment. Quite simply, the principal reason for the dismissal will be the misconduct, not redundancy. At first glance, therefore, S.140(1) appears to be otiose. However, the explanation appears to be that S.140(1) deals with a situation where the employer is entitled to dismiss for gross misconduct, but in fact dismisses for redundancy. It will only come into play where there is a dismissal for redundancy of an employee who is guilty of gross misconduct (of which the employer may not be aware at the time of dismissal). The employee will then be disqualified from receiving a redundancy payment if the dismissal takes one of the forms set out in S.140(1). However, this is subject to the exceptions discussed below.

Industrial action during the notice period 9.19

There are two important exceptions to S.140(1). These apply where the misconduct warranting summary dismissal occurs *after* notice of redundancy has been given.

The first exception deals with participation in a strike. Section 140(1) does 9.20 not apply if an employee who has been given notice of redundancy is dismissed for taking part in a strike during the obligatory notice period (defined below) in circumstances which entitle the employer to treat the contract of employment as terminable without notice – S.140(2). Where this provision applies, the employee's right to a redundancy payment will be unaffected by the strike. Strikes in this context are defined in S.235(5) as strikes about terms or conditions of employment.

The obligatory period of notice is the period ending on the date of expiry of the employer's notice which is equal in length to the statutory notice period under S.86 ERA or to the employee's contractual notice entitlement, whichever is the longer – S.136(4). In other words, the obligatory period is the same length as the minimum notice the employer may give to terminate the contract lawfully. If the employer chooses to give more notice than the minimum required by statute or the contract, the obligatory period is still the minimum period, but is calculated backwards from the date of expiry of the notice. For example, if an employee has three years' service he or she will be entitled to three weeks'

229

statutory notice. If the employer gives six weeks' notice of redundancy then – provided the employee has no separate contractual entitlement to notice – the last three weeks of the employer's six weeks' notice will be the obligatory period. If, however, the same employee has a contractual entitlement to four weeks' notice under his or her contract, it is the last four weeks of the employer's notice which will be the obligatory period. Since the obligatory period is likely to differ from one employee to the next, it follows that some employees will forfeit their redundancy pay while others will not.

9.21 Section 140(2) only applies when an employee goes on strike after having been given notice of redundancy – it does not operate if an employee is dismissed for redundancy when already on strike. This is illustrated by the following case:

- **Simmons v Hoover Ltd** 1977 ICR 61, EAT: about 150 employees, including S, had been on strike for some two and a half months when the employer sent them letters giving one week's notice of redundancy. The strike was settled and the other employees returned to work, but S had found another job and claimed a redundancy payment instead. The EAT held that striking was a repudiatory breach of contract entitling the employer to dismiss S without notice. He was therefore barred from any entitlement to a redundancy payment by virtue of S.140(1) and S.140(2) did not apply.

Section 140(2) also applies where an employee who has given a notice of intention to claim a lay-off or short-time redundancy payment is dismissed for taking part in a strike after the service of the notice. But if an employee is dismissed he or she is barred from claiming lay-off or short-time redundancy – S.151. Any claim for a redundancy payment would have to be based on the express dismissal by the employer, who will not be able to rely on S.140(1) to disqualify the employee.

9.22 **The second exception deals with other misconduct during the notice period.** As we have seen, S.140(2) deals solely with strikes. Other types of industrial action fall within S.140(3) and (4), which give tribunals a wide discretion to award the whole or part of a redundancy payment where an employee is dismissed for other misconduct during the obligatory notice period (or after the employee has served notice of intention to claim a redundancy payment because of lay-off or short-time). Thus, where the employee is dismissed for other types of industrial action the tribunal may award that amount of the redundancy payment that it considers 'just and equitable' in the circumstances.

9.23 **Extension of notice period after strike**
As explained above, if an employee goes on strike during the obligatory notice period the employer cannot rely on S.140(1) to exclude the right to a redundancy payment. But the employer does have another option: namely, requiring the employee to make up the working days lost through the strike by working

230

through an extended notice period as a prerequisite to the employer agreeing to pay a redundancy payment.

Section 143 contains the rather complicated statutory scheme. Briefly, if an employee goes on strike when under notice of dismissal for redundancy, the employer may serve a written notice of extension requesting him or her to extend the employment contract by the number of working days lost because of the strike. The employer's written notice must:

- indicate the employer's reasons for making the request

- state that the employer will contest liability to make a redundancy payment if the employee does not comply with the request, unless the employer is satisfied that the employee cannot comply with the request – e.g. because of sickness or injury – or that it is not reasonable in the circumstances for the employee to comply with it – S.143(2).

9.24 The employee will be taken to have complied with the notice of extension by actually turning up for work on each working day during the specified extension period – S.144(1). If the employee complies with the notice of extension, then the notice of termination is deemed to have effect as if the period specified had been extended by the period set out in the employer's written request. If the employee does not fully comply with the request but turns up on only some of the days during the period of extension, the contract is treated as continuing up to the last day on which the employee turns up to work – S.143(7)–(8). If the employee does not comply at all, then the original notice takes effect. (The importance of knowing when the contract terminates will arise in relation to matters such as pension rights and the protection of pay during the notice period.)

If the employee does not comply precisely with the employer's request – i.e. does not turn up on all the days requested – he or she will lose entitlement to a redundancy payment (unless the employer agrees to pay one anyway) and must apply to a tribunal for an 'appropriate payment'. The tribunal may then award a redundancy payment in whole or in part if it is satisfied that the employee was unable, because of sickness, injury or the like, to comply with the employer's request, or that it was reasonable for the employee not to comply with it – S.143(3)–(6). The amount of the award is a matter for the tribunal's discretion.

Lay-off and short-time

9.25 Sections 147–154 ERA provide the means whereby employees can claim redundancy pay from their employer after they have been laid off or put on short-time for a specified period. Industrial action affects this right since S.154(b) states that, when calculating the number of weeks during which the employee was laid off or on short-time, no account shall be taken of any week when the lay-off was caused wholly or mainly by a strike or lock-out. Note that the strike or lock-out need not involve the particular employer or employee. Indeed, the strike or lock-out can occur in a different company, in a different trade or industry, and even in a different part of the world. The strike or lock-out must, however, be one that comes within the definitions contained in S.235(4) and (5). This means that employees *are entitled* to count a week when they were laid off because of a strike or lock-out that was *not* related to terms and conditions of employment. Likewise, employees can count weeks when the lay-off was on account of industrial action short of a strike.

9.26 Guarantee payments

Where employees are laid off in accordance with their contracts, they are usually entitled to claim a statutory guarantee payment for each workless day for a limited duration – S.28 ERA. However, the laid-off employee will lose this entitlement where the failure to provide work occurs in consequence of a strike, lock-out or other industrial action involving any employee of the employer or an associated employer – S.29(3). The exclusion is not restricted to industrial action arising out of a trade dispute – a purely 'political' strike will bring the exclusion into play. Note that there is no need for the laid-off employee to be involved in the industrial action to be deprived of guarantee pay. It is enough that other employees of the employer or an associated employer are involved – Ibbett and ors v Birds Eye Foods Ltd ET Case No.2171/78.

9.27 Involvement in industrial action

Industrial action only precludes a guarantee payment if it involves employees of the employer or of an associated employer. In Newman and ors v Edward Hanson Ltd ET Case No.6817/80 the employer supplied contract labour to the British Steel Corporation. When there was a national steel strike it laid off its workforce. It argued that the strike 'involved' its employees. The tribunal said that 'involving' must have a narrower meaning than 'affecting': it must mean that the employees 'had an interest in' or were 'participating' in the strike. The employees were in no way participating in any dispute with the British Steel Corporation and they were therefore entitled to guarantee payments.

However, whether or not there was 'involvement' for the purposes of the Act in any particular case is a question of fact for the tribunal to decide. For example, in McMonagle and ors v Cementation Mining Co ET Case No.19126/84 it was held that a refusal to cross picket lines was involvement in industrial action. Subcontractors to the National Coal Board did not physically participate in the 1984 miners' strike, but they were members of the National Union of Mineworkers and they refused to cross picket lines. They were held to have been 'involved' in the strike. Similarly, in Garvey v J and J Maybank (Oldham) Ltd 1979 IRLR 408, ET, the employer was a paper merchant who used road haulage contractors as well as its own fleet of lorries. During a road haulage strike its own drivers refused to obey the employer's order to cross the picket-lines set up by the road haulage drivers. The tribunal held that the employees had thereby become 'involved' in a dispute with their own employer, so that employees laid off in consequence were not entitled to a guarantee payment.

In Slack v Jones t/a JJ Engineering ET Case No.33319/79 the employer was a **9.28** subcontractor on a maintenance contract for a brewery. He refused to cross a picket-line at the brewery because he was afraid of being 'blacked' and he sent his employees home without pay. A tribunal dismissed the employees' claims for guarantee payments, not on the basis that the claimants were involved in industrial action but on the ground that the employer had not failed to provide work. The work was there to be done on the other side of the picket line and it was the pickets, not the employer, who were preventing access to it. However, this decision is difficult to reconcile with that in Peplow v Bennett Swiftline (Birmingham) Ltd ET Case No.37871/81, where the tribunal awarded guarantee payments when a subcontractor laid off his workforce because of a strike on a customer's premises. The tribunal took the view that the strike, which did not involve the employees, was an 'occurrence' affecting the normal working of the business.

Causation
9.29
The lay-off must be in consequence of industrial action. Even if the employer establishes that there was relevant action for the purposes of resisting a guarantee payment, it must still be shown that the failure to provide work was caused by that action. However, tribunals have taken the view that the action need not be the sole cause. Two examples:

- **Thomson v Priest (Lindley) Ltd** 1978 IRLR 99, ET: T claimed a guarantee payment for a lay-off, which the employer claimed was occasioned by a strike at the factory of an associated employer. T argued that the strike was only one of a number of factors causing the lay-off and that the strike alone would not have resulted in the lay-off. The tribunal dismissed his claim. It held that the strike need not be the sole cause of the lay-off. The correct test is to ask whether, but for the strike, there would have been a lay-off. In the instant case there were certainly a number of economic factors contributing to the lay-off, but these had remained constant for several months. The immediate cause of the lay-off was the strike and therefore T was not entitled to a guarantee payment

- **Lawrence and ors v Landywood Cabinet Co Ltd** ET Case No.5574/86: L was laid off when his employer encountered a shortage of parts. The employer claimed that the shortage was a result of the employees' own industrial action in terminating an unsatisfactory bonus scheme. The tribunal, by a majority, decided that the employees were not taking industrial action by exercising their right under a collective agreement to cancel the bonus scheme but,

233

even if they had been taking action, that action had not been the cause of the lay-off. There were other factors – such as the seasonal lull in work and the disruptive effects of a new foreman – that were the overwhelming cause of the slow-down in production. L was therefore entitled to his guarantee pay.

9.30 Continuity of employment

An employee becomes entitled to most (but not all) statutory employment rights only after a qualifying period of continuous employment with an employer. Many rights also increase in size or value in line with the length of continuous employment – for example, the entitlement to a redundancy payment or to statutory notice. The statutory scheme governing the calculation of periods of continuous employment is considered in detail in IDS Employment Law Handbook, 'Continuity of Employment' (2001). Briefly, continuity is calculated on a week-by-week basis and any complete week which does not count as continuous employment breaks continuity. This section deals specifically with the situation where an employee is absent from work because he or she is involved in a strike or lock-out. Broadly speaking, under S.216 ERA periods of absence from work on account of a strike or lock-out do not break continuity, but nor do they count in calculating a period of continuous employment.

9.31 Meaning of 'strike'

Any week during which, or during part of which, an employee takes part in a strike does not count towards a period of continuous employment – S.216(1). However, such periods spent on strike do not break continuity either – S.216(2). 'Strike' is defined in S.235(5) for the purpose of calculating continuity of employment as '(a) the cessation of work by a body of employed persons acting in combination, or (b) a concerted refusal, or a refusal under a common understanding, of any number of employed persons to continue to work for an employer in consequence of a dispute, done as a means of compelling their employer or any employed person or body of employed persons, or to aid other employees in compelling their employer or any employed person or body of employed persons, to accept or not to accept terms or conditions of or affecting employment'. It makes no difference whether the strike is official or unofficial, supported or not supported by a properly held ballot. Any strike that meets the above definition will be a strike for the purpose of S.216.

A stoppage of work that does not come within the above definition will not be a strike and S.216 will not apply. The definition only covers strikes over terms and conditions of employment, so a 'political' strike, for example, would not come within the definition of 'strike' in S.235(5). Thus, in Adewusi v George Wimpey and Co Ltd ET Case No.13034/72 a tribunal decided that an employee's withdrawal of labour on Mayday and on other days to protest at the passing of the Industrial Relations Act 1971 did not amount to a strike. The employee's absences therefore had no impact on his period of continuous employment. Similarly, continuity is not affected by industrial action short of a strike.

Dismissal of strikers

9.32

Section 216 preserves the continuity of employment of an 'employee' taking part in a strike. This has led to the contention that if an employee is dismissed while on strike, and is subsequently re-employed, his or her continuous employment will be broken as he or she was no longer an 'employee' during the break in employment. However, in Bloomfield and ors v Springfield Hosiery Finishing Co Ltd 1972 ICR 91, NIRC, the National Industrial Relations Court held that striking employees continue to be employees even if dismissed unless the employer replaces them on a permanent basis or they take other jobs on a permanent basis or the employer closes down the business or workplace permanently. In this context 'employee' means somebody who, but for his or her action in ceasing or refusing to continue to work, would be an employee. In other words, the dismissal of strikers who are subsequently re-employed does not of itself break continuity. An example:

- **Hanson v Fashion Industries (Hartlepool) Ltd** 1981 ICR 35, EAT: H, an employee with seven years' service, took part in a strike that lasted nine weeks. The employer dismissed all the strikers but re-engaged them on new contracts when the dispute was over. H's new contract stated that no employment with a previous employer would count towards her continuity of employment and that her employment began on the date of the new contract. The EAT held that H's continuity was preserved during the strike action by virtue of what now is S.216. The fact that H was dismissed did not affect this conclusion.

The situation appears to be different if an employee is dismissed while taking part in a strike that does not come within the S.235(5) definition (see above). If an employee is dismissed during such a strike and is then re-engaged when the strike is over, he or she will find that the original contract of employment was terminated and that he or she cannot rely on S.216(2) to protect his or her continuity of employment. Thus, if the break between the dismissal and the re-engagement was greater than one week, the employee's continuity will be broken. However, since the vast majority of strikes do fit the S.235(5) definition, and those that do not tend to be of very short duration, the matter may be largely academic.

The Court in the Bloomfield case (above) stated that striking employees cease 9.33 to be employees if they have taken on another job on a permanent basis during the strike. This implies that employees can take temporary jobs elsewhere during a strike without breaking continuity, provided they intend to return to their old jobs once the strike is over. Tribunals have applied this distinction between temporary and permanent jobs in the following cases:

235

- **Weathers v Marshall Fowler Ltd** ET Case No.11346/73: W took a temporary job during a lock-out but returned to his original job as soon as the lock-out was over. A tribunal found that continuity was preserved because of his intention to return

- **Yates v Ruston Diesels Ltd** ET Case No.21453/83: Y took a new job during a stoppage but subsequently left it to return to his old one. There was evidence, though, that he had initially treated the new job as permanent – by joining the staff pension scheme. A tribunal held that his continuity was therefore broken.

9.34 'Taking part' in a strike

Section 216 only applies to preserve continuity where an employee's absence from work is on account of his or her 'taking part' in a strike. If absence is for this reason, and the employee returns to work, continuity of employment is not broken, although the period of absence does not count towards the employee's period of continuous employment. If, however, an employee is absent but is not taking part in the strike, continuity may be broken if the contract does not subsist. Much will depend on the duration of the absence and the reason for it. It is therefore important to establish whether an employee who is absent during a strike is 'taking part' in that strike, or is absent for another reason.

The question of whether or not an employee is taking part in a strike is dealt with fully in Chapter 8 in relation to industrial action dismissals. In this regard, the case law on 'taking part' in industrial action for the purposes of Ss.237, 238 and 238A TULR(C)A applies equally to situations where the continuity of employment of an employee is in issue. Although those cases are authority for what constitutes 'taking part' in a strike for the purposes of S.216 ERA, it should nevertheless be remembered that S.216 is confined to industrial action amounting to a *strike* as defined in S.235(5) ERA (see above under 'Meaning of "strike"'), whereas Ss.237, 238 and 238A TULR(C)A extend to all industrial action, including action short of a strike.

9.35 Employees do not always return to work immediately once a strike is over. Often employers agree with unions to have a phased return to work, so that some sections of the workforce return before others. In such a situation, those employees who are neither taking part in a strike nor back at work will be caught in a precarious kind of limbo. The question may then arise as to whether the period between the strike ending and the resumption of work breaks continuity. The situation arose in Clarke Chapman-John Thompson Ltd v Walters 1972 ICR 83, NIRC, where the employees were dismissed while on strike. The employer arranged a phased return to work after the strike was over, which meant that W was not re-employed until two weeks later. The Court got round the problem outlined above by ruling that the reason the employee was away from work during the two weeks in question was that the employer had no work for him. This was a 'temporary cessation of work' and counted under S.212(3)(b) as a period of continuous employment. If such an interpretation had not been possible, and no other provision could assist, the two-week gap would have broken continuity.

Effect of strikes on period of continuous employment 9.36

When an employee takes part in a strike, the start of his or her period of continuous employment is deemed to be 'postponed' by a certain number of days – S.211(3). This is the actual number of days (not the number of working days) falling within the period 'between the last working day before the strike and the day on which work [is] resumed' – Ss.211(3) and 216(2). There is an absence of case authority explaining precisely how the postponement of the deemed start date of an employee's period of continuous employment works in this context. However, it is probable that, in computing the number of days that fall to be deducted from the start of an employee's period of continuous service on account of a strike, neither the working day before the strike nor the actual day on which work was resumed following the strike is deducted. It is the number of days in the period between those two dates that are added up and then deducted from the actual date an employee's continuous employment began in order to give the deemed starting date.

It may be useful to illustrate how this works in circumstances where an employee works a five-day week, Monday to Friday. If the employee takes part in a strike that starts on a Monday and ends on a Wednesday, then four days fall to be deducted from the start of his or her period of continuous employment. That is because the employee's last working day before the strike was a Friday (which does not fall to be deducted) and the day he or she resumed work after the strike was the following Wednesday (which also does not fall to be deducted). The intervening period of actual days (as opposed to working days) comprises Saturday, Sunday, Monday and Tuesday – hence a total of four days. If an employee begins and ends a strike on the same day (other than a Monday), no days are deducted from the period of the employee's continuous employment since there is no intervening period between the last working day before the start of the strike (which does not fall to be deducted) and the day on which the employee resumes work (which again does not fall to be deducted). But a bizarre consequence follows if it happens that an employee employed on a five-day working week takes part in a one-day strike that both begins and ends on a Monday. In such circumstances, the last working day was a Friday and the day on which work was resumed was a Monday. Although neither of those days falls to be deducted, in between there are two actual (non-working) days – Saturday and Sunday: it would seem on a strict reading of Ss.211(3) and 216(2) that the employee's deemed starting date so far as his continuous employment is concerned would therefore be postponed by two days.

237

9.37 Once it is established that the employee took part in the strike, it seems that under S.216(2) he or she will lose all the days that the strike lasted, even if he or she only took part in it for a day. In other words, an employee who joined the strike late or went back to work early will lose the same number of days from his or her period of continuous employment as one who stayed out for the whole duration of the strike. Similarly, a part-time employee would lose the same number of days from his or her period of continuous employment as a full-time colleague even if, for example, he or she normally only worked one day a week.

It should be noted that, if construed literally, the statutory provisions allow an employee to suffer a double deduction. This is because S.216(1) states that any week during the whole or part of which an employee takes part in a strike does not count towards his or her period of continuous employment. And S.216(2) goes on to provide that if the employee takes part in a strike, his or her start date is postponed by the appropriate number of days (see above). This means that a striking employee stands to be penalised twice in respect of any period during the whole or part of which he or she was on strike. It is strongly arguable, however, that this double deduction is not intended and that a tribunal should apply the provisions postponing the employee's start date and allow the actual strike weeks to stand.

9.38 Lock-outs

At first sight, the treatment of lock-outs so far as the effect on continuity is concerned is similar to that of strikes and is governed by S.216(3). That subsection states that 'the continuity of an employee's period of employment is not broken by a week if during the week... the employee is absent from work because of a lock-out by the employer'. 'Lock out' is defined in S.235(4) as: '(a) the closing of a place of employment, (b) the suspension of work, or (c) the refusal by an employer to continue to employ any number of persons employed by him in consequence of a dispute, done with a view to compelling persons employed by the employer, or to aid another employer in compelling persons employed by him, to accept terms or conditions of or affecting employment'. There is a lock-out within this definition whether or not the employer dismisses the employees.

But there is one crucial difference in the way the statutory provisions deal with the effect of lock-outs on continuous employment. This arises from the way in which the relevant provisions treat continuity when an employee's contract subsists throughout a strike or lock-out. Neither a strike nor a lock-out necessarily causes the contract of employment to be terminated, so it is possible for the contract to subsist throughout an employee's absence from work on account of either of these events – see Express and Star Ltd v Bunday and ors 1988 ICR 379, CA. Given that S.212(1) provides that each week during which an employee's employment is governed by a contract of employment counts towards his or her continuity of employment, then (unless the statute provides otherwise) an employee whose contract subsisted throughout a week during the whole or part of which he or she was on strike or locked out would be entitled to include that week when calculating the period of his or her continuous employment. But in the case of a strike the statute does indeed provide otherwise, since, as we have seen above, S.216(1) specifically states that 'a week does not count under S.212 if during the week, or any part of the week, the employee takes part in a strike'. However, no such provision is made in the case of a lock-out. There is nothing, therefore, to prevent the ordinary rule in S.212(1) from applying. In consequence, if an employee's contract subsists during a lock-out, any week during which the lock-out occurs counts towards the period of continuous employment by virtue of S.212(1) and continuity remains entirely unaffected.

This raises the question: what is the effect of a lock-out on an employee's **9.39** continuity if the contract does not subsist – e.g. because the employer dismisses the employee immediately prior to the lock-out and re-engages him or her once it is at an end? In such cases, S.216(3) applies. This provides that although the lock-out does not itself break continuity, the number of days falling within the period 'between the last working day before the lock-out and the day on which work [is] resumed' are deducted from the start of the employee's period of continuous employment. This mirrors what happens in the case of strikers – whether or not their contracts subsist throughout the strike: see 'Effect of strikes on period of continuous employment' above. What does not happen, however, in the case of a locked-out employee is that he or she does not stand to suffer a double deduction in the way that strikers potentially do. For whereas the number of days during which the lock-out occurred falls to be deducted from the start of the period of the employee's continuous employment, no question arises of the entire week during the whole or part of which an employee was locked out not counting towards the total period of his or her continuous employment. This is because of the absence in the case of lock-outs of any provision equivalent to S.216(1).

The way in which the calculation is made of the number of days to be deducted from an employee's start date for the purpose of S.216(3) is exactly the same as that which applies to employees taking part in strikes. For an explanation of this, see 'Effect of strikes on period of continuous employment' above.

Agreement concerning continuity   **9.40**

Sometimes employers and unions agree, as part of the negotiated return to work, that strikers' continuity of employment will not be adversely affected by a strike or lock-out. Although such an agreement might well be binding so far as contractual rights are concerned, it will have no relevance to the calculation of an employee's period of continuous employment for the purposes of statutory rights. In other words, it is not open to the employer and employee to agree

239

that continuity is not broken in circumstances when, by virtue of the application of the provisions of the ERA, it clearly is.

9.41 Notice rights

As a general rule, employees' pay is protected during the statutory notice period (i.e. the minimum notice period to which employees are entitled under S.86 ERA) – Ss.88 and 89 ERA. Employees who do not work for some or all of the days of their notice period will still be entitled to their pay provided that they are:

- ready and willing to work but no work is available

- incapable of work because of sickness or injury

- absent from work wholly or partly because of pregnancy or childbirth, or on adoption, parental or paternity leave; or

- absent from work in accordance with the terms of their employment relating to holidays.

Thus pay is protected even though normal sick pay entitlement has run out or other employees are only receiving guarantee pay.

9.42 However, taking strike action has a serious effect on this entitlement to notice pay. First, a strike (or for that matter any industrial action amounting to a serious breach of contract) will entitle the employer to dismiss the employee summarily. Since Ss.88–89 apply only to dismissals with notice, an employee dismissed without notice for taking industrial action will have no right to any notice pay. This is so even if the employee's statutory notice period has begun at the time of the summary dismissal – in such cases the employer need not pay for the unexpired period of notice falling after the termination of the employment – S.91(4).

Secondly, where the *employee* gives notice to terminate the contract and then goes on strike, S.91(2) disqualifies him or her from receiving any payment under Ss.88–89 for the remainder of the statutory notice period. This is so even if the employee returns to work after an hour. Where, on the other hand, it is the *employer* who has given notice, an employee who goes on strike does not lose his or her basic right to notice pay, but he or she will forfeit payment for the days not worked while on strike because he or she is not 'ready and willing to work'. In this situation, assuming the employer chooses not to dismiss the employee for the repudiatory breach, his or her pay is still protected for the days when he or she is not on strike. It follows that where an employee tries to return to work and is not allowed to do so, he or she must be paid, because he or she is now ready and willing to work.

240

Time-off rights

While members of recognised independent unions are given the right under S.170 TULR(C)A to take reasonable (unpaid) time off to participate in union activities, S.170(2) specifically provides that they are not entitled to take time off to participate in union activities which consist of industrial action – such as, for example, attending mandatory union meetings held for the purpose of disrupting the employer's production schedules.

Union officials, on the other hand, who are acting in their official capacity in relation to a dispute, for example, by representing members who are taking action, are entitled to paid time off for specified activities under Ss.168 and 169 TULR(C)A. The amount of time off and the circumstances in which the employee is permitted to take time off are those which are reasonable in the circumstances having regard to the relevant provisions of the Acas Code of Practice on 'Time Off for Trade Union Duties and Activities' (2003) – S.168(3).

In Oxford and County Newspapers v McIntyre and anor EAT 95/86 the EAT **9.44** held that a union meeting to consider proposals for strike action was capable in law of constituting a union duty under S.168 TULR(C)A and therefore it would not interfere with a tribunal's decision that the complainants were performing union duties for which they were entitled to paid time off (even though no conclusion was reached at that meeting as to whether to strike and the question was left open for the membership to decide). The EAT did indicate, however, that time off for planning industrial action directly damaging to the employer – even where it amounts to a union duty – might sometimes reasonably be refused.

The McIntyre case should be contrasted with the situation where an official is actually *participating* in industrial action. Participation will prevent the official from claiming either paid or unpaid time off, even for the time that he or she acts as a go-between in negotiations – see, for example, Mottershead v Nu-Swift International Ltd ET Case No.35494/80. But, as the Code of Practice says, an official may be representing members who are taking industrial action without taking part him or herself, and in those circumstances normal arrangements for time off with pay should apply.

The right to time off for union duties and activities is dealt with in IDS Employment Law Handbook, 'Trade Unions' (2000), Chapter 6.

10 Industrial pressure to dismiss

Redeployment

Causation

Contributory conduct

Joinder of third parties

Right not to be subjected to detriment

An employer can be faced with a situation in which his workforce demands, for **10.1** whatever reason, that a certain employee be dismissed, and backs up this demand by taking, or threatening to take, industrial action. S.107 of the Employment Rights Act 1996 (ERA) states that in such a case an employer who responds to the action by dismissing the employee in question will not be able to rely on the industrial pressure as the reason for the dismissal if the employee subsequently brings a claim before a tribunal.

Reason for dismissal
10.2

Section 107 provides that in deciding the main reason for dismissal and whether it was reasonable to dismiss:

- no account shall be taken of any pressure to dismiss exerted by way of industrial action or any threats of industrial action

- any such question is to be decided as if no such pressure has been exerted.

Section 107 creates a legal fiction whereby the real reason for dismissal has to be ignored. So, if the only reason for the dismissal which the employer can show is pressure from industrial action, the tribunal is bound to find the dismissal unfair because the employer has failed to establish a potentially fair reason as required by S.98(1) ERA – Hazells Offset Ltd v Luckett 1977 IRLR 430, EAT. However, if the employer had another reason for dismissal – even if it was not the principal reason – the tribunal will ignore the industrial pressure and determine the fairness of the dismissal on the merits of the subsidiary reason.

The subsidiary reason must have existed *at the time of dismissal*. In Trend v **10.3** Chiltern Hunt Ltd 1977 ICR 612, EAT, the employer had in mind to dismiss an employee for misconduct but refrained from doing so until fellow employees presented a petition calling for the strongest action possible against him. The employer was left with no doubt that the petitioners were prepared to take action. The EAT held that either the threat contained in the petition led to dismissal and the employer could not establish misconduct as the reason – S.107

243

applied and the dismissal was unfair because the employer was unable to establish a reason – or the misconduct was not a good ground on its own for dismissal.

Even if the employer can show a subsidiary reason for dismissal, the dismissal may well be unfair since the tribunal will have to be satisfied that the employer acted reasonably in treating that subsidiary reason as a fair reason for dismissal – S.98(4). But, as in the Trend decision, the very fact that it is a *subsidiary* reason may mean that it is unlikely to have had sufficient bearing on the decision to dismiss to make the dismissal for the subsidiary reason fair. In reaching a decision on the question of reasonableness, the tribunal must ignore the fact that industrial pressure was brought to bear – S.107(1)(c).

10.4 Pressure to dismiss

Not all pressure is caught by S.107. The section will only apply where the pressure consists of actual or threatened industrial action *and* its purpose is to force dismissal. Two cases illustrate this:

- **Leggett v Department of Health and Social Security** EAT 520/80: L had a long history of inharmonious working relationships. He had received several warnings about this and had been transferred to different offices a number of times. Eventually, his colleagues signed a letter complaining about him and demanding that 'action [be] taken against him as both sections are against working alongside him any more'. L was then suspended and later dismissed. The EAT held that the letter constituted pressure on management but it was doubtful if, by itself, it amounted to a threat of industrial action. In any event, it did not amount to pressure to *dismiss* so S.107 did not apply. This was a fair dismissal for misconduct

- **Knowles v Bacofoil Ltd** ET Case No.2738/80: K was a shift supervisor who spent too much time acting as honorary secretary of the company's social club to the detriment of his shift and the production bonuses of the shift operatives. They complained to their shop steward with a threat of taking industrial action and demanded that K's conduct be investigated by management. The tribunal held that the shift was not demanding K's dismissal and, in any case, it was not shop-floor pressure but K's conduct that caused his dismissal.

Dismissal need not be expressly demanded for S.107 to apply. Often the employees will simply be refusing to work with an individual. Whether S.107 applies in this situation will depend on all the circumstances. In the Leggett case (above), for example, the judge held that the demand that some action be taken was perfectly consistent with a demand that L's employment be relocated at another office. However, he did acknowledge that, for some employers, the only possible action that could be taken would be to dismiss. The leading case is:

- **Ford Motor Co Ltd v Hudson and ors** 1978 ICR 482, EAT: H and three others were ostracised by their workmates for complaining that their shop steward was not properly serving their interests. For over four months they were paid but not allowed to work. They were then offered jobs in different departments, but when these were refused all four employees were dismissed. On appeal, the EAT held that it is a question of fact whether pressure to dismiss was exerted on the employer. In order for S.107 to apply, it is not necessary that those exerting the pressure explicitly sought the dismissal of the employee. The proper test is whether *the pressure was such that dismissal was a foreseeable consequence*. An important factor is the likely reaction of an employee when ordered to transfer to another department.

Similarly, in Drake v Dunlop Ltd ET Case No.28844/78 D's colleagues refused **10.5** to work with him after an accident at work and threatened industrial action if he returned to his old job. He was then employed doing odd jobs in other departments but still at his old rate of pay, which meant that he was being paid more than his colleagues who were employed on more responsible work. This in turn caused unrest among the workforce, with the result that D was dismissed some ten months after his original colleagues threatened industrial action. The tribunal, applying the 'foreseeability of dismissal' test from the Ford case, held that S.107 applied.

The pressure to dismiss must be directed at the claimant. S.107 has no application if the pressure to dismiss relates to someone else. In Bray v Sealink UK Ltd EAT 493/85 two unregistered seamen worked for a shipping company on different ships. On one ship the crew threatened industrial action if the unregistered seaman was not dismissed. There was no pressure to dismiss on the other ship but the employer foresaw similar problems and so dismissed the other seaman. The issue for the EAT was whether, in order to fall within S.107, the pressure had to be for the dismissal of the employee claiming unfair dismissal, or whether pressure to dismiss another employee would suffice. The EAT held that the reference in S.107 to 'the employee' meant that the pressure must be to dismiss the person seeking relief and so the section did not apply in this case.

Redeployment 10.6

An employer may try to defuse the situation by redeploying the employee to another department, as either a temporary or a permanent measure. The employer must, however, make sure that he has a right under the employment contract to make such a transfer. If there is no right, the employer will be acting in breach of contract if he insists on the move. An employer may choose to dismiss the employee for the refusal to transfer. Alternatively, an employee may resign and claim constructive dismissal. In this situation, it is all the more likely that industrial pressure to move a colleague will amount to pressure to dismiss.

245

And if it is the *only* reason the employer can show for the move, then S.107 will apply and the employer will effectively have no reason for dismissal. An example:

- **Colwyn Borough Council v Dutton** 1980 IRLR 420, EAT: D was a driver in the litter collection department. His colleagues refused to drive with him because of his record of dangerous driving. They warned the employer that if any of them were disciplined for refusing to work with D they would take industrial action. D was offered other non-driving duties as a relief loader but, when he refused that offer, he was dismissed. At the tribunal, the employer tried to argue that there was no pressure to dismiss since the employees were only pressing for D to be taken off driving duties – they were perfectly content for him to continue as an employee of the Council. The EAT, however, pointed out that D could not be required under his contract of employment to take up the job of relief loader. The employees were therefore in effect pressuring the employer to terminate D's contract as a driver and to offer him alternative employment. This amounted to pressure to dismiss under S.107.

10.7 Where the employer does have the contractual right to transfer an employee, it may still be that pressure to have the employee moved will amount to pressure to have him or her dismissed. The EAT, in the Ford Motor case (above), said that, no matter what the contractual position, it will be relevant to the question of foreseeability that the circumstances were such that no self-respecting employee could, without great loss of face, have agreed to the move in the circumstances under which the move was demanded. An example:

- **British Leyland (UK) Ltd v Smith** EAT 443/77: S had been a tool setter for 16 years when he suddenly found himself out of favour with his fellow employees. The disagreement was over negotiations between union and management. S's colleagues brought pressure to bear on their employer to discipline S. The employer proposed various compromises – all of which involved, in effect, a downgrading. S refused to accept them. He was then ordered to move to a different job without loss of pay. When he refused, the employer dismissed him. The EAT held that even if S could be required under his contract of employment to change jobs, his dismissal for refusing to do so was still unfair since, first, S had acted reasonably in disobeying the order when to obey would have meant loss of face and, secondly, the employer did not order the transfer for good operational reasons but solely to appease the industrial pressure being brought to bear.

As mentioned above, employers need also be aware of the possibility of unfair constructive dismissal claims being brought against them where the employee objects to redeployment. For example, where the employer gives in to industrial pressure from (parts of) the workforce and moves an employee into a different role, this may amount to a breach of the implied term of mutual trust and confidence. This term, implied into every contract of employment, provides

246

that employers (and employees) will not, without reasonable or proper cause, conduct themselves in a manner calculated or likely to destroy or seriously damage the relationship of trust and confidence between the parties. Accordingly, a breach of the implied term would allow the employee to resign and claim unfair constructive dismissal. For more information on the implied term of mutual trust and confidence, see IDS Employment Law Handbook, 'Contracts of Employment' (2009), Chapter 2.

Causation   10.8

The pressure to dismiss must be the cause of the dismissal for S.107 to apply. In Trend v Chiltern Hunt Ltd 1977 ICR 612, EAT, the employees presented the employer with a petition calling for the strongest possible action to be taken against T as they did not wish to work with him. The employer decided to dismiss the employee the next day. However, as well as being unpopular with his colleagues, T was also guilty of various acts of misconduct. Considering his record, the tribunal was of the view that the employer was bound to have dismissed T at some stage. Nevertheless, it held that S.107 applied since it was the presentation of the petition which actually caused his dismissal. The EAT, upholding the tribunal decision, felt it was particularly relevant that earlier in the month the employer had the option to make T redundant or offer him other employment. Since it chose the latter, it was unlikely that his previous conduct justified termination.

Similarly, in James Ferries and Co Ltd v Johnstone EAT 489/84 a manager was guilty of provocation and violence against his subordinates and fellow employees and was eventually dismissed after employee pressure and limited industrial action. The EAT held that the real reason for the dismissal was the employer's fear of industrial action and so S.107 applied.

In both of the above cases the pressure from employees was the last straw 10.9 which led to the dismissal and was therefore the causative factor. By contrast, in Boreland v Gloucestershire County Council EAT 645/92 any industrial pressure from the claimant's co-workers, which had resulted in her suspension, was not the reason she was eventually dismissed by the employer. The tribunal found, and the EAT agreed, that the claimant's dismissal, taking place a year after the industrial pressure, had been on the ground of redundancy; by that time the employer's requirement for the work that she had been employed for had simply ceased or diminished.

Contributory conduct   10.10

The fact that an employee is dismissed in a case where S.107 applies does not prevent the tribunal finding that the employee's own conduct contributed to the dismissal and reducing the compensatory award accordingly. In some cases the

247

employee's behaviour in provoking the antagonism of his or her colleagues may constitute contributory fault. In Colwyn Borough Council v Dutton 1980 IRLR 420, EAT, where it was the incompetence of the employee that brought about the pressure to dismiss, the EAT expressed the view that the employee could be said to have contributed to his own dismissal. And in Sulemanji v Toughened Glass Ltd and anor 1979 ICR 799, EAT, the tribunal ruled that the employee's behaviour was such that his award should be reduced by 100 per cent on account of his contributory conduct. The EAT upheld the decision, stating that while a finding of a 100 per cent reduction in S.107 cases would be rare, it was one that the tribunal was entitled to make.

In other cases, it may be the employee's unreasonable refusal to cooperate with the employer's attempts to resolve the workplace conflict that warrants a finding of contributory conduct. In Ford Motor Co Ltd v Hudson and ors 1978 ICR 482, EAT, for example, the EAT stated that it was open to a tribunal to hold that an employee had been unduly uncooperative and unreasonable in refusing to transfer to another job and that the tribunal would be entitled to hold that the employee had contributed to his or her dismissal if this were the case.

10.11 Joinder of third parties

If an employer dismisses an employee on account of industrial pressure *and the reason for the pressure was that the employee was or was not a union member*, then either the employer or the dismissed employee can request that those who brought the pressure to bear be joined (or sisted, in Scotland) as a party to the unfair dismissal proceedings – S.160(1) TULR(C)A. In the majority of cases it will be a union that is the relevant party. If the request is made before the unfair dismissal hearing commences, the tribunal *must* grant it, but if it is made once the hearing has begun, then it is within the tribunal's discretion whether or not to order joinder. No request may be made after an award of compensation or an order for redeployment has been made – S.160(2). Once joined, the third party can play a full part in the hearing.

The effect of a joinder is that the tribunal may, as it considers 'just and equitable' in the circumstances, make any award against a third party instead of against the employer or apportion the award between the two – S.160(3).

10.12 Right not to be subjected to detriment

Section 148(2) TULR(C)A contains parallel provisions to S.107 ERA, covering the situation where an employer is forced by industrial pressure to subject an employee to a detriment on union membership grounds. Thus, if an employer takes detrimental action short of dismissal against an employee to avoid industrial action by other workers, he cannot use this pressure as a defence when faced with a complaint under S.146 TULR(C)A, which prohibits employers from subjecting employees to a detriment on grounds related to union membership or activities. As with dismissal cases, the employer or the employee is entitled to join a third party to the action – S.150. For more information on protection against trade union victimisation, see IDS Employment Law Handbook, 'Trade Unions' (2000), Chapter 9.

Case list

(Note that employment tribunal cases are not included in this list.)

A

AB and ors v South West Water Services Ltd 1993 1 All ER 609, CA 7.29

Allen v Flood and anor 1898 AC 1, HL 2.30

American Cyanamid Co v Ethicon Ltd 1975 AC 396, HL 7.4

Anderson and ors v British Coal Corporation, unreported 28.1.93, QBD 1.22

Anglian Windows Ltd v GMB 2007 EWHC 917, QBD 5.12, 5.15, 5.24, 5.40, 5.72

Arrowsmith v Jenkins 1963 2 QB 561, Div Ct 6.28

Associated British Ports and anor v Transport and General Workers' Union
and anor 1989 ICR 557, CA and HL 2.37, 2.45, 5.81

Associated British Ports and ors v Transport and General Workers'
Union 1989 IRLR 291, ChD 3.10, 3.27, 5.60

Athinaiki Chartopoiia AE v Panagiotidis and ors 2007 IRLR 284, ECJ 8.60

Atkins and ors v Abram Alloys Ltd EAT 370/89 8.58

Austin Rover Group Ltd v Amalgamated Union of Engineering Workers (Technical,
Administrative and Supervisory Section) 1985 IRLR 162, QBD 7.20

Austin v Commissioner of Police of the Metropolis 2005 EWHC 480 (QB), QBD 6.36

B

Balfour Kilpatrick Ltd v Acheson and ors 2003 IRLR 683, EAT 2.7, 8.8, 8.11, 8.19

Barretts and Baird (Wholesale) Ltd and ors v Institution of Professional
Civil Servants and ors 1987 IRLR 3, QBD 2.48, 7.1

Baxter and ors v Limb Group of Companies 1994 IRLR 572, CA 9.17

Bent's Brewery Co Ltd and ors v Hogan 1945 2 All ER 570, Liverpool Spring Assizes 3.28

Bigham and anor v GKN Kwikform Ltd 1992 ICR 113, EAT 8.68

Blackpool and The Fylde College v National Association of Teachers in Further and
Higher Education 1994 ICR 648, CA 5.10

Bloomfield and ors v Springfield Hosiery Finishing Co Ltd 1972
ICR 91, NIRC 9.32

Bolton Roadways Ltd v Edwards and ors 1987 IRLR 392, EAT 8.58, 8.62, 8.71

Boreland v Gloucestershire County Council EAT 645/92 10.9

Bowater Containers Ltd v Blake EAT 552/81 1.19, 8.49

Boxfoldia Ltd v National Graphical Association (1982) 1988 ICR 752, QBD 2.19, 7.25

Bray v Sealink UK Ltd EAT 493/85 10.5

Brimelow v Casson 1924 1 Ch 302, ChD 2.29

British Airports Authority v Ashton and ors 1983 ICR 696, QBD 6.10

British Airways plc v Unite the Union 2009
EWHC 3541, QBD 1.12, 5.17, 5.30, 5.73, 7.12

British Broadcasting Corporation v Hearn and ors 1977 ICR 685, CA 3.16

British Industrial Plastics Ltd and ors v Ferguson and ors 1940 1 All ER 479, HL 2.35

British Leyland (UK) Ltd v Smith EAT 443/77 10.7

British Railways Board v National Union of Rail, Maritime and Transport Workers,
unreported 17.9.92, QBD 4.10, 7.9

British Railways Board v National Union of Railwaymen 1989 ICR 678, CA 5.33, 5.63

British Telecommunications plc v Communication Workers Union
   2004 IRLR 58, QBD   3.13, 5.15, 5.24, 5.59
British Telecommunications plc v Ticehurst and anor 1992 ICR 383, CA   2.17, 9.9, 9.10
Broome v Director of Public Prosecutions 1974 ICR 84, HL   6.5, 6.28
Burgess and ors v Stevedoring Services Ltd 2002 IRLR 810, PC   2.18, 8.46

C

Clarke Chapman-John Thompson Ltd v Walters 1972 ICR 83, NIRC   9.35
Coates and anor v Modern Methods and Materials Ltd 1982 ICR 763, CA   8.43, 8.56
Colwyn Borough Council v Dutton 1980 IRLR 420, EAT   10.6, 10.10
Con-Mech (Engineers) Ltd v Amalgamated Union of Engineering Workers
   (Engineering Section) (No.3) 1974 ICR 464, NIRC   7.23
Connex South Eastern Ltd v National Union of Rail, Maritime and Transport
   Workers 1999 IRLR 249, CA   1.23, 5.59
Conway v Wade 1909 AC 506, HL   3.28
Cooper and ors v Isle of Wight College 2008 IRLR 124, QBD   225
Cory Lighterage Ltd v Transport and General Workers' Union and ors 1973
   ICR 339, CA   3.11
Courtaulds Northern Spinning Ltd v Moosa 1984 IRLR 43, EAT   8.77
Cream Holdings Ltd v Banerjee 2005 1 AC 253, HL   7.6
Crofter Hand Woven Harris Tweed Co Ltd v Veitch and anor 1942 AC 435, HL   2.53
Crosville Wales Ltd v Tracey and ors 1993 IRLR 60, EAT   8.72
Crowther v British Railways Board EAT 762 and 1118/95   8.51, 8.77

D

Danilenkov v Russia (Application No.67336/01), ECtHR   1.11, 9.4
DC Thomson and Co Ltd v Deakin and ors 1952 Ch 646, CA   2.24, 2.28, 2.33
Demir and anor v Turkey 2009 IRLR 766, ECtHR   1.11
Dimbleby and Sons Ltd v National Union of Journalists 1984 IRLR 161, HL   7.2
Dimskal Shipping Co SA v International Transport Workers' Federation 1992
   ICR 37, HL   2.55
Director of Public Prosecutions v Fidler and anor 1992 1 WLR 91, Div Ct   6.32
Director of Public Prosecutions v Jones and anor 1999 2 AC 240, HL   6.20, 6.39
Director of Public Prosecutions v Orum 1989 1 WLR 88, Div Ct   6.43
Djavit An v Turkey 2005 40 EHRR 45, ECtHR   6.2
Doctor and ors v Labour Pump Co Ltd EAT 38/85   8.58
Drew v St Edmundsbury Borough Council 1980 ICR 513, EAT   8.51, 9.2
Duport Steels Ltd and ors v Sirs and ors 1980 ICR 161, HL   3.27, 7.14

E

EDF Energy Powerlink Ltd v National Union of Rail, Maritime and Transport
   Workers 2010 IRLR 114, QBD   5.12, 7.17
Edwards and ors v Cardiff City Council 1979 IRLR 303, EAT   8.76
Elsey v Smith (Procurator Fiscal) 1983 IRLR 292, High Court of Justiciary   6.31
Emerald Construction Co Ltd v Lowthian 1966 1 WLR 691, CA   2.34
Enerji Yapi-Yol Sen v Turkey (Application No.68959/01), ECtHR   1.11, 9.4
Engineering Utilities and Installations Ltd v Rosser EAT 553/84   8.73
English, Welsh and Scottish Railway Ltd and anor v National Union of Rail,
   Maritime and Transport Workers 2004 EWCA Civ 1539, CA   5.7, 5.68

Examite Ltd v Whittaker and ors 1977 IRLR 312, CA　3.9
Express and Star Ltd and ors v National Graphical Association (1982) and anor 1986
　IRLR 222, CA　7.21, 7.22
Express and Star Ltd v Bunday and ors 1988 ICR 379, CA　1.25, 8.38, 8.41, 9.38
Express Newspapers Ltd v McShane and anor 1980 ICR 42, HL　3.26, 3.28

F

Falconer v Associated Society of Locomotive Engineers and Firemen and National
　Union of Railwaymen 1986 IRLR 331, Sheffield County Court　7.29
Fenn v Mirror Group Newspapers Ltd EAT 28/81　9.16
Fisher and ors v York Trailer Co Ltd 1979 ICR 834, EAT　8.54
Ford Motor Co Ltd v Hudson and ors 1978 ICR 482, EAT　10.4, 10.10

G

Galt (Procurator Fiscal) v Philp and ors 1984 IRLR 156, High Court of
　Justiciary　6.30, 6.31
Gate Gourmet London Ltd v Transport and General Workers'
　Union and ors 2005 IRLR 881, QBD　6.6, 6.11, 6.13, 7.12, 7.19
Gill and ors v Ford Motor Co Ltd; Wong and ors v BAE Systems
　Operations Ltd 2004 IRLR 840, EAT　9.6
Glenrose (Fish Merchants) Ltd v Chapman and ors EAT 245/89　1.19, 8.44, 8.50, 8.57
Glenrose (Fish Merchants) Ltd v Chapman and ors EAT 467/91　8.74
Golden Sunrise (Pies) Ltd v W and S Hamill EAT 640/80　8.72
Gouriet v Union of Post Office Workers and ors 1977 3 All ER 70, HL　7.16
G v Chief Superintendent of Police, Stroud 1986 86 Cr App Rep 92, Div Ct　6.50

H

Hadmor Productions Ltd and ors v Hamilton
　and anor 1982 ICR 114, HL　2.41, 3.5, 3.20, 7.14
Hanson v Fashion Industries (Hartlepool) Ltd 1981 ICR 35, EAT　9.32
Hazells Offset Ltd v Luckett 1977 IRLR 430, EAT　10.2
H Campey and Sons Ltd v Bellwood and ors 1987 ICR 311, EAT　8.54
Health Computing Ltd and anor v Meek and ors 1981 ICR 24, ChD　3.20, 3.28
Heath and anor v JF Longman (Meat Salesmen) Ltd 1973 ICR 407, NIRC　8.62
Heatons Transport (St Helens) Ltd v Transport and General Workers' Union
　1972 ICR 308, NIRC and HL　2.11, 7.22
Highland Fabricators Ltd v McLaughlin 1985 ICR 183, EAT　8.73
Hindle Gears Ltd v McGinty and ors 1985 ICR 111, EAT　8.58, 8.59, 8.63
Hirst and Agu v Chief Constable of the West Yorkshire Police 1987
　85 Cr App Rep 143, Div Ct　6.29
Howitt Transport Ltd and anor v Transport and General Workers' Union 1973
　ICR 1, NIRC　7.20
Hulse and anor v E Hillier and Son (Engineering) Ltd and ors EAT 273/94　8.56, 8.58
Hunter v Canary Wharf Ltd 1997 2 All ER 426, HL　6.23

I

In re Corby Group Litigation 2009 QB 335, CA　6.26
International Transport Workers' Federation and anor v Viking Line ABP and anor
　2008 ICR 741, ECJ　1.8

253

J

J and R Kenny Cleaning Services v Transport and General Workers' Union,
    unreported 8.6.89, CA   6.4
J Lyons and Sons v Wilkins (No.2) 1899 1 Ch 255, CA   6.32
JT Stratford and Son Ltd v Lindley and anor 1965 AC 269, HL   2.34, 3.11
Jakeman and ors v South West Thames Regional Health Authority and London
    Ambulance Service 1990 IRLR 62, QBD   9.13
James Ferries and Co Ltd v Johnstone EAT 489/84   10.8
Jenkins v P and O European Ferries (Dover) Ltd 1991 ICR 652, EAT   8.57
Judge v Bennett 1887 4 TLR 75, Div Ct   6.31

K

Kavanagh v Hiscock and anor 1974 ICR 282, Div Ct   6.46
Kaya and Seyhan v Turkey (Application No.30946/04), ECtHR   1.11, 9.4
Kent Free Press v National Graphical Association and ors 1987 IRLR 267, QBD 7.20
Knowles and anor v Fire Brigades Union 1996 IRLR 617, CA   8.46

L

Laffin and anor v Fashion Industries (Hartlepool) Ltd 1978 IRLR 448, EAT   8.76
Larkin and ors v Long 1915 AC 814, HL   3.11
Laval un Partneri Ltd v Svenska Byggnadsarbetareförbundet and ors 2008 IRLR
    160, ECJ   1.8
Leggett v Department of Health and Social Security EAT 520/80   10.4
Lewis and Britton v E Mason and Sons 1994 IRLR 4, EAT   1.19, 8.47, 8.49, 8.58, 8.64
Livingstone v Raywards Coal Co 1880 5 App Cas 25, HL   7.28
London Borough of Islington v Hutchings EAT 34/01   9.2
London Underground Ltd and ors v National Union of Rail, Maritime and Transport
    Workers 2001 ICR 647, CA   5.10
London Underground Ltd v National Union of Rail, Maritime and Transport
    Workers 1996 ICR 170, CA   5.37, 5.39
London Underground Ltd v National Union of Rail, Maritime and
    Transport Workers, unreported 22.12.98, QBD   3.18, 5.80, 7.8
London Underground Ltd v National Union of Railwaymen 1989 IRLR 341, QBD   5.60
Lonrho plc v Al-Fayed and ors 1991 3 All ER 303, HL   2.54
Lookers of Bradford Ltd v Mavin and ors EAT 332/80   8.65
Lumley v Gye 118 ER 749, Court of Queen's Bench   2.24, 2.30

M

McCormick v Horsepower Ltd 1981 ICR 535, CA   8.60
McKenzie v Crosville Motor Services Ltd 1990 ICR 172, EAT   8.57
McLaren v National Coal Board 1988 IRLR 215, CA   8.75
MacPherson v London Borough of Lambeth 1988 IRLR 470, ChD   9.14
Mainland Car Deliveries Ltd v Cooper and ors EAT 492/96   8.50
Majrowski v Guy's and St Thomas's NHS Trust 2006 ICR 1199, HL   6.54
Manifold Industries Ltd v Sims and ors 1991 ICR 504, EAT   8.39, 8.57, 8.67
Marfax Ltd v Amalgamated Union of Enigineering Workers,
    unreported 16.7.86, QBD   7.14
Marsden and ors v Fairey Stainless Ltd 1979 IRLR 103, EAT   8.71
Mercury Communications Ltd v Scott-Garner and anor 1984 ICR 74, CA   3.21, 7.7

Merkur Island Shipping Corporation v Laughton and ors 1983 ICR 490, HL   2.24, 2.31
Mersey Dock and Harbour Company v Verrinder and ors 1982 IRLR 152, ChD   6.22
Messenger Newspapers Group Ltd v National Graphical Association (1982)
   1984 IRLR 397, QBD   4.17, 7.29
Metrobus Ltd v Unite the Union 2010 ICR 173, CA   1.12, 5.2, 5.14, 5.67, 5.73, 7.12
Middlebrook Mushrooms Ltd v Transport and General
   Workers' Union and ors 1993 ICR 612, CA   2.47, 6.17, 6.63
Midland Plastics v Till and ors 1983 ICR 118, EAT   1.16, 8.44, 8.47
Miles v Wakefield Metropolitan District Council 1987 ICR 368, HL   9.7, 9.8, 9.11
Ministry of Justice v POA (formerly Prison Officers Association) 2008
   ICR 702, QBD   7.9, 7.13
Monsanto plc v TGWU 1987 ICR 269, CA   5.80
Moss and ors v McLachlan 1985 IRLR 76, Div Ct   6.49

N

NWL Ltd v Woods 1979 ICR 867, HL   7.5
Nagy v Weston 1965 1 All ER 78, Div Ct   6.28
National Union of Rail, Maritime and Transport Workers v Midland
   Mainline Ltd 2001 IRLR 813, CA   5.27, 5.36, 5.63
Naylor and ors v Orton and Smith Ltd and anor 1983 ICR 665, EAT   8.44, 8.51
Newham London Borough Council v National and Local Government
   Officers Association 1993 ICR 189, CA   3.28, 5.62, 5.77
News Group Newspapers Ltd and ors v Society of Graphical and Allied
   Trades '82 1986 ICR 716, CA   7.27
News Group Newspapers Ltd and ors v Society of
   Graphical and Allied Trades '82 and ors (No.2)
   1987 ICR 181, QBD   2.11, 2.51, 6.9, 6.15, 6.26, 7.18
New Venture Carpets Ltd v Vincent and ors EAT 733/83   8.57, 8.59
Norbrook Laboratories Ltd v King 1984 IRLR 200, NICA   3.27, 6.21, 7.28

O

OBG Ltd and ors v Allan and ors and other cases 2007 IRLR 608, HL   2.23, 2.25, 2.28,
                                           2.31, 2.33, 2.34, 2.36, 2.39,
                                           2.42, 2.44, 2.48, 2.54, 3.4
Oxford and County Newspapers v McIntyre and anor EAT 95/86   9.44

P

P (A Minor) v National Association of Schoolmasters/
   Union of Women Teachers 2003 ICR 386, HL   3.16, 5.29, 5.33, 5.35, 5.63, 7.35
P and O European Ferries (Dover) Ltd v Byrne 1989 ICR 779, CA   8.66
Phonographic Performance Ltd v Amusement Caterers (Peckham) Ltd 1963
   3 WLR 898, ChD   7.21
Piddington v Bates 1960 3 All ER 660, Div Ct   6.5, 6.47
Plessey Co plc and anor v Wilson and ors 1982 IRLR 198, Ct Sess (Inner House)   3.6
Pointon and ors v BBA Friction Ltd EAT 1380/00   8.58
Post Office v Union of Communication Workers 1990 ICR 258, CA   5.2, 5.38, 5.59, 5.80
Power Packing Casemakers Ltd v Faust and ors 1983 ICR 292, CA   1.19, 8.43, 8.45
Presho v DHSS 1984 IRLR 74, HL   8.55
Prudential Assurance Co Ltd v Lorenz and ors 1971 11 KIR 78, ChD   3.7

255

Q

Quinn v Leathem 1901 AC 495, HL   1.3

R

R (on the application of Laporte) v Chief Constable of Gloucestershire
    2007 2 AC 105, HL   6.48, 6.49, 6.50
R v Howell (Errol) 1982 QB 416, CA   6.47
R v Rimmington; R v Goldstein 2006 1 AC 459, HL   6.27
RCA Corporation v Pollard 1983 Ch 135, CA   2.44
RDF Media Group plc and anor v Clements 2008 IRLR 207, QBD   9.5
RJB Mining (UK) Ltd v National Union of Mineworkers 1995 IRLR 556, CA   5.79
Ramalheira and ors v Bloomsbury Health Authority EAT 698/87   8.63
Rasool and ors v Hepworth Pipe Co Ltd 1980 ICR 494, EAT   1.24, 8.43
Rayware Ltd and anor v Transport and General Workers' Union and anor 1989
    ICR 457, CA   6.10
Richard Read (Transport) Ltd v National Union of Mineworkers (South Wales Area)
    1985 IRLR 67, QBD   7.20
Robinson v Harman 1848 1 Exch 850, Court of Exchequer   7.28
Rookes v Barnard 1964 AC 1129, HL   1.4, 2.42, 2.45, 2.50, 7.29

S

Sanders and ors v Ernest A Neale Ltd 1974 ICR 565, NIRC   9.16
Scott v Strathclyde Fire Board EAT 0050/03   9.6
Seaboard World Airlines Inc v Transport and General Workers' Union and ors 1973
    ICR 458, NIRC   1.16
Secretary of State for Employment v ASLEF and ors (No.2) 1972 ICR 19, CA   2.16
Sehmi v Gate Gourmet London Ltd; Sandhu and ors v Gate Gourmet London Ltd
    2009 IRLR 807, EAT   8.59
Shell UK Ltd v McGillivray 1991 SLT 667, Ct Sess (Outer House)   3.6
Shipping Company Uniform Inc v International Transport Workers Federation
    and ors 1985 ICR 245, QBD   4.6
Simmons v Hoover Ltd 1977 ICR 61, EAT   2.13, 9.21
Sim v Rotherham Metropolitan Borough Council 1986 ICR 897, ChD   9.11, 9.12
Smithkline Beecham plc v Avery 2009 EWHC 1488, QBD   6.58
Smith v Lex Wilkinson Ltd EAT 661/84   8.67
Sorenson v Denmark; Rasmussen v Denmark 2008 46 EHRR 29, ECtHR   4.24
South East Kent Health Authority v Gillis and ors EAT 927/83   8.50
South Wales Miners Federation and ors v Glamorgan Coal Co Ltd 1905
    AC 239, CA   2.35
Sulemanji v Toughened Glass Ltd and anor 1979 ICR 799, EAT   10.10
Sunderland Polytechnic v Evans 1993 ICR 392, EAT   9.6

T

Taff Vale Railway Co v Amalgamated Society of Railway Servants 1901 AC 426, HL   1.3
Tanks and Drums Ltd v Transport and General Workers' Union 1992 ICR 1, CA   5.55
Taylor and ors v National Union of Mineworkers (Derbyshire Area) and ors 1984
    IRLR 440, ChD   7.30
Thomas and ors v National Union of Mineworkers (South Wales
    Area) and ors 1985 ICR 886, ChD   6.12, 6.22, 6.23, 6.31

Thompson and ors v Eaton Ltd 1976 IRLR 308, EAT   8.44
TimePlan Education Group Ltd v National Union of Teachers 1997 IRLR 457, CA   2.35
Tomczynski v JK Millar Ltd 1976 ITR 127, EAT   8.71
Torquay Hotel Co Ltd v Cousins and ors 1969 2 Ch 106, CA   2.31
Tracey and ors v Crosville Wales Ltd 1997 ICR 862, HL   8.77
Tramp Shipping Corp v Greenwich Marine Inc 1975 ICR 261, CA   1.21, 8.42
Transport and General Workers' Union v Associated British Ports Ltd 2001
   EWCA Civ 2032, CA   3.8, 5.83
Trend v Chiltern Hunt Ltd 1977 ICR 612, EAT   10.3, 10.8
Tynan v Balmer 1966 2 WLR 1181, Div Ct   6.19

U

Union Traffic Ltd v Transport and General Workers' Union and ors
   1989 ICR 98, CA   6.9. 6.16
UNISON v United Kingdom 2002 IRLR 497, ECtHR   3.18
Universe Tankships Inc of Monrovia v International Transport Workers'
   Federation and ors 1982 ICR 262, HL   2.55, 3.7, 3.15
University College London Hospitals NHS Trust v UNISON 1999
   ICR 204, CA   3.17, 3.18, 3.22
University of Central England and anor v National and Local Government
   Officers' Association 1993 IRLR 81, QBD   5.42

V

Vascroft Contractors Ltd v Falvey and Clarke EAT 176/94   8.51, 8.57
Veakins v Kier Islington Ltd 2010 IRLR 132, CA   6.54

W

Wandsworth London Borough Council v National Association of
   Schoolmasters/Union of Women Teachers 1994 ICR 81, CA   3.12, 3.21
Ward Lock and Co Ltd v Operative Printers' Assistants' Society and anor
   1906 22 TLR 327, CA   6.21, 6.30
Webb and ors v Sundaw Products Ltd and anor EAT 477/79   8.39, 9.16
West Midlands Travel Ltd v Transport and General Workers' Union 1994
   IRLR 578, CA   5.64
Westminster City Council v UNISON 2001 ICR 1046, CA   3.21, 5.11, 5.15, 5.71
Wilkins and ors v Cantrell and Cochrane (GB) Ltd 1978 IRLR 483, EAT   8.19
Willerby Holiday Homes Ltd v Union of Construction, Allied Trades and
   Technicians 2003 EWHC 2608, QBD   5.16
Williams and ors v National Theatre Board Ltd 1982 ICR 715, CA   8.70, 8.72
Williams v Western Mail and Echo Ltd 1980 IRLR 222, EAT   8.58
Wilson and anor v United Kingdom; Palmer and ors v United Kingdom; Doolan
   and ors v United Kingdom 2002 IRLR 568, ECtHR   1.12
Wilson v Housing Corporation 1998 ICR 151, QBD   2.38
Wiluszynski v Tower Hamlets London Borough Council 1989 ICR 493, CA   9.7, 9.11
Winnett v Seamarks Brothers Ltd 1978 ICR 1240, EAT   8.47, 8.58, 8.64
Wood Group Engineering Contractors Ltd v Byrne EAT 447/92   8.57

Index

A

Acas conciliation
trade union immunity, 3.24–3.25
Action against government
trade union immunity, 3.12
Action on expiry of notice
breach of contract, 2.19
Aggravated trespass
picketing, 6.33
Armed forces
criminal liability for industrial action,
2.56
Authorisation
unofficial action
dismissal during, 8.9
Automatically unfair dismissal
protected official action, 8.22–8.23

B

Ballots
costs, 5.3
effectiveness, period of
continuing industrial action, 5.80
generally, 5.79
intervening legal proceedings,
5.81–5.84
entitlement to vote
denial of, 5.32–5.36
determining constituency, 5.26–5.31
existing members, 5.39
generally, 5.24–5.25
new members, 5.37–5.38
introduction, 5.1
legislation concerning, 5.2
notice to employer
appropriate period, 5.68
content of notice, 5.8–5.9
errors in notice, 5.16–5.18
generally, 5.6–5.7
level of detail, 5.10–5.15
relevant notice, meaning of, 5.69
preliminary considerations
generally, 5.4–5.5
independent scrutineer, 5.21–5.23

notice of ballot to employer,
5.6–5.18
sample voting paper, 5.19–5.20
requirements
ballot results, 5.64
calling industrial action, 5.77–5.78
conduct of ballot, 5.61–5.63
contents of ballot paper, 5.53–5.60
employee information, 5.70–5.76
informing employer of ballot result,
5.66–5.67
introduction, 5.52
merchant seamen, 5.65
notice to employer, 5.68–5.69
restriction on industrial action
following, 5.2
separate workplace ballots
common factors, 5.44–5.49
generally, 5.40–5.42
overseas members, 5.50–5.51
reasonable belief in single
workplace, 5.43
trade union immunity, 4.3
unofficial action, endorsement of, 2.9
Breach of contract
dismissal during non-protected official
action, 8.45–8.46
exceptions
action on expiry of notice, 2.19
generally, 2.14–2.15
implied terms, 2.16–2.18
generally, 2.13
legal consequences, 2.20–2.21
procuring or inducing
Civil Service, 2.32
generally, 2.30–2.31
inducement, 2.33
intention, 2.34–2.36
knowledge, 2.34–2.36
non-contractual obligations,
2.37–2.38
procurement, 2.33
Breach of the peace
picketing, 6.46–6.51

259

C

Causation
guarantee payments, 9.29
industrial pressure for dismissal,
10.8–10.9

Causing loss by unlawful means
generally, 2.39–2.40
intention, 2.48
interference with economic interest,
2.41
lawful interference, 2.47
statutory immunity, and, 2.49
unlawful means, 2.42–2.46

Civil liability
picketing
introduction, 6.18
private nuisance, 6.21–6.23
trade union liability, 6.24
trespass to highway, 6.19–6.20

Civil Service
procuring or inducing breach of
contract, 2.32

Claw-back
trade union immunity, 3.2

Code of Practice
picketing, 6.2

Committee of the union
meaning, 2.4

Common law
trade union liability, 2.11–2.12

Compensation
dismissal during non-protected official
action, 8.77–8.78

Conspiracy
generally, 2.52
injure by lawful means, 2.53
injure by unlawful means, 2.54
picketing, 6.52
trade union immunity, and, 3.3

Contempt of court
injunctions for unlawful action,
7.20–7.23

Continuity of employment
employment rights
agreements concerning, 9.40
dismissal of strikers, 9.32–9.33
effect of strikes on, 9.36–9.37
generally, 9.30
lock-outs, 9.38–9.39

strike, meaning of, 9.31
taking part in strike, 9.34–9.35

Contributory conduct
industrial pressure for dismissal, 10.10

Costs
ballots, 5.3

Criminal liability
offences committed during industrial
action, 2.57
picketing
aggravated trespass, 6.33
breach of the peace, 6.46–6.51
conspiracy, 6.52
dispersal orders, 6.45
introduction, 6.25
obstruction of highway, 6.28–6.29
public nuisance, 6.26–6.27
public order offences, 6.34–6.44
S.241 offences, 6.30–6.32
prohibited action, 2.56

D

Damages
remedies for unlawful action
exceptions to limitations, 7.26
heads of damage, 7.28–7.29
limitations, 7.24–7.25
protected property, 7.27

Defences
industrial torts, 2.29

Demarcation disputes
trade union immunity, 3.12

Demonstrations
picketing, and, 6.15

Detriment
continuity of employment, 9.2–9.5
industrial pressure for dismissal, 10.12

Direct action
versus indirect action, 2.27–2.28

Dismissals
industrial pressure for
causation, 10.8–10.9
contributory conduct, 10.10
detriment, right not to be subject to,
10.12
introduction, 10.1
joinder of third parties, 10.11
pressure to dismiss, 10.4–10.5
reasons for dismissal, 10.2–10.3

redeployment, 10.6–10.7
introduction, 8.1–8.2
non-protected official action
    breach of contract, 8.45–8.46
    compensation, 8.77–8.78
    dismissal of relevant employees,
        8.66–8.67
    ending industrial action, 8.50
    generally, 8.33–8.36
    individuals, 8.49
    lock-outs, 8.37–8.40
    other industrial action, 8.43–8.44
    reasonableness of dismissal,
        8.74–8.76
    relevant employees, 8.52–8.60
    selective re-engagement, 8.68–8.73
    strikes, 8.37, 8.41–8.42
    threats of action, 8.47–8.48
    time limits, 8.79–8.80
    timing of dismissal, 8.61–8.65
    trade union activities, 8.51
protected official action
    automatically unfair dismissal,
        8.22–8.23
    introduction, 8.20
    protected industrial action,
        8.24–8.25
    protected period, 8.26
    qualifying period, 8.31
    reasonable steps for resolution of
        disputes, 8.27–8.28
    reinstatement, 8.29
    time limits, 8.32
    tribunal procedure, 8.30
unofficial action
    action in support of dismissed
        employees, 8.16
    authorisation, 8.9
    effect of S.237 on, 8.17
    employer-provoked strikes, 8.18
    endorsement, 8.9
    exceptions, 8.4–8.5
    general rule, 8.3
    health and safety, 8.19
    meaning, 8.6–8.8
    repudiation, 8.10–8.13
    timing of dismissal, 8.14–8.15
Dispersal orders
    picketing, 6.45

E
Economic duress
    tortious liability, 2.55
Employee information
    ballots, 5.70–5.76
Employer-provoked strikes
    unofficial action, dismissal during, 8.18
Employment rights
    continuity of employment
        agreements concerning, 9.40
        dismissal of strikers, 9.32–9.33
        effect of strikes on, 9.36–9.37
        generally, 9.30
        lock-outs, 9.38–9.39
        strike, meaning of, 9.31
        taking part in strike, 9.34–9.35
    detriment short of dismissal, 9.2–9.5
    guarantee payments
        causation, 9.29
        generally, 9.26
        involvement in industrial action,
            9.27–9.28
    introduction, 9.1
    notice rights, 9.41–9.42
    pay
        generally, 9.6–9.8
        partial performance, 9.11–9.12
        remedies, 9.13–9.14
        withdrawal of goodwill, 9.9–9.10
    redundancy payments
        extension of notice period after
            strike, 9.23–9.24
        industrial action during notice
            period, 9.19–9.22
        introduction, 9.15
        lay-offs, 9.25
        misconduct, 9.18
        reasons for dismissal, 9.16–9.17
        short-time, 9.25
    time-off rights, 9.43–9.44
Endorsement
    unofficial action
        dismissal during, 8.9
        trade union liability, 2.9–2.10
Entitlement to vote
    ballots
        denial of, 5.32–5.36
        determining constituency, 5.26–5.31
        existing members, new jobs, 5.39

261

generally, 5.24–5.25
new members, 5.37–5.38

G
Goodwill, withdrawal of
pay, 9.9–9.10
Government, action against
trade union immunity, 3.12
Guarantee payments
causation, 9.29
generally, 9.26
involvement in industrial action,
9.27–9.28

H
Harassment
picketing
harassing a person at home,
6.61–6.62
introduction, 6.53
offence of harassment, 6.54–6.68
Health and safety
unofficial action, dismissal during, 8.19
Highways
picketing
obstruction of highway, 6.28–6.29
trespass to highway, 6.19–6.20
Human rights
picketing, 6.2

I
Immunity
causing loss by unlawful means, 2.49
**In contemplation or furtherance of a trade
dispute**
picketing, and, 6.4
trade union immunity, 3.26–3.28
Independent scrutineer
ballots, 5.21–5.23
Indirect action
direct action versus, 2.27–2.28
Individuals
dismissal during non-protected official
action, 8.49
remedies for unlawful action by,
7.33–7.35
Inducing breach of contract, procuring or
Civil Service, 2.32
generally, 2.30-2.31

inducement, 2.33
intention, 2.34–2.36
knowledge, 2.34–2.36
non-contractual obligations, 2.37–2.38
procurement, 2.33
trade union immunity, and, 3.3
Industrial action
concerted action, 1.19–1.20
lawfulness of, 3.1
meaning, 1.16–1.17
pressure on employer, 1.18
restrictions following ballots, 5.2
Industrial pressure for dismissal
causation, 10.8–10.9
contributory conduct, 10.10
detriment, right not to be subject to,
10.12
introduction, 10.1
joinder of third parties, 10.11
pressure to dismiss, 10.4–10.5
reasons for dismissal, 10.2–10.3
redeployment, 10.6–10.7
Industrial torts
causing loss by unlawful means
generally, 2.39–2.40
intention, 2.48
interference with economic interest,
2.41
lawful interference, 2.47
statutory immunity, and, 2.49
unlawful means, 2.42–2.46
conspiracy
generally, 2.52
injure by lawful means, 2.53
injure by unlawful means, 2.54
defences to, 2.29
direct v indirect action, 2.27–2.28
economic duress, 2.55
intimidation, 2.50–2.51
meaning, 2.22
procuring or inducing breach of
contract
Civil Service, 2.32
generally, 2.30–2.31
inducement, 2.33
intention, 2.34–2.36
knowledge, 2.34–2.36
non-contractual obligations,
2.37–2.38

procurement, 2.33
status, 2.23
statutory immunity, 2.26
unified theory, rejection of, 2.24–2.25

Injunctions
unlawful action
contempt of court, 7.20–7.23
generally, 7.3
grounds for seeking, 7.11–7.12
interim injunctions, 7.4–7.10
judicial discretion, 7.14
procedure, 7.16–7.19
scope of, 7.15

Intention
causing loss by unlawful means, 2.48
procuring or inducing breach of
contract, 2.34–2.36

Interference with economic interest
causing loss by unlawful means, 2.41
trade union immunity, and, 3.3

Intimidation
tortious liability, 2.50–2.51
trade union immunity, and, 3.3

J

Joinder of third parties
industrial pressure for dismissal, 10.11

Lawful interference
causing loss by unlawful means, 2.47

L

Lay-offs
redundancy payments, 9.25

Legal proceedings
period of effectiveness of ballots, and,
5.81–5.84

Legality of action
three-stage test, 1.13

Liability
breach of contract
exceptions, 2.14–2.19
generally, 2.13
legal consequences, 2.20–2.21
procuring or inducing, 2.30–2.38
criminal liability, 2.56–2.57
industrial torts
causing loss by unlawful means,
2.39–2.49
conspiracy, 2.52–2.54

defences to, 2.29
direct v indirect action, 2.27–2.28
economic duress, 2.55
intimidation, 2.50–2.51
meaning, 2.22
procuring or inducing breach of
contract, 2.30–2.38
rejection of unified theory, 2.24–2.25
status, 2.23
statutory immunity, 2.26
introduction, 2.1
trade unions
common law liability, 2.11–2.12
endorsement of unofficial action,
2.9–2.10
repudiation, 2.6–2.8
statutory liability, 2.3–2.5
tortious liability, 2.2

Limitations
damages for unlawful actions,
7.24–7.25

Lock-outs
continuity of employment, 9.38–9.39
dismissal during non-protected official
action, 8.37–8.40

M

Marches
picketing, and, 6.15

Merchant seamen
ballots, 5.65
criminal liability for industrial action,
2.56

Misconduct
redundancy payments, 9.18

N

Non-protected official action
dismissal during
breach of contract, 8.45–8.46
compensation, 8.77–8.78
dismissal of relevant employees,
8.66–8.67
ending industrial action, 8.50
generally, 8.33–8.36
individuals, 8.49
lock-outs, 8.37–8.40
other industrial action, 8.43–8.44

reasonableness of dismissal,
8.74–8.76
relevant employees, 8.52–8.60
selective re-engagement, 8.68–8.73
strikes, 8.37, 8.41–8.42
threats of action, 8.47–8.48
time limits, 8.79–8.80
timing of dismissal, 8.61–8.65
trade union activities, 8.51
Notice
employment rights
generally, 9.41–9.42
redundancy payments, 9.19–9.24
Notice to employer
action on expiry of
breach of contract, 2.19
ballots
appropriate period, 5.68
content of notice, 5.8–5.9
errors in notice, 5.16–5.18
generally, 5.6–5.7
level of detail, 5.10–5.15
relevant notice, meaning of, 5.69
trade union immunity, 4.3
Notification to employer
ballot results, 5.66–5.67
Nuisance
picketing
private, 6.21–6.23
public, 6.26–6.27

O
Obstruction of highway
picketing, 6.28–6.29
Offences
industrial action constituting,
2.56–2.57
picketing
aggravated trespass, 6.33
breach of the peace, 6.46–6.51
conspiracy, 6.52
dispersal orders, 6.45
harassment, 6.54–6.68
introduction, 6.25
obstruction of highway, 6.28–6.29
public nuisance, 6.26–6.27
public order offences, 6.34–6.44
S.241 offences, 6.30–6.32

Official action, non-protected
dismissal during
breach of contract, 8.45–8.46
compensation, 8.77–8.78
dismissal of relevant employees,
8.66–8.67
ending industrial action, 8.50
generally, 8.33–8.36
individuals, 8.49
lock-outs, 8.37–8.40
other industrial action, 8.43–8.44
reasonableness of dismissal,
8.74–8.76
relevant employees, 8.52–8.60
selective re-engagement, 8.68–8.73
strikes, 8.37, 8.41–8.42
threats of action, 8.47–8.48
time limits, 8.79–8.80
timing of dismissal, 8.61–8.65
trade union activities, 8.51
Official action, protected
dismissal during
automatically unfair dismissal,
8.22–8.23
introduction, 8.20
protected industrial action,
8.24–8.25
protected period, 8.26
qualifying period, 8.31
reasonable steps for resolution of
disputes, 8.27–8.28
reinstatement, 8.29
time limits, 8.32
tribunal procedure, 8.30
Overseas disputes
trade union immunity, 3.23
Overseas members
separate workplace ballots, 5.50–5.51
Overtime, refusal of
breach of contract, and, 2.16–2.18

P
Pay
employment rights
generally, 9.6–9.8
partial performance, 9.11–9.12
remedies, 9.13–9.14
withdrawal of goodwill, 9.9–9.10

Picketing
civil liability
introduction, 6.18
private nuisance, 6.21–6.23
trade union liability, 6.24
trespass to highway, 6.19–6.20
Code of Practice, 6.2
criminal liability
aggravated trespass, 6.33
breach of the peace, 6.46–6.51
conspiracy, 6.52
dispersal orders, 6.45
introduction, 6.25
obstruction of highway, 6.28–6.29
public nuisance, 6.26–6.27
public order offences, 6.34–6.44
S.241 offences, 6.30–6.32
harassment
harassing a person at home,
6.61–6.62
introduction, 6.53
offence of harassment, 6.54–6.68
human rights, 6.2
meaning, 6.1
secondary picketing, 6.63
statutory protection
demonstrations, and, 6.15
generally, 6.3
in contemplation or furtherance of a
trade dispute, 6.4
loss of, 6.16–6.17
marches, and, 6.15
number of pickets, 6.12–6.14
place of picket, 6.7–6.11
purpose of picket, 6.5–6.6
trade union immunity, 4.13
Police
criminal liability for industrial action,
2.56
Postal workers
criminal liability for industrial action,
2.56
Private nuisance
picketing, 6.21–6.23
Procuring or inducing breach of contract
Civil Service, 2.32
generally, 2.30–2.31
inducement, 2.33

intention, 2.34–2.36
knowledge, 2.34–2.36
non-contractual obligations, 2.37–2.38
procurement, 2.33
trade union immunity, and, 3.3
Protected official action
dismissal during
automatically unfair dismissal,
8.22–8.23
introduction, 8.20
protected industrial action,
8.24–8.25
protected period, 8.26
qualifying period, 8.31
reasonable steps for resolution of
disputes, 8.27–8.28
reinstatement, 8.29
time limits, 8.32
tribunal procedure, 8.30
Public nuisance
picketing, 6.26–6.27
Public order offences
picketing, 6.34–6.44
Public sector employees
criminal liability for industrial action,
2.56

R
Redeployment
industrial pressure for dismissal,
10.6–10.7
Redundancy payments
extension of notice period after strike,
9.23–9.24
industrial action during notice period,
9.19–9.22
introduction, 9.15
lay-offs, 9.25
misconduct, 9.18
reasons for dismissal, 9.16–9.17
short-time, 9.25
Re-engagement, selective
dismissal during non-protected official
action, 8.68–8.73
Reinstatement
dismissal during protected official
action, 8.29

Remedies
  pay, 9.13–9.14
  unlawful action
    action by individuals, 7.33–7.35
    action by union members, 7.30–7.32
    damages, 7.24–7.29
    injunctions, 7.3–7.23
    introduction, 1.15, 7.1–7.2
Repudiation
  trade union liability
    generally, 2.6–2.8
    unofficial action, 2.9
  unofficial action
    dismissal during, 8.10–8.13
    trade union liability, 2.9
Right to strike
  generally, 1.3

S
Scrutineer
  ballots, 5.21–5.23
Secondary action
  trade union immunity, 4.4–4.9
Secondary picketing
  see Picketing
Selective re-engagement
  dismissal during non-protected official action, 8.68–8.73
Separate workplace ballots
  common factors, 5.44–5.49
  generally, 5.40–5.42
  overseas members, 5.50–5.51
  reasonable belief in single workplace, 5.43
Short-time
  redundancy payments, 9.25
Statutory immunity
  causing loss by unlawful means, 2.49
Statutory liability
  trade unions, 2.3–2.5
Strikes
  breach of contract, and, 2.13–2.15
  continuity of employment
    dismissal of strikers, 9.32–9.33
    effect of strikes on, 9.36–9.37
    strike, meaning of, 9.31
    taking part in strike, 9.34–9.35

dismissal
  during non-protected official action, 8.37, 8.41–8.42
  during unofficial action, 8.18
industrial action short of, 1.23–1.25
meaning, 1.21–1.22
right to
  generally, 1.3
  international obligations, 1.6–1.12
  legal developments, 1.4–1.5

T
Telecommunication workers
  criminal liability for industrial action, 2.56
Third parties, joinder of
  industrial pressure for dismissal, 10.11
Threats of action
  dismissal during non-protected official action, 8.47–8.48
Time limits
  dismissal
    during non-protected official action, 8.79–8.80
    during protected official action, 8.32
Time off
  employment rights, 9.43–9.44
Tortious liability
  economic duress, 2.55
  intimidation, 2.50–2.51
  trade unions, 2.2
Trade disputes
  trade union immunity
    Acas conciliation, 3.24–3.25
    action against government, 3.12
    demarcation disputes, 3.12
    excluded disputes, 3.11
    meaning, 3.8
    overseas disputes, 3.23
    subject matter of dispute, 3.13–3.20
    wholly or mainly, 3.21–3.22
    with workers, 3.8–3.10
Trade union activities
  dismissal during non-protected official action, 8.51
Trade union immunity
  claw-back provisions, 3.2
  in contemplation or furtherance, 3.26–3.28

lawfulness of industrial action, 3.1
loss of
    ballots, 4.3
    dismissals during unofficial action,
    4.10–4.11
    enforcing union membership,
    4.23–4.24
    introduction, 1.14, 4.1–4.2
    notice of industrial action, 4.3
    secondary action, 4.4–4.9
    union-only clauses, 4.14–4.18
    union recognition clauses, 4.19–4.22
    unlawful picketing, 4.13
scope of
    double liability, 3.7
    generally, 3.3–3.6
trade disputes
    Acas conciliation, 3.24–3.25
    action against government, 3.12
    demarcation disputes, 3.12
    excluded disputes, 3.11
    meaning, 3.8
    overseas disputes, 3.23
    subject matter of dispute, 3.13–3.20
    wholly or mainly, 3.21–3.22
    with workers, 3.8–3.10
Trade union officials
meaning, 2.4
Trade unions
common law liability, 2.11–2.12
endorsement of unofficial action,
    2.9–2.10
immunity
    see also **Trade union immunity**
    claw-back provisions, 3.2
    in contemplation of furtherance,
    3.26–3.28
    lawfulness of industrial action, 3.1
    loss of, 4.1–4.24
    scope of, 3.3–3.7
    trade disputes, 3.8–3.25
liability
    common law liability, 2.11–2.12
    picketing, 6.24
    statutory liability, 2.3–2.5
    tortious liability, 2.2
membership
    enforcement of, 4.23–4.24

remedies for unlawful action by,
    7.30–7.32
repudiation, 2.6–2.8
statutory liability, 2.3–2.5
tortious liability, 2.2
Trespass
picketing
    aggravated trespass, 6.33
    trespass to highway, 6.19–6.20
Tribunal procedure
dismissal during protected official
    action, 8.30

U
Unified theory, rejection of
industrial torts, and, 2.24–2.25
Union only clauses
trade union immunity, 4.14–4.18
Union recognition clauses
trade union immunity, 4.19–4.22
Unlawful picketing
trade union immunity, 4.13
Unofficial action
dismissal during
    action in support of dismissed
        employees, 8.16
    authorisation, 8.9
    effect of S.237 on, 8.17
    employer-provoked strikes, 8.18
    endorsement, 8.9
    exceptions, 8.4–8.5
    general rule, 8.3
    health and safety, 8.19
    meaning, 8.6–8.8
    repudiation, 8.10–8.13
    timing of dismissal, 8.14–8.15
    trade union immunity, 4.10–4.11
endorsement of
    trade union liability, 2.9–2.10

V
Voting papers
ballots
    contents, 5.53–5.60
    sample, 5.19–5.20
Voting rights
ballots
    denial of, 5.32–5.36
    determining constituency, 5.26–5.31

267

existing members, new jobs, 5.39
generally, 5.24–5.25
new members, 5.37–5.38

W
Work to rule
  breach of contract, and, 2.16–2.18